Kim Glück, Sophia Thubauville (eds.)
Saving and Being Safe Away from Home

Culture and Social Practice

Kim Glück, born in 1986, is a social anthropologist specializing in Ethiopian studies. After studying social anthropology and history in Frankfurt am Main, Germany, and in Montpellier, France, she completed her doctorate in Mainz, Germany. She conducts research in Ethiopia as well as in the Ethiopian diaspora in the USA and Israel. Her research interests include migration and diaspora studies, performance studies and anthropology of the future.

Sophia Thubauville, born in 1979, is a social anthropologist at the Frobenius-Institut für kulturanthropologische Forschung in Frankfurt am Main, Germany. Thubauville is an active member of the European Librarians in African Studies (ELIAS) and of the Commission for Migration of the International Union of Anthropological and Ethnological Science (IUAES). She is also spokesperson for the DGSKA working group "Family in the Field". Her research focuses on migration, anthropology of the future, higher education, gender, and Ethiopia-India relations.

Kim Glück, Sophia Thubauville (eds.)
Saving and Being Safe
Away from Home
Savings and Insurance Associations in Ethiopia
and Its Diaspora

[transcript]

This book and some of the underlying research was funded by the DFG project "On the saf(v)e side: informal economic associations and future aspirations in the Ethiopian diaspora" (2021–2024).

Bibliographic information published by the Deutsche Nationalbibliothek
The Deutsche Nationalbibliothek lists this publication in the Deutsche Nationalbibliografie; detailed bibliographic data are available in the Internet at https://dnb.dnb.de/

This work is licensed under the Creative Commons Attribution-ShareAlike 4.0 (BY-SA) which means that the text may be remixed, build upon and be distributed, provided credit is given to the author and that copies or adaptations of the work are released under the same or similar license.
https://creativecommons.org/licenses/by-sa/4.0/
Creative Commons license terms for re-use do not apply to any content (such as graphs, figures, photos, excerpts, etc.) not original to the Open Access publication and further permission may be required from the rights holder. The obligation to research and clear permission lies solely with the party re-using the material.

First published in 2024 by transcript Verlag, Bielefeld
© Kim Glück, Sophia Thubauville (eds.)

Cover layout: Kordula Röckenhaus, Bielefeld
Cover illustration: Kim Glück, Kiryat Gat, 2022
Copy-editing: Kay Celtel
Printed by: Majuskel Medienproduktion GmbH, Wetzlar
https://doi.org/10.14361/9783839471272
Print-ISBN: 978-3-8376-7127-8
PDF-ISBN: 978-3-8394-7127-2
ISSN of series: 2703-0024
eISSN of series: 2703-0032

Printed on permanent acid-free text paper.

Contents

Acknowledgements 7

Introduction
Kim Glück and Sophia Thubauville 9

Saving and being safe in Ethiopia

***Iddir* funerary insurance as uncaptured civil society**
Its emergence, transformation, and relations with the state in Ethiopia
Alula Pankhurst 27

Informal savings and insurance associations
Advancing solidarity and key for a 'good life'
Abraham Asnake 45

Wijjo and *kochoo*
Indigenous rotating saving and cooperation institutions among Mareko and Arsi-Oromo
Yohannes Tesfaye Getachew and Zelalem Mulatu Demu 63

The activities, benefits, and challenges of Awada women's self-help groups
in empowering women in Sidama region, southern Ethiopia
Dagne Shibru Abate and Hanna Getachew Amare 71

Saving and being safe in the Ethiopian diaspora

'Wealth in people'
Equbs as forms of investment among Ethiopian immigrants in the US
Worku Nida 93

Solidarity until the end
Insurance associations (*iddir*) of Ethiopians in southern California
Sophia Thubauville 113

Islands of hope
Informal savings associations among Ethiopian Israelis and the Ethiopian-Eritrean
diaspora community in Israel
Kim Glück 127

"Trust a man after you bury him"
Trust and the status of informal saving associations among Ethiopians
in the United Arab Emirates
Kelemework Tafere Reda 153

Savings (*equb*) and insurance (*iddir*) associations of Eritreans in Germany
Sebhatleab Tewolde Kelati 167

Saving and being safe beyond Ethiopia

Spatial manifestation of self-governance groups
Addis Ababa x Nairobi
Yasmin Abdu Bushra 185

Caring for the future
Social insurances, and the notion of time and trust
Sabine Klocke-Daffa 205

Author's biographies 227

Acknowledgements

This book and some of the underlying research was funded by the DFG project "On the saf(v)e side: informal economic associations and future aspirations in the Ethiopian diaspora" (2021–2024). The DFG also funded the workshop "Saving (for) the future – Informal savings and insurance associations as future-making practices" in March 2023 in Jinka, Ethiopia, where the chapters of the book were presented and discussed as presentations. Therefore, of course, our first thanks go to the DFG for this generous support.

Further thanks go to our research partners, without whom the research could not have taken place. The project's partner institutions also played an important role here: the Universities of Jinka and Hawassa in Ethiopia, the Africa Studies Center at UCLA, the University of California at Riverside, Ono College in Israel, and the University of Applied Science in Frankfurt. They have all supported the work of the project that led to this book over the last three years.

A big thank you also goes to Marius Heimer, who was the student assistant of our project. Finally, special thanks are extended to Kay Celtel for the wonderful copy-editing.

Frankfurt am Main, March 2024
Kim Glück and Sophia Thubauville

Introduction

Kim Glück and Sophia Thubauville

In recent years several anthropologists have emphasized that social anthropology could make an enormous contribution to the study of the future (Appadurai 2013; Bryant/Knight 2019; Collins 2008; Rollason 2014), and that it need not be confined to the present and past. Further calls have also been made for anthropological studies to focus more on the 'good' (Fischer 2014; Robbins 2013), rather than on the harsh dimensions of life (power, domination, inequality, and oppression), which are the subject of what Sherry Ortner (2016) calls 'dark anthropology'. One very promising way to gain new insights into these important and novel fields of anthropological research is to look at how people work towards a 'good life' and a 'good future' through informal practices of saving and insurance. These practices are particularly interesting because they are based on values of 'good life' that are shaped by the past and present but are at the same time oriented towards the future.

Even though the first studies on informal economic institutions, such as savings and insurance associations, described them as useful only for an intermediate stage of development and suspected that they would disappear as soon as developed financial institutions were available (Geertz 1962:242), such informal economic institutions seem as vibrant today as ever. While in the past informal institutions were associated with rural, poor, and female population groups that had limited access to formal financial institutions, recent research shows that these institutions are now popular with successful and urban elites, and that they have huge funds. Members of such institutions seem to be drawn from all socio-economic classes in their countries of origin, and the institutions themselves provide financial and social support in diaspora communities (Ardener 2014:3). In a recent article, Shirley Ardener – who has been following the changes and continuities of informal savings associations in Cameroon and in comparative perspective for more than four decades – foresees that they have a promising future (Ardener 2014:6). This view is also underlined by recent research and publications, especially by economists. In "Transforming Africa", Dana Redford and Grietjie Verhoef (2022) present current savings groups activities across Africa and how they contribute to financial inclusion and resilience. Another active researcher in this field is Caroline Shanaz Hossein, who describes ROSCAs (rotating savings and credit associations) as an integral part of the 'Black social economy' in the Black diaspora (Hossein 2018; Hossein et al. 2023) as well as of 'social and solidarity economics' in the Global South (Hossein/Christabell 2022).

Saving and insuring are always future-oriented activities. Ethiopia is a particularly good place to investigate savings and insurance associations as they are particularly popular there and are also widespread in its diaspora, even in countries with diversified and comprehensive formal financial institutions (Solomon Addis Getahun 2007; Getachew Mequanent 1996; Taa 2003; Salamon et al. 2009).

Ethiopia is currently in a challenging situation. Since the appointment of Abiy Ahmed as prime minister in 2018, Ethiopia has been undergoing a fundamental transformation. Abiy Ahmed has initiated a series of reforms intended to represent a paradigm shift towards greater political 'openness' (Ishiyama/Basnet 2022:1). This endeavour raised hopes that the changes initiated, would usher in a new era characterized by peace and the promotion of democratic principles in Ethiopia and the Horn of Africa in general. There was optimism that these political changes would also have a positive impact on domestic and foreign policy (e.g., in relation to the Ethiopian–Eritrean conflict). Yet, despite the positive outlook for the country's future, these changes seem to have sparked a surge in ethnic turmoil and acts of violence (ibid.). Hopes for peace and further economic growth under the current government have not been fulfilled so far. Instead, the country is economically and politically fractured following the long-running conflict in the north and other ethnic clashes in other parts of the country. In addition, due to strong population growth, unemployment is high, especially among young people (Mains 2011). To many of them migration seems to offer the hope of access to a 'good life', and certain savings associations contribute to making this step possible. Yet, Ethiopians already living in the diaspora have different ideas about a 'good life' and a 'good future', and some even dream of returning home (Chait 2011).

Saving and insuring: Towards a 'good life' and a 'good future'

In support of an anthropology that has a clear focus on the future, Marilyn Strathern argues that "peoples' actions are all the time informed by possible worlds which are not yet realized" (Strathern 2005:51). She emphasizes that anthropologists learn a lot about the future to which humans aspire and their practices of shaping the future by observing and investigating the present. Arjun Appadurai (2004) moreover suggests that anthropologists can examine the future by describing the desires of human beings. Alexandra D'Onofrio (2017:190) argues that imaginings are not only abstract products of human consciousness but are embodied and embedded in human actions today. She thus agrees with Appadurai that, by working towards their imaginary goals, "humans are future-makers and future is a cultural fact" (2013:85).

Aside from Appadurai, other scientists have also recently called for more studies on the 'good life'[1], and are establishing links between the idea of a 'good life', people's wishes and an anthropology of the future. In his article 'Beyond the Suffering Subject', Joel Robbins argues that "analysts must recognize the good as something that at least sometimes goes beyond what is given, what is already taken for granted there in social life and the world in which social life unfolds" (2013:457). He continues to call on anthropologists to include human desires in their reports. In his monograph on the 'good life', Edward Fischer (2014) stresses the importance of people's ambitions. For him, striving itself is already an important part of the 'good life'. Finally, Ortner agrees, in her article on the dominance of 'dark anthropology', that it is important to place 'good' at the centre of anthropological research. She rightly asks, "what is the point of opposing neoliberalism [which is according to her the origin of 'dark anthropology'] if we cannot imagine better ways of living and better futures?" (Ortner 2016:49).

Building on this, Rebecca Bryant and Daniel Knight bring a temporal dimension to the discussion of the 'good life'. They point to certain parameters that influence visions of the 'good life', such as anticipation, expectation, speculation, potentiality, hope and destiny. These parameters reflect different time periods (present and future) and various implications of visions of the future for our present actions. Bryant and Knight argue for a multitemporality of the present and refer to the temporal dynamics of our actions, i.e. how visions of the future or ideas of the 'good life' influence our present actions (2019:2, 15). Further, they highlight that even though orientations involve imagining, planning, and striving for the future, they can also lead to a decline or exhaustion of these aspirations. In these cases, hope can turn to indifference, ambitious planning to disappointment, and imaginative thinking to weariness (Bryant/Knight 2019:19). Bryant also says that the future awakens the present and those expectations of the future infuse our everyday life (Bryant 2020:16). Here, anticipation is more than just waiting for something to hopefully occur, as Bryant points out, it is the very active act of looking ahead, of imagining, and in that sense pulling the future into the present, which in turn becomes possible by becoming active in the present (Bryant 2020:17).

How can these new approaches to the anthropology of the future and 'good life' be combined with a focus on informal saving and insuring? Appadurai (2004) and Geeta Patel (2007) stress that saving and insurance practices – such as buying insurance, buying pensions, or paying social security contributions – are food for thought

---

1 With the 'good' we mean here something conceived rather than perceived to be good by our research participants, as represented by statements of people's imaginations of value, morality, and well-being (Robbins 2013:457). Exploring the 'good life' does not mean ignoring and overlooking all the negatives and failures involved in striving for a 'good life' (Treiber 2017:170).

when it comes to understanding people's desires, ideas, and fantasies about future life. By exploring ways to lead a successful life, the study of savings and insurance practices can also contribute to the current debate on the 'good life' (Fischer 2014) and, thus, close a known gap in future studies: as Appadurai (2013:292) argues, "studies on the future in anthropology tend to focus on utopian and millennial movements and cultural trauma, visions of the 'good life', afterlife, and just life present a gap". Studying the visions of the 'good life' in Ethiopia, its diaspora communities and beyond is a direct response to Appadurai's call.

Research on informal saving and insurance associations in Ethiopia

The focus of the first part of our collection covers savings and insurance associations within Ethiopia. Since the 1960s, Ardener (Ardener/Burman 1996; Ardener 1964; 2010; 2014) has conducted comprehensive research on informal savings and insurance associations, or so-called rotating savings and credit associations (ROSCAs), in Cameroon and in a worldwide perspective. What ROSCAs have in common is that their members meet regularly and that fixed amounts of money are collected and distributed during those meetings. The number of members varies greatly, but they usually share a common economic or social background.

Figure 1: Illustration of a Rotating Saving Group

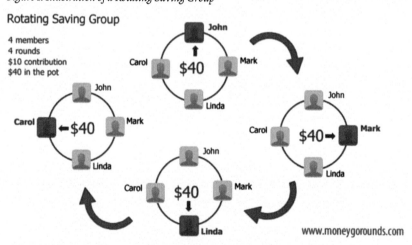

Source: https://www.collaborativefinance.org/rosca/social-saving/

Like all informal savings and insurance associations worldwide, the most common Ethiopian associations – *equbs*[2] (rotating savings associations) and *iddirs* (mutual self-help associations) – may have their origins in a system of neighbourhood assistance (Low 1999). The rotating arrangement, as in the *equb*, is found in indigenous working groups, such as those found among the Gurage (Shack 1966:80ff; Levine 1965; Nida 2007) and the Oromo (Lewis 1965). Some of the functions of the *iddir* in Ethiopia can be traced back to the *mahibers*, associations of Ethiopian Orthodox Christians who meet regularly in the homes of members for food, drink and discussion. In contrast to the indigenous associations mentioned above, however, *equb* and *iddir* practices are based on a regular distribution of money and in kind payments. Thus, it seems plausible that their emergence went hand in hand with the emergence of monetarization. Consequently, Jean Comhaire (1966) argues that the emergence of such associations in Addis Ababa, as elsewhere in Africa, took place in the 1930s and coincided with the end of traditional economic practices and trade. Other authors argue that they are products of the Italian invasion (Pankhurst/Endreas Eshete 1958), which also took place in the 1930s. Either way, the informal savings and insurance associations in Ethiopia arose in a context of monetarization and literacy that is closely linked to urbanization and that drove a need to create clearer community links and obligations (de Weerdt et al. 2007:169).

Today, these groups exist throughout Ethiopia under different names and with certain variations (Elliesie 2017). The *equb* is a classic example of a ROSCA. Associations can consist of friends, acquaintances, neighbours, relatives or colleagues (Haileleul Getahun 2001:112). Such groups exist in all income brackets, and the sums paid in and out can also vary considerably, although poor people often contribute a much higher percentage of their income to their *equb* than economically better off people (Konjit Hailu Gudeta et al. 2022; Mammo Tirfe 1999:191). Another difference between the groups concerns the disbursement of the money. Funds can either be raffled or paid out to the participant who needs them most. In most cases, the entire disbursement payment is made to one member of the group, but in some cases, part of the fund is invested in a general fund used for social services. In addition to its economic role, the association is also used as a forum for discussion and conflict resolution (Haileleul Getahun 2001:112). There are several reasons why people prefer an *equb* to formal savings options. For example, Mammo Tirfe argues that due to the strong social ties between members, delays to payments are almost unknown. The *equb* is, in addition, flexible and adaptable to the needs of its members; no adminis-

---

2   In the interest of enhancing readability, adjustments have been made to the grammatical cases and singular/plural forms of the Amharic terms *iddir* and *equb* to align them with English grammatical conventions. The Amharic singular form has been used throughout the volume and adapted to the English grammatical structure.

trative costs are incurred, there are no interest rates, and members believe that the mandatory savings lead to self-discipline (Mammo Tirfe 1999:191).

The second very common type of association in Ethiopia is the *iddir*. This type of informal insurance association is a union of people who help each other when certain well-defined events occur (de Weerdt et al. 2007:157). These associations vary greatly in size. *Iddirs* are mostly organized on the basis of a city's quarters, which are mostly mixed in Ethiopia (de Weerdt et al. 2007:165–168). They collect money from members to ensure access to a minimum level of social security, most often used to cover funeral expenses. According to Alula Pankhurst, funerals are the most important and therefore most expensive celebrations in the highlands of Ethiopia (Pankhurst 2008). The disbursement system within *iddirs* is strictly regulated. For example, Joachim de Weerdt states that *iddir* groups have drawn up statutes and contribution and payment documents (de Weerdt et al. 2007:161). In addition to the payment of expenses and the organization of funerals (*iddirs* may possess tents, large pots and other utensils needed for funeral ceremonies), some associations guarantee social security through additional loans in the event of disasters, such as house demolitions or serious illness. Another important function of *iddirs* is their engagement in community development, such as the construction of schools or roads (Desalegn Amsalu et al. 2020; Haileleul Getahun 2001:112f). *Iddirs* are very inclusive and accommodate all income levels. In Addis Ababa at least 85 per cent of households, in some parts of the city even over 90 per cent, belong to at least one *iddir* (Pankhurst 2008:176).[3]

Informal saving and insurance associations in Ethiopia's diaspora and beyond

The second part of this volume focuses on savings or insurance associations outside of Ethiopia, in its diaspora and beyond. The Ethiopian diaspora societies, internally diversified as they may be, follow and share some cultural practices in their new homelands that partly preserve and reproduce their national and/or ethnic identities. As with migration from rural to urban areas within Ethiopia, new community links are needed after migration abroad. Therefore, savings and insurance associations are also actively used in the Ethiopian diaspora.

The Ethiopian diaspora is a comparatively new phenomenon; it formed from the mid-1970s onwards. In the absence of a colonial past, the destinations of Ethiopia's migrants are shaped by a combination of factors such as geographical proximity,

---

3   The importance and prevalence of *iddir* groups in Ethiopia is also evident in the amount of scholarly literature dealing with them, which is listed in a 69-page annotated bibliography (Desalgen Amsalu et al. 2020).

migrant networks, destination country politics and other historical connections (Girmachew Adugna 2021). During the imperial period (1930–1974), emigration from Ethiopia was practically non-existent (Solomon Addis Getahun 2007:3). Only a few members of the imperial nobility, selected by the emperor himself, studied abroad in America and Europe, with the intention of bringing the education and knowledge gained there into the Ethiopian state apparatus. The situation changed in the mid-1970s when the military junta, the Derg (1974–1987), took over, upsetting the balance of power. The Derg persecuted and killed political opponents, especially members of the nobility and the former imperial political class. During this violent period of political repression, mass emigration out of Ethiopia began. Within just six years of the socialist revolution, 1,743,800 Ethiopians had fled their homes (Solomon Addis Getahun 2007:48). At the same time, the north of the country, especially the regions of Wollo, Tigray, and Northern Shoa, were hit by drought. Famine and starvation were the result. Thousands fled to neighbouring countries, such as Sudan. These political, economic, and, in the case of the Ethiopian Jewish community (also known under the self-designation Beta Israel,[4] which is translated as 'House of Israel'), religious reasons led to the increased emigration and flight of Ethiopians between the 1970s and 1990s (Fassil Demissie 2016:126–128).

Today, it is estimated that 3 million Ethiopians live abroad (Dereje Feyissa 2019). The largest Ethiopian diaspora is in the USA, with 246,000 people, followed by 155,300 in Israel, about 124,347 in Saudi Arabia and 90,000 in the United Arab Emirates (Chacko/Gebre 2017; Solomon Addis Getahun 2007). The real number of Ethiopians in the diaspora is estimated to be at least twice as high. Most Ethiopian migrants take an indirect route to the West. Ethiopians emigrated, and continue to emigrate, in waves in response to the violence or political repression of the different governments in Ethiopia, which in the past, as now, has led to clear political and social differences among migrant Ethiopians (cf. Thubauville/Glück 2024).

So far only a few publications have explored savings and insurance associations in Ethiopia's diaspora. Two articles (Salamon et al. 2009 and Getachew Mequanent 1996) and some pages of a doctoral thesis (Taa 2003) have provided the first insights into the adaptation, role, and significance of informal savings and insurance associations in the Ethiopian diaspora. Hagar Salamon et al. (2009) have described the

---

4   The use of this designation is, in the case of Ethiopian Jews, rather complex. It depends on which immigrant generation (1st, 2nd, 3rd) one belongs to, i.e., whether one was born in Ethiopia (1st generation, would most likely refer to the term Beta Israel) or in Israel as a descendant of Ethiopian Jewish parents (2nd and 3rd generation, would most likely refer to themselves as Ethiopian Israelis or Israelis). There is also the Falash Mura group, who converted from Judaism to Christianity in Ethiopia. They represent the current group of Jewish migration from Ethiopia to Israel. For further discussion of the designation process, see Glück (this volume), Kaplan (2013) and Hamilton/Benti (2007).

rotating savings associations of Ethiopian women in Israel from a gender perspective, and Getachew Mequanent (1996) and Busha Taa (2003) have focused on the role of informal savings and insurance associations in the integration of Ethiopian immigrants into the Canadian host society.

The articles in the second part of this publication want to make a new contribution to this debate. They inquire into how the practices of *equb* and *iddir* vary in the different host countries, and how they are related to ideas of 'good life' and future-making. We are particularly interested in how people in the Ethiopian diaspora imagine their future, how they envision it, what ideas and plans they have for their lives and to what extent are these influenced, adapted, and changed by the realities of life in the respective host countries.

Future orientation means planning, hoping, and imagining, that is, working towards a certain goal/end, or saving for something in our case. This goal could be the much-vaunted 'good life', which is envisioned in the host country or in a new/old home country, through second migration or by returning, dead or alive, to Ethiopia. By mapping out the different research sites in the following papers, we highlight the characteristics of *equb* and *iddir* and the extent to which they are future-oriented practices, which are driven by the search for a 'good life'.

Contributions

The initial focus of research on informal savings and insurance associations worldwide and in Ethiopia was strongly linked to their (possible) economic contribution to the strengthening or development of disadvantaged groups, such as women, the illiterate, and the 'unbanked' (i.e. poor) (Ardener/Burman 1996). Much of this research was carried out by or on behalf of non-governmental organizations, including ACORD, CANGO, DAG, and Oxfam (CANGO 2007; Fantahun Kerebo 2011; Gebre Yntiso Deko et al. 2014; Low 1999), and its focus on the economic performance of associations came about through a more general development paradigm. Much of the existing literature also refers to the historical formation, forms, and functions of informal savings and insurance associations in Ethiopia itself. Such associations are well described in Ethiopia, but studies on them in the Ethiopian diaspora are few. The contributions in this edited volume hope to broaden this literature by exploring informal savings associations outside Ethiopia and by a concern with the actions that individuals take in the present to shape their future. Although, it is rather the visions of the future, dreams of a better or different life, that shape and influence activities in the present. By hoping for something, by imagining something, one becomes active in the present. Here, we adapt Bryant's assumption that the future awakens the present (Bryant 2020:16).

To what extent are the visions of the future in turn influenced by the idea of a 'good life'? Moreover, what does safety mean in the different study locations: legal status; social network; financial independence? These and other questions are discussed as well as the question of how these very individual ideas of certainty interact with the pursuit of a 'good life'. Answering this question requires a comprehensive analysis of the various socio-political contexts of Ethiopian diaspora communities and a thorough exploration of the factors that cause feelings of uncertainty. In addition, the study will explore the complex interplay between savings and insurance practices and perceptions of safety.

All contributions to this volume were presented and discussed at the international workshop "Saving (for) the future – Informal savings and insurance associations as future-making practices" held at Jinka University, Ethiopia, in April 2023. We would like to thank the local organizers and participants and the German Research Foundation for their generous support of the workshop.

The contributions to the anthology divide into three parts: Ethiopia, its diaspora, and areas beyond. The first contribution is by Alula Pankhurst, who gives a comprehensive historical overview of the emergence of informal insurance associations, *iddirs*, in Ethiopia. He argues that *iddirs* emerged in the 20th century in the course of Ethiopia's urbanization, monetization, and increasing literacy rates. According to him, the associations have been so successful and able to spread during different political eras because they represent an uncaptured civil society, not controlled by the state.

The contributions by Abraham Asnake, Yohannes Tesfaye Getachew, and Zelalem Mulatu Demu, as well as Dagne Shibru Abate and Hanna Getachew Amare, give us an ethnographic insight into different forms of informal savings and insurance associations in southern Ethiopia.

Abraham Asnake's contribution takes us to Hawassa, the capital of the Sidaama Regional State in southern Ethiopia, and sheds light on the use of informal savings and insurance associations as a means of realizing local peoples' vision of a 'good life'. He shows the different facets of his interlocutors' notions of the 'good life' and how *equb* comes into play as an informal savings association to achieve this. He also shows the role savings associations play in migration (rural to urban and vice versa or even abroad) and how the obligations in *equbs* promote commitment and group cohesion.

Yohannes Tesfaye Getachew and Zelalem Mulatu Demu refer in their contribution to the socio-economic impact of indigenous rotating savings and cooperative associations among the Mareko and Arsi-Oromo in south-central Ethiopia. In contrast to all other contributions in this volume, the described associations do not circulate money but goods and labour and can therefore be considered forerunners of the urban associations. Participation in these cooperatives provides participants with social security, which translates into a self-determined life, especially for women, and represents an active shaping of their present life and future prospects.

In their contribution, Dagne Shibru Abate and Hanna Getachew expand the scope of informal savings systems to include self-help groups, which, while structured differently from traditional ROSCAs, share a common goal of improving the participants' lives with a future-oriented focus. The authors specifically examine the organization of Awada self-help groups in southern Ethiopia and demonstrate how these groups serve as a means of financial emancipation for women by using the pooled savings for investments, which in turn provide opportunities for empowerment.

The second part of this edited volume highlights informal savings and insurance associations in the Ethiopian diaspora, primarily the USA, the Middle East (UAE and Israel), and Europe (Germany). Worku Nida's contribution takes us to the American West Coast, more precisely to L.A. and Seattle. Nida examines how ROSCAs, especially *equbs*, serve as investment mechanisms to improve living conditions and secure future prospects. Drawing on the concept of 'wealth in people' (cf. Guyer 1993), he argues that the practice of *equb* is a means of creating multiple forms of values, i.e. material wealth (in the form of things) through saving and immaterial wealth (social networks, relationships) through the fostering of social capital.

Sophia Thubauville's contribution focuses on insurance associations, *iddirs*, in southern California. She shows that most of these institutions have been created within the last decade with the aim of providing a decent burial according to Ethiopian cultural norms in the USA. Central to the establishment of the associations is the solidarity from below that people extend to each other. However, as the article shows this solidarity has its limits, which are continuously negotiated and which should help to make these institutions sustainable and attractive for future generations of Ethiopians in the USA.

In her contribution, Kim Glück shows the practice of *equb* in Israel, looking at both the Ethiopian-Jewish community as well as the Ethiopian–Eritrean migrant community. Despite their different socio-political positions, as Israeli citizens or asylum seekers, both groups use informal savings systems and adapt them to their everyday lives and challenges in Israel. She shows that it is above all the hope for a better life, the understanding of which she critically scrutinizes, that keeps *equbs* thriving in Israel.

Kelemework Tafere's contribution sheds light on the situation of Ethiopian migrant workers in the cosmopolitan city of Dubai in the United Arab Emirates. Here, between precarious working conditions and insecure residence permits, the formation of and activity in informal savings associations proves to provide a necessary social network that goes far beyond the financial opportunities opened up by *equb* savings. Trust (in the *equb*, in the social network, in people, and in oneself) is shown to be the main factor that strengthens solidarity among migrants and improves their living situation.

The third part of our edited volume looks at examples beyond Ethiopia and its diaspora. Yasmin Bushra's contribution examines self-governed community organizations in urban areas. She looks at *iddirs* in Addis Ababa and neighbourhood associations in Nairobi and describes how the rapid growth of urban spaces and the extent to which the state or public institutions are unable to meet the demands of the steadily increasing urban population encourages the activity of self-managed community organizations. *Iddir* groups in Addis Ababa and neighbourhood associations in Nairobi are able to compensate for the state deficit, partly by working with state institutions and by shaping urban space on their own initiative and according to their needs.

Informal insurance systems are common in diaspora communities and are often the preferred and familiar future-oriented practices, as the contributions in this edited volume show. However, at the same time, market-oriented and formal insurance companies are on the rise in African countries. Adapted to regional and especially socio-cultural conditions, insurance companies enjoy great popularity especially in the southern African countries of South Africa, Botswana, and Namibia. Sabine Klocke-Daffa's contribution expands the regional and thematic scope of this edited volume and explores this social insurance industry in Southern Africa, especially in Namibia. She analyses the reasons for the emergence of life insurance, sheds light on their rapid rise and outlines the different socio-economic and temporal facets associated with caring for the afterlife.

Figures

Figure 1: Illustration of a Rotating Saving Group

Bibliography

Appadurai, Arjun (2004): "The Capacity to Aspire. Culture and the Term of Recognition." In: Vijayendra Rao/Michael Walton (eds.), *Culture and Public Action. A Cross-Disciplinary Dialogue on Development Policy*, Palo Alto: Stanford University Press, pp. 59–83.

Appadurai, Arjun (2013): *The Future as a Cultural Fact. Essays on the Global Condition*, London, New York: Verso.

Ardener, Shirley (1964): "The Comparative Study of Rotating Credit Associations." *Journal of the Royal Anthropological Institute* 94/2, pp. 201–229.

Ardener, Shirley (2010): "Microcredit, Money Transfers, Women, and the Cameroon Diaspora." *Afrika Focus* 23/2, pp. 11–24.

Ardener, Shirley (2014): "Credit Unions and Money Clubs (ROSCAs)." *Anthropology Today* 30/4, pp. 3–6.

Ardener, Shirley/Burman, Sandra (1996): *Money-Go-Rounds. The Importance of Rotating Savings and Credit Associations for Women*, Oxford: Berg.

Bryant, Rebecca (2020): "The Anthropology of the Future." *Ethnofoor* 32/1, pp. 11–22.

Bryant, Rebecca/Knight, Daniel M. (2019): "Hope". In: Rebecca Bryant/Daniel M. Knight (eds.), *The Anthropology of the Future*, Cambridge: Cambridge University Press, pp. 132–157.

CANGO (2007): "Ethiopia. The Path to Self-Resiliency." Accessed August, 9, 2023, (https://reliefweb.int/sites/reliefweb.int/files/resources/8223B0899505C 62685257340007158C4-Full_Report.pdf).

Chacko, Elizabeth/Gebre, Peter H. (2017): "Engaging the Ethiopian Diaspora. Policies, Practices and Performance." In: Jack Mangala (ed.), *Africa and its Global Diaspora*, London: Palgrave Macmillan, pp. 219–249.

Chait, Sandra M. (2011): *Seeking Salaam. Ethiopians, Eritreans, and Somalis in the Pacific Northwest*, Seattle: University of Washington Press.

Collins, Samuel Gerald (2008): *All Tomorrow's Cultures. Anthropological Engagements with the Future*, New York, Oxford: Berghahn.

Comhaire, Jean (1966): "Wage Pooling as a Form of Voluntary Association in Ethiopian and Other African towns." In: Institute of Ethiopian Studies (ed.), *Proceedings of the Third International Conference of Ethiopian Studies* III, Institute of Ethiopian Studies: Addis Ababa, pp. 44–47.

Dereje Feyissa (2019): "Ethiopia Brief." Accessed August 11, 2023, (https://www.mid eq.org/en/resources-index-page/ethiopia-brief/).

Desalegn Amsalu/Bisaillon, Laura/Yordanos Tiruneh (2020): "'I Have Risen from the Place I Always Used to be': An Annotated Bibliography of the Ethiopian Iddir." Accessed August 11, 2023, (https://papers.ssrn.com/sol3/papers.cfm?abstract_i d=3662537).

D'Onofrio, Alexandra (2017): "Reaching for The Horizon. Exploring Essential Possibilities of Migration And Movement Within Past–Present–Future and Through Participatory Animation." In: Juan Francisco Salazar et al. (eds.), *Anthropologies and Futures. Researching Emerging and Uncertain Worlds*, London: Bloomsbury, pp. 198–207.

Elliesie, Hatem (2017): "Traditional Forms of Social Protection in Africa: Selected Examples from Ethiopian and Eritrean Societies." *Recht in Afrika* 20, pp. 58–73.

Fantahun Kerebo for ACORD (2011): *Iddirs Beyond Funeral*, Film, 21:54 minutes.

Fassil Demissie (2016): "Living Across Worlds and Oceans – An Introduction." *African and Black Diaspora: An International Journal* 9/2, pp. 125–133

Fischer, Edward F. (2014): *The Good Life. Aspiration, Dignity, and the Anthropology of Well-Being*, Stanford, California: Stanford University Press.

Gebre Yntiso Deko/Dagne Shibiru/Temesgen Chibsa (2014): "Self-Help Groups in Ethiopia: Activities, Opportunities and Constraints." Accessed August 9, 2023 (h ttp://esap2.org.et/wp-content/uploads/2014/11/Report-11_SHGs_July2014.pdf).

Geertz, Clifford (1962): "The Rotating Credit Association: A 'Middle Rung' in Development." *Economic Development and Cultural Change* 10/3, pp. 241–263.

Getachew Mequanent (1996): "The Role of Informal Organizations in Resettlement Adjustment Process: A Case Study of Iqubs, Idirs and Mahabers in the Ethiopian Community in Toronto." *Refuge* 15/3, pp. 30–38.

Girmachew Adugna (2021): "Once Primarily an Origin for Refugees, Ethiopia Experiences Evolving Migration Patterns." Migration Policy Institute. Accessed August 11, 2023 (https://www.migrationpolicy.org/article/ethiopia-origin-refugees-evolving-migration).

Guyer, Jane (1993): "Wealth in People and Self-Realization in Equatorial Africa." *Man* 28/2, pp. 243–265.

Haileleul Getahun (2001): *Assault on Rural Poverty. The Case of Ethiopia*, Lanham, New York, Oxford: University Press of America.

Hamilton, Ruth Simms/Getahun Benti (2007): "Redefining a Collective Identity in the Struggle for State and National Identity in Ethiopia and Israel. The Case of Ethiopian Jews (Beta Israel)". In: Ruth Simms Hamilton (ed.), *Routes of Passage. Rethinking the African Diaspora* Vol. 1, Part 2, East Lansing, Michigan: Michigan State University Press, pp. 135–167.

Hossein, Caroline S. (2018): *The Black Social Economy in the Americas: Exploring Diverse Community-Based Markets*, New York: Palgrave.

Hossein, Caroline S./Austin, W. S. D./Edmonds, K. (2023): *Beyond Racial Capitalism: Co-operatives in the African Diaspora*, Oxford: Oxford University Press.

Hossein, Caroline S./Christabell P. J. (2022): *Community Economies in the Global South: Case Studies of Rotating Savings and Credit Associations and Economic Cooperation*, Oxford: Oxford University Press.

Ishiyama, John/Basnet, Post (2022): "Ethnic Versus National Identity in Ethiopia. Is Ethnic Identity Growing and Among Whom?" *African Security Review* 31/5, pp. 1–17.

Kaplan, Steven (2013): "Ethiopian Immigrants in Israel. The Discourses of Intrinsic and Extrinsic Racism." In: Efrayim Sicher (ed.), *Race, Color, Identity. Rethinking Discourses About "Jews" in the Twenty-first Century*, New York; Oxford: Berghahn books, pp. 167–181.

Konjit Hailu Gudeta/Atsede Tesfaye Hailemariam/Bantie Workie Gessese (2022): "Saving Groups in Urban Ethiopia." In: Dana T. Redford/Grietjie Verhoef, *Transforming Africa. How Savings Groups Foster Financial Inclusion, Resilience and Economic Development*, Bradford: Emerald Publishing, pp. 117–133.

Levine, Donald N. (1965): *Wax and Gold. Tradition and Innovation in Ethiopian Culture*, Chicago: The University of Chicago Press.

Lewis, Herbert S. (1965): *A Galla Monarchy. Jimma Abba Jifar, Ethiopia, 1830–1932*, Madison: The University of Wisconsin Press.

Low, Alaine (1999): *A Bibliographical Survey of Rotating Savings and Credit Associations*, Oxford: Oxfam and CCCRW.

Mains, Daniel (2011): *Hope is Cut. Youth, Unemployment, and the Future in Urban Ethiopia*, Philadelphia: Temple University Press.

Mammo Tirfe (1999): *The Paradox of Africa's Poverty. The Role of Indigenous Knowledge, Traditional Practices and Local Institutions – The Case of Ethiopia*, Lawrencehill, Asmara: Red Sea Press.

Nida, Worku (2007): "African Religious Beliefs and Practices in Diaspora. An Ethnographic Observation of Activities at an Ethiopian Orthodox Christian Church in Los Angeles." In: Jacob K. Olupona/Regina Gemignani (eds.), *African Immigrant Religions in America*, New York, London: New York University Press, pp. 207–226.

Ortner, Sherry B. (2016): "Dark Anthropology and its Others. Theory Since the Eighties." *HAU: Journal of Ethnographic Theory* 6/1, pp. 47–73.

Pankhurst, Alula (2008): "The Emergence, Evolution and Transformations of Iddir Funeral Associations in Urban Ethiopia." *Journal of Ethiopian Studies* 41/1–2, pp. 143–186.

Pankhurst, Richard/Endreas Eshete (1958): "Self-Help in Ethiopia." *Ethiopia Observer* 2/1, pp. 358.

Patel, Geeta (2007): "Imagining Risk, Care and Security. Insurance and Fantasy." *Anthropological Theory* 7/1, pp. 99–118.

Redford, Dana T./Verhoef, Grietjie (2022): *Transforming Africa. How Savings Groups Foster Financial Inclusion, Resilience and Economic Development*, Bradford: Emerald Publishing.

Robbins, Joel (2013): "Beyond the Suffering Subject. Toward an Anthropology of the Good." *Journal of the Royal Anthropological Institute* 19, pp. 47–62.

Rollason, Will (2014): *Pacific Futures. Projects, Politics and Interests*, Oxford, New York: Berghahn.

Salamon, Hagar/Kaplan, Steven/Goldberg, Harvey (2009): "What Goes Around, Comes Around. Rotating Credit Associations Among Ethiopian Women in Israel". *African Identities* 7/3, pp. 399–415.

Shack, William A. (1966): *The Gurage. A People of the Ensete Culture*, London: Oxford University Press.

Solomon Addis Getahun (2007): *The History of Ethiopian Immigrants and Refugees in America, 1900–2000*, New York City: LFB Scholarly.

Strathern, Marilyn (2005): *Kinship, Law and the Unexpected: Relatives are Always a Surprise*, Cambridge: Cambridge University Press.

Taa, Busha J. (2003): *The Role of Knowledge in the Integration Experience of Ethiopian Immigrants to Toronto*, PhD thesis, University of Toronto.

Thubauville, Sophia/Glück, Kim (eds.) (forthcoming 2024): *Home and Future Making in the Ethiopian Diaspora*, Addis Ababa: Centre français des étdues éthiopiennes.

Treiber Magnus (2017): *Migration aus Eritrea. Wege, Stationen, informelles Handeln*, Berlin: Reimer.

Weerdt, Joachim de/ Dercon, Stefan/ Bold, Tessa/Pankhurst, Alula (2007): "Membership-Based Indigenous Insurance Associations in Ethiopia and Tanzania." In: Martha Chen/Renana Jhabvala/Ravi Kanbur/Carol Richards (eds.), *Membership-Based Organizations of the Poor*, London, New York: Routledge, pp. 157–176.

Saving and being safe in Ethiopia

Iddir funerary insurance as uncaptured civil society
Its emergence, transformation, and relations with the state in Ethiopia

Alula Pankhurst

Abstract *This chapter addresses the history and development of the iddir funerary insurance association and its spread and transformation in Ethiopia through several regimes from the early twentieth century till the present. This form of association is nowadays so ubiquitous throughout the country that it is commonly assumed to be an age-old institution with rural roots. However, I provide evidence that in fact it is an institution that emerged in a context of urbanization, migration, and monetization of the economy, specifically in Addis Ababa, and only gradually spread to rural areas. I further suggest that a major rationale for its increasingly rapid spread, throughout most of the country, was as a form of social capital that was organised voluntarily by individuals independently of state structures, and therefore was built on localised trust in a context of growing suspicion of state control. Whereas iddirs have at times sought to extend their roles beyond merely funerary functions to become involved in wider development activities, whenever the state has sought to organise them and interfere in their activities, they have retracted to their original burial and insurance roles.*

Introduction

The *iddir* – a funerary insurance association that has become ubiquitous throughout Ethiopia and has spread in the diaspora – is often assumed to be an ancient quintessentially Ethiopian traditional institution with deep rural roots. In this paper I argue that, in fact, *iddirs* are dynamic evolving institutions with clear parallels in other African countries and worldwide. I contend that they emerged in Addis Ababa in the early twentieth century as a result of urbanization, migration, and monetization of the economy, and only gradually spread to rural areas. There is less evidence regarding the *equbs*, which have remained more informal and share the characteristics of rotating savings and credit associations (ROSCAs) worldwide, and the origins of which in Ethiopia are discussed by Yohannes Tesfaye Getachew and Zelalem Mulatu Demu in another chapter of this book (see also Nida this volume). The major transformations seen among *iddirs* – their formalization, the writing of their rules and formulation of their statutes, their registration and functional specialization, and the development of sub-types – have all occurred in urban contexts. The involvement of *iddirs* in development activities also began in Addis Ababa and is largely limited to the capital city and other major towns.

I further argue that a major rationale and impetus for the expansion of these institutions was that they provided a form of social capital that was organized by individuals who formed voluntary associations independently of state structures. The nature of *iddirs* as uncaptured civil society was a major reason for their rapid expansion, especially in periods when the state tried to control local governance. While there have been times when these institutions have sought to become involved in wider development activities, when the state has tried to organize them and interfere in their activities, they have retracted and limited themselves to their burial and insurance roles.

Institutions with clear parallels worldwide

Some authors, especially those who emphasize links with traditional rural institutions suggest that *iddirs* are uniquely Ethiopian (Dejene Aredo 1993). However, some (Alemayehu Seifu 1968; Koehn/Koehn 1975) have noted parallels in studies of West African urbanization (Little 1965; Meillassoux 1968). Similar institutions include *engozi* societies in Uganda (Walford/Olikira 1997), hometown associations in Nigerian towns (McNulty/Lawrence 1996), and voluntary levy schemes at a village level in Guinea Bissau that are traditional communal funds with which villagers organize social events (such as funerals and parties) (Chabot et al. 1991). Insurance mechanisms for funerals exist across the developing world, and rotating credit associations are likewise very common, as shown by Shirley Ardener (1964), who has also written about their transformations (2014) and their importance for women (Ardener/Burman 1995).

However, the extent to which institutions similar to *iddirs* in other African countries focus on burial, were established by migrants, and have a voluntary, formalized and lasting structure deserves further study. In any case, even if there are parallels with other countries, there is no evidence of borrowing or influence, and it would seem rather that while the processes relating to urbanization and the monetization of the economy were broadly similar in all contexts, the particular way in which *iddirs* emerged was particular to the Ethiopian context. The only example of a specific comparison between *iddirs* in Ethiopia and funeral associations in Tanzania shows that the burial societies in Ethiopia have a much longer history, greater endurance, and are made up of larger groups with great asset holdings than those in Tanzania, which are much smaller, short-lived, and without substantial assets, but which offer more insurance (Dercon et al. 2006).

Urban origins in Addis Ababa

Iddirs are such a widespread institution throughout much of Ethiopia that it is commonly assumed that they are an age-old type of association with rural origins.[1] Popular opinion and the view of most writers concur in assuming that they were built on traditional forms of cooperation existing in rural areas throughout Ethiopia.[2] While institutions and rules for burial, mutual help, and cooperation in production, distribution, and exchange are commonplace in many rural societies, there is little conclusive evidence that rural institutions are the basis for *iddir* associations. The assumption of such a connection does not consider the specific nature of these institutions, nor the differing rural and urban contexts.[3]

Iddirs are not simply funerary institutions with rules of conduct; they are voluntary associations with organizational structures, monetary contributions, and written records. Membership requires the payment of contributions and adherence to rules, non-compliance with which involves sanctions and could theoretically lead to ostracism. Likewise, *equbs* are formed by members who join voluntarily and contribute fixed sums of money at specific intervals; they have membership lists, rules about disbursement, and fines for non-compliance.

One of the most fundamental transformations that occurred within the institution of *iddir* in Addis Ababa was the collection of regular cash contributions from members prior to any death. This differentiated *iddirs* even more significantly from rural mutual help and funerary institutions, which tend to deal with death or misfortune on a case-by-case basis, with provisions in kind at the time when a death

---

1   This contribution focuses mainly on *iddirs*, for which there is more evidence about their origins, development, spread and transformations than for similar savings associations.

2   In the late imperial period, Korten expressed the view that *iddirs* were "A modern formalization of collective assistance that was practised in the traditional structure" (1972:87). He concluded that *iddirs* "basically mirror the traditional village patterns of mutual assistance and social control" (1972:88). Likewise, Fekadu Gadamu (1974) suggested that migrants "transplanted their rural local-level social structures to towns along with some modifications that added functions". Similarly, Dejene Aredo (1993) suggested that the *iddir* evolved from its precursors, i.e. from different types of mutual assistance. Likewise, Getinet Assefa concluded that "rural institutions and associations are the forefathers of urban institutions" (2000:5).

3   As Alemayehu Seifu first pointed out: "Some believe that *eder* [*iddir*] is a traditional association having a long history. But these people confuse two things: the spirit of mutual help and the type of association through which it was manifested" (1968:9).

30 Saving and being safe in Ethiopia

occurs. Another thing that distinguishes *iddirs* from other mutual help and funerary institutions is their formal and bureaucratic aspects: their use of writing and the existence of lists of members, written bylaws, regular meetings, fines for nonattendance, differentiated rules about amounts of money given to the bereaved, periodically elected executive committee members with specialized responsibilities, and equipment held by the group. This gives *iddirs* a corporate or group identity as an organization that goes beyond institutional customary funerary rules. These characteristics suggest that *iddirs* are unlikely to have emerged outside a context of urbanization, monetization, literacy, and possibly also a context of formalization related to notions of modernization. While *equbs* are less formalized and have an almost purely savings role, the use, collection, keeping and distribution of money and the keeping of records of members contributions mean that the development of this institution may well also linked to monetization of the economy.

The few writers who have argued that *iddirs* are essentially an urban phenomenon have tended to link their emergence with the Italian occupation period.[4] Urbanization, demand for labour resulting in a rapid increase in the number of migrants, as well as the disruptions and periods of fighting during the occupation no doubt increased the need for better organization of burials, and created conditions that were conducive to the expansion of the number of *iddirs*. However, there is evidence that at least a few *iddirs* existed in Addis Ababa prior to the occupation. A census of 4000 *iddirs* in Addis Ababa in 2001 found 21 established before the occupation (Tenagne Tadesse 2002), while a survey of 303 *iddirs* found eight that existed before 1935 (Pankhurst et al. 2008). For example, the Hibret Minch *iddir* produced a pamphlet stating that its history went back to 1907 and was established by Soddo Kistane hideworkers, who became migrant traders in Addis Ababa and needed to bury their dead. The most conclusive evidence, however, comes from the ledger book of the Nebbar Kolfe *iddir*, in which the first entry of expenses records

---

4 Richard Pankhurst and Endreas Eshete suggested that the insititution of *iddir* "is said to have become important [...] at the time of the Italian occupation when life became disorganized and large numbers of people were killed leaving no relative to bury them" (1958:358). Alemayehu Seifu took the argument further, suggesting that there were no *iddirs* before the Italian occupation and that *iddirs* emerged later in the occupation. He wrote: "Many elder people maintain that there was no association such as *eder* [*iddir*] before the Italian occupation and that it came into existence only during the latter days of the occupation period" (1968:9). He argued that, because of war, rural life became difficult, and towns became more attractive, resulting in accelerated urbanization, and that the new conditions facing migrants led them to create the *iddir* institution. The link with the Italian occupation was also stressed by Mekuria Bulcha (1976:361–3), who developed the arguments about both the rapid urbanization and the disruptions of the occupation period. In the reader-produced *Urbanization in Ethiopia*, Ottaway (1976:359) also notes that *iddir* "came into being in Addis Ababa, probably at the time of the Italian occupation".

the purchase of burial cloths in 1917. However, the first list of members seems to be from 1933, and the word *iddir* was apparently only first used in writing in 1941 (Pankhurst 2001:17). A review of Amharic dictionaries suggests that the term *iddir* did exist in Amharic at the end of the 19th century in the sense of 'custom', but that the idea about it being related to group decisions and sanctions only emerged in the 1920s, and that the current usage, which sees *iddirs* primarily as organizations essentially concerned with funerals, probably only emerged in the post-occupation period (Pankhurst 2010).

Single or multiethnic origins?

The question of whether the first *iddirs* were established by one ethnic group or members of several remains controversial. The earliest article on Ethiopian self-help groups suggests that *iddir* is "believed to have been first practiced among the Gurages" (Pankhurst/Endreas 1958:358). However, Alemayehu Seifu (1968) argues, albeit without providing evidence, that *iddirs* started on the basis of vicinity and that those based on occupation or 'tribe' emerged later. The suggestion of Gurage origins has been repeated by several authors. Fekadu Gadamu (1974) provides an argument based on a plausible sociological rationale of differing social structures. He suggests that migrants from non-centralized "acepaholous social and political systems" were not tied into the patronage system of the Ethiopian state and that, therefore, migrants from the south needed to form associations for burial. He argues that the polyethnicization came later, with the transition from *iddirs* based on migrants' associations related to particular ethnic groups to *iddirs* based on residential area.

The account of the Hibret Minch *iddir* lends credence to the suggestion of a Gurage origin, and even more specifically points to the Kistane craftworkers. In an interview, one elderly founding member of an *iddir* established towards the end of the occupation period, Ato Sahlemariam Desta[5] (who is not himself Gurage), suggested that it was commonly assumed at the time of the occupation that the institution was established by the Gurage. The view that the institution was introduced by Gurage migrants in Addis Ababa is also given credence in the article on *iddir* in the *Encyclopaedia Aethiopica* (Bustorf/Schaefer 2005:225). However, evidence from the Nebbar Kolfe *iddir* suggests that it was formed from the merger of two *iddir* established by two leaders – Ato Welde Aregay Belete, who was Amhara, and Ato Daba Duresa, who was Oromo. According to the *iddir*'s ledger, the merger seems to have taken place at least in 1941. An entry in 1947 refers to the formation of a

---

5   Ato Sahle Mariam who was 87 at the time of the interview (12 December 2001).

32   Saving and being safe in Ethiopia

united *iddir* in 1941, with the two leaders referred to as *shenecha* (Tesfa 2008).[6] The issue of ethnicity was seemingly not salient at the time, and the feudal structure of allegiance to important men may have been more significant in the establishment of this particular *iddir*. This evidence suggests that Fekadu Gadamu's thesis may need some modification to take account of the formation of *iddirs* on the basis of patronage in relation to respected leaders. Certainly, the Derg regime saw *iddirs* as being led and dominated by the so-called feudal elites of *balabbats* and sought to replace them with *kebele* structures. However, further research is needed to understand how principles of organization relating to ethnic identity, loyalty to leaders, and settlement within neighbourhoods were involved and were combined in the formation of the *iddir* institution. The formation of *kebele* and housing cooperations during the Derg period was a means of countering the ethnic-based *iddirs*, and the regime made attempts to insist that *iddir* be formed on a *kebele* or *ketana* (sub-*kebele*) basis. However, the *iddirs* resisted this, and formal name changes allowed many to continue much as before.

In the post-Derg period there is evidence of a resurgence of ethnicity-based *iddir*, both in terms of formerly ethnicity-based *iddir* reasserting themselves and new *iddir* being formed (Shiferaw Tesfaye 2002). This resurgence was, in part, due to the policy of decentralization based on ethnicity.

However, discussing the case of Dire Dawa, Feleke Tadele (1998) argues that *iddirs* have become increasingly polyethnic in recent years, though there is a tendency for one ethnic group to dominate any given *iddir*, as was suggested earlier by Fekadu Gadamu (1974). In 2000, a compilation from the records of the Addis Ababa City Administration Office for the Registration of Associations and Security found that 41 out of 794 *iddirs* (i.e. 5.2 per cent) were considered "ethnic" (Mesfin Bantayehu/Social Beyene 2000:18).

According to Fekadu Gadamu (1974), during the 1950s *iddirs* became ethnically mixed for three basic reasons: 1) expanding urban in-migration and increasing value of land meant that residential segregation could not be maintained; 2) social relations with members of groups other than their own became vital for migrants looking to exploit various urban resources; and 3) a "thin veneer of national culture" emerged that facilitated inter-ethnic relationships. Fekadu Gadamu showed that nine out of ten of the *iddirs* that he studied had become multiethnic. This suggests that his thesis that the institution of *iddir* became polyethnic has some merit. However, *iddirs* that maintained a largely monoethnic nature continued to exist, and

---

6   The term comes from the word for five in Oromo: "an administrative committee of five involved in cooperative cattle tending" (Tilahun Gamta 1989:518). In homicide cases, a council of five elders is selected to undertake the proceedings (Areba Abdella/ Berhanu Amenew 2008:179).

in the late 1950s and early 1960s they probably became even more important as a result of the emergence of migrant associations (*meredaja mahibers*) with an interest in raising funds for their homelands. However, legislation introduced after the attempted coup in 1966, in which leaders of the Mecha Tulema Association were allegedly involved and which resulted in suspicion of associations, prompted a move away from obvious ethnic affiliation among *iddirs*. The legislation required *iddirs* to register and to include a clause in their statutes stating that they were not based on ethnicity, religion, age or sex (Mekuria Bulcha 1976). Many of the *meredaja mahibers* reverted to or became merely burial associations and *iddirs* began to include non-involvement in politics in their statutes and to change their names from ethnic to more neutral ones; indeed, in Akaki, they were obliged to do so (Fekadu Gadamu 1974).

The expansion and transformation of *iddirs* in the 20th century

In a society where state control tended to be strong and increasingly so, the space for voluntary associations to flourish has been constrained, and relations with the state have influenced the development of institutions such as *iddirs*.

The imperial period

The accounts of two early *iddirs* from the imperial period reveal the importance of patronage of the country's leaders. The booklet recounting the history of the Hibret Minch *iddir* suggests that the sight of Gurage Kistane craftworker traders gathering to bury a dead person was viewed with suspicion, and that the blessing, support and contribution of Fitawrari Habte Giorgis was important in the establishment of the *iddir*. Likewise, it was said that the endorsement Emperor Haile Sellassie and his gift of a tent and 100 birr to a group of mourners near the palace was important in establishment of Tallaqu *iddir*, the "great *iddir*", named thus due to the Emperor's involvement (Pankhurst 2010). As there was no legal basis for benevolent associations at that time, migrant groups wishing to help their home areas in the early post-liberation era could only appeal directly to the Emperor, as the exceptional case of the Gurage road building association which asked permission of the Emperor to build a road demonstrated (Fecadu Gadamu 1972).

The 1955 Constitution provided a legal basis for the right to form associations. However, migrants' associations remained few until the 1960 Civil Code added certain provisions. Furthermore, the 1962 Labour Relations Decree and 1963 Labour Relations Proclamation concerning Professional Associations created a conducive environment for specific sections of the urban population, notably factory workers, to organize themselves and form *iddirs*. During Ethiopia's first three elections (in

1957, 1961, and 1965), there was a perceived danger that politicians might join *iddirs* for their own purposes (Fekadu Gadamu 1974). Instead, associations began to be seen as pressure groups for development, and members of parliament began to work with them on developmental issues, notably after the second elections. In 1957, the Ministry of National Community Development was established and sought to create model centres of community development in collaboration with *iddirs*.

The governmental tide turned against associations with the above-mentioned attempted coup against the Emperor in 1966. The government's response was the enactment of the 1966 Associations Registration Regulation, by which all associations had to register and obtain certificates. In addition, 27 associations, including some Muslim ones, were banned. Many *meredaja mahibers* disappeared or turned into purely burial associations, and the new legislation required associations to include a clause in their statutes stating clearly that they were open to all and that they did not engage in political activities.

Despite this setback a new phase of closer contact between state organizations and voluntary associations began in the late 1960s and early 1970s. The initiative came mainly from the Municipality of Addis Ababa (followed by those of Akaki and Nazaret), which sought to involve *iddirs* in policing and crime prevention, as well as sanitation. The Municipality also tried to organize *iddirs* on a *woreda* basis within umbrella committees, for each of the ten *woredas* of the capital, and the potential for an overall umbrella organization was being explored. In November 1972 a three-day seminar was organized for all the *iddirs* in Addis Ababa, and a proposal for a confederation of 395 *iddirs* was put forward. Addis Ababa's mayor was also to set up a commission to coordinate the activities of the *iddirs* (Fekadu Gadamu 1974). These plans did not materialize and were lost in the political turmoil at the time of the revolution. A committee was established but out of 30 members, most were government representatives from various ministries, and it would seem that they were more interested in controlling *iddirs* than in genuinely engaging with them. Observers noted that weaknesses in the collaborations between the government and *iddirs* included that the focus was mainly on what Koehn (1976) referred to as "pattern maintenance functions", in other words on areas that were conservative rather than developmental. For instance, *iddirs* were mobilized for ceremonial events such as a parade for the Emperor's 80th birthday and in demonstrations against miniskirts and student activism. The Municipality also sought to involve *iddirs* in assisting with policing and sanitation. According to Koehn and Koehn (1975) this was mainly because the leadership of the *iddirs* was conservative, belonging to the landed elite and with little education or commitment to development. Koehn (1976) suggests that the *iddirs* were largely a conservative force, which was why they were seen as appropriate partners by the imperial regime. In practice, their involvement in development activities, apart from the creating of community development centres, was relatively limited.

Fekadu Gadamu (1974) notes that the young urban, educated elites were reluctant to take part in *iddirs*, which they perceived as 'traditional'.

The Derg period

The view of *iddirs* as controlled by reactionary forces soon meant that they were at best avoided or ignored and at worst interfered with or banned. From the early days of the revolution there were conflicts of interest between the *iddirs* and the new structures – particularly the newly established *kebeles* and the housing cooperatives (Ottaway 1976) – that the revolutionary government was seeking to put in place. Established *iddir* leaders, who were members of the earlier elite were not allowed to take up leadership positions in the new structures, and conflicts over loyalties occurred. There were various ways in which the *iddirs* were either bypassed, ignored, or co-opted and exploited for government purposes. For example, *iddir* were expected to 'donate' tents and other property to the Somali war effort. Halls that belonged to *iddirs* were used by *kebeles*. More or less subtle methods of exerting control were employed, such as changing times when *iddirs* could meet (Mulunesh Tenagashaw 1973), using *iddirs* to call meetings for the *kebele*, collecting double levies and recruiting militia, and pressurizing *iddir* leaders to become members of the Workers Party. There were also attempts to form *kebele iddirs* on the grounds that the old ones were too costly, and there were attempts to zone *iddir* (Sime Tadele 1986). There was further pressure for *iddirs* not be based on ethnicity or have religious names and to be formed on the basis of the newly instituted *kebele*, territorial divisions, or even the sub-divisions into *ketena*.

Under the Derg, the *iddirs* were thus largely marginalized, and they tended to stick to or revert to their burial functions as a strategy to avoid interference by the government. However, paradoxically, the *iddir* as an organized form of institution continued to expand rapidly, notably in peri-urban areas and into the countryside. Moreover, the process of formalization, with written statutes and bylaws, electoral procedures, diversification of leadership positions, and better financial management and accounting continued apace. In the case of individual *iddirs* too, the monthly contributions showed increasing trends. It may also be suggested that with the change in generations and the far-reaching effects of the revolutionary period, notably the literacy campaigns, the leadership of *iddirs* were transformed, and a younger, more literate generation began to replace the older generation, which was perceived as a reactionary force.

The EPRDF[7] period

During the EPRDF period the government and some non-governmental organizations showed renewed interest in *iddirs* as potential vehicles for development. This was largely due to a global change in paradigm which recognized that neither state nor market forces can be the only actors in successful and sustainable development. With the regime's emphasis on ethnicity, and the promotion of ethnically based associations, *iddirs* with an underlying ethnic constituency resurfaced, and new ones were formed. In this respect, the 1990s were reminiscent of the early 1960s, when migrants' associations flourished. There was also a sense that *iddirs* might be mobilized to tackle pressing problems that required popular participation, notably the campaign against HIV/AIDS. *Iddir* representatives were invited to participate in the workshop organized by the Committee of Legal Affairs in the House of Peoples' Representatives on the draft National Law of the Ombudsman and Human Rights and on proclamation 147/1998 of the Cooperatives Regulation, organized by the Cooperatives Unit of the Addis Ababa City Government (Getinet Assefa 2000). Likewise, the establishment of a special programme for Civil Society Capacity Building, one of 14 programmes within the Ministry of Capacity Building, showed that the question of local organizations was being given increasing government attention. There was also considerable donor interest in the promotion civil society and a recognition by government of the potential for gaining access to international grants and loans for the purpose of civil society mobilization. In Addis Ababa, several zones showed an interest trying to mobilize *iddirs* to tackle pressing problems requiring popular participation, notably the campaign against AIDS. With the reorganization of the city into *Kifle ketema*, complete with Capacity Building Offices, there was further interest in establishing *Mikir bet*, councils of *iddir* reminiscent of the attempts in the early 1970s. Officials from the *Kifle ketema* established contacts with the *iddirs* and collected information in a move toward establishing such councils (Pankhurst 2004).

Some NGOs also attempted to develop partnerships with *iddirs* in a few major cities (Shiferaw Tesfaye 2002). In particular, an increasing number of NGOs have been working with *iddirs* specifically on HIV/AIDs issues. Most of the work focuses on prevention, in particular information, education and communication, though gradually there has been an increasing concern with working with people living with AIDS and AIDS orphans.

There was also a resurgence of *iddir* umbrella organizations (Getinet Assefa 2000). NGOs, notably ACORD and Concern, involved several *iddir* in joint credit and savings associations and development projects providing kindergartens, mills, etc. The Addis Ababa City Administration also sought to establish *iddir Mikir bet*.

---

7   Ethiopian People's Revolutionary Democratic Front

However, there remained a degree of distrust of government among the *iddirs*, and many of their members refused to engage in anything but funerary activities.

Recent evidence

Throughout their existence, *iddirs* have played a key role in times of hardship, and they continued to do so through the COVID pandemic of 2020–23, even if their resources have been severely constrained, and funerary celebrations sometimes limited and the food consumed reduced, sometimes just to the *nifro* boiled grain usually given to mourners when they return from the burial as they enter the compound.

Iddirs have also played a role in contexts of crisis in the absence of government, including in recent times, and also in situations of conflict. For instance, when Lalibela was besieged by the Tigray Defence Force for five months in the second half of 2021, *iddirs* formed coalitions and, along with the Ethiopian Orthodox Church, identified those most in need and helped to distribute food to them.

Growth in number, spatial diffusion, and density of *iddirs*

In the post-occupation period, the number of *iddirs* grew rapidly. The 2001 census in Addis Ababa found 954 *iddirs* formed in the 33 years of the post-occupation imperial period, representing 24 per cent of the total. A 2003 survey found that 153 *iddirs* formed before the downfall of the imperial regime in 1974, and these represented 50 per cent of the sample. According to official records there were 395 *iddirs* registered in Addis Ababa in 1970; in 1973 there were 541 (Koehn/Koehn 1975).

There was further expansion during the Derg period. The 2001 census found that 1478 *iddirs* had been established during the 17 years of Derg rule from 1974 to 1991, representing 37 per cent of the sample, whereas the 2003 survey found 70 *iddir* formed in this period, representing 23 per cent of the sample. There was an even greater increase just during the first decade of the EPRDF period from 1991 to 2001. The 2001 census found 1,464 *iddir* formed, representing 36 per cent of the total. The 2003 survey found 56 *iddir* formed during until 2003 representing 18 per cent of the sample.

Outside Addis Ababa, *iddirs* are known to have been common in other urban areas of Ethiopia in imperial times. In 1972, Akaki town was reported to have 56 *iddirs*, of which 40 were already members of a confederation (Fekadu Gadamu 1974). In Dire Dawa in 1994, there were 366 *iddirs*, representing almost 50 per cent of the households surveyed. Feleke Tadele (1998) suggested that there was a rapid increase in the number of *iddirs* in Dire Dawa just after the change of government, in part due to the lack of peace and stability.

Overall, national figures on the prevalence of *iddirs* do not exist. However, in the World Values Survey of Ethiopia carried out in 2007, 61 per cent of the sample said they were members of an *iddir*. In a study of 15 villages by the Ethiopian Rural Household Survey, *iddirs* were found in all the sites except in Tigray, and nearly 90 per cent of households reported belonging to at least one *iddir* (Dercon et al. 2008). The 2001 census of *iddir* in Addis Ababa estimated that 85 per cent of households were members (Tenagne Tadesse 2003:12). A survey carried out in 2004 for the World Bank in nine *woredas* found membership ranging from a minimum of 48 per cent to a maximum of 100 per cent. A 2005 report by the Wellbeing in Developing Countries Research Project (WeD) found that 242 households (92 per cent) out of a sample of 262 households in the Kolfe area of Addis Ababa belonged to an *iddir*.

Individuals and/or households may belong to several *iddirs*, and studies reveal that between 20 per cent and 40 per cent of households belong to more than one *iddir*, and that *iddirs* may range in size from about ten to over 600 households. The question of whether membership of *iddirs* is open to all wealth categories has been discussed from the earliest writings on the institution, although most writers do not define the wealth categories. Pankhurst and Endreas Eshete (1958:358) noted that even the very poor were not necessarily excluded, as provision was frequently made for certain members to render services, such as grave digging instead of money. Mekuria Bulcha (1973:14) suggested that membership was limited to the poor. Fekadu Gadamu (1974:78) suggested that Western educated people and members of the higher echelons of government did not join *iddirs*, though that was beginning to change. Some *iddirs* are known to exempt the very poor and very old from payments or even provide them with services without payment (Damen Haile Mariam 2001:722). Dercon et al. (2008:15) suggest that wealthier households are more likely to join *iddirs* and to join more than one *iddir* but that the differences in membership between rich and poor are not large.

The rapid and increasing expansion of *iddirs* in terms of spatial and geographical coverage and density, and the proportion of households that are members is quite remarkable. The logic that initially drove the development of *iddirs* was a response to the problems of migrants in Addis Ababa. During the occupation, disruptions – including the resettlement of Ethiopians to other parts of the town, resistance, and fighting – were seen as reasons for the upsurge in the establishment of *iddirs*. During the 1950s, the consolidation of *iddirs* was attributed by Fekadu Gadamu (1974) to the lessening of residential clustering by migrants, interest in relations with neighbours and workmates, and a "thin veneer of national urban culture". A further reason was the establishment of legislation conducive to the formation of associations from the mid-1950s, which allowed for the rapid development of *meredaja mahiber*, migrants associations seeking to promote development in the areas in which they settled. Attempts by the Ministry of National Community Development and the Municipality of Addis Ababa to mobilize *iddirs* in the early 1970s probably also promoted their expansion.

Despite the Derg's opposition to *iddirs* and the formation of state-controlled, local-level associations in the form of *kebele* and cooperatives, paradoxically *iddirs* continued to flourish and expand at an even greater rate. Arguably, this was because *iddirs* represented an 'uncaptured' space for civil society action that was not successfully controlled by the state since *iddirs* found many ways of resisting. The expansion of *iddirs* from urban to rural areas during the Derg has also been attributed to the 1985 famine, the collapse of indigenous institutions, and the experiences of rural inhabitants in urban famine shelters in northern Ethiopia (Bustorf/Schaefer 2005). Feleke Tadele (1998) has suggested that, the disruption and uncertain conditions that marked the early EPRDF period was a further reason for the expansion of *iddirs*. The rapid efflorescence of ethnically-based associations in the early years after the change of government also probably acted as a spur for the formation of *iddirs* based on ethnic identity in the early 1990s (Shiferaw Tesfaye 2002). The expansion of *iddirs* from urban to rural areas has also increased rapidly in the past decades, with *iddirs* becoming established in areas where they did not previously exist.

The WIDE longitudinal evidence

A review of the data from the Wellbeing Illbeing Dynamics in Ethiopia (WIDE) research, which compares studies of 15 villages from 1995 with situation reports from 2010–13, which include five more sites, provides some evidence for a relatively recent spread of *iddirs* from towns and from the centre of the country to the peripheries.[8] Claims made by two villages in the 1995 studies of 19th century or early 20th century origins for their *iddirs* should probably be disregarded as projections from the present into the past.[9] The claim that, in the Gurage site near the town of Imdibir,

---

[8] The evidence is difficult to interpret not just due to current projections into the past but because *iddirs* are often confused with a number of customary institutions involved in burial but offering other support in hard times, for example, when cattle die or are lost or when there is a fire, or in dispute resolution. These usually provide only food at the time death, and include the *Qire* in Wello, *Desh* in Gojjam, *Yejoka* in Gurage, *Sera* in Oromia, *Afocha* in Harerge, and various labour-sharing or pooling associations such as *Wijo* for butter (cf. Yohannes Tesfaye Getachew and Zelalem Mulatu Demu this volume), and *Mesqel* ox purchase groups, notably in Kambata and Wolayta.

[9] In the Korodegaga site in Arsi, it was suggested that *iddirs* "may have been set up during the reign of Menelik after private ownership of land was started", but the authors start by saying, "Respondents cannot remember when *iddir* were established". In the Adado site in Gedeo, in a list of dates of institutions, it was suggested that an *iddir* was established in 1918, though the profile also speaks of *iddir*-like customary institutions.

the *iddirs* were established prior to 1940 may also be questioned, though a date of around 1960 mentioned in 2010 may be more plausible.[10]

There is some evidence of *iddirs* being established during the Derg in some sites. At Amhara sites in Yetmen in Gojjam, it was noted that some were established during the Derg; and in Kormargefya in North Shewa, some were said to have been established after the 1984 famine. In Oromia sites in Oda Haro, near Bako, the oldest *iddirs* were established following the villagization of the mid-1980s; and in Oda Dawata in Arsi, separate Muslim and Christian *iddirs* were established during the Derg. There is also evidence of more recent transformation towards urban-type *iddirs*. For instance, in Shumsheha, near Lalibela (where there were traditional *qire* institutions for burial), the largest *iddir* was established in 2004 and was in the process of becoming like an urban *iddir*, with contributions of money rather than food. Similarly, in Adele Keke in Harerge, Oromia village, in 2011, *iddir* that contributed cash on death were planning to start monthly contributions like urban *iddirs*. In the two agro-pastoralist sites which were added to the study in 2003 – Luka in South Omo in the Tsemai area of the Southern Region and Gelcha in the Kerayu area of Oromia – there were still no *iddirs* in the villages in 2011, though some people living close to towns or with urban connections had joined urban *iddirs*. In Tigray, there were no *iddirs* in Geblen in 2010, though some women were trying to set one up, and only three in Harresaw in 2011, which were said to have been established "recently".

Conclusions

In this article I suggest that rather than being traditional customary institutions *iddirs* are, in fact, dynamic institutions that emerged in a context of urbanization and monetization of the economy and the expansion of literacy first in Addis Ababa in the early 20th century. I contend that their expansion over time and space, and the extent to which *iddirs* become involved in activities beyond merely funerary insurance depends largely on their relations with state institutions.

I suggest that the rapid expansion of *iddirs*, to the extent that they have become an almost ubiquitous organization even in remote areas, is in large measure due to the fact that they are grassroots institutions that are largely uncontrolled by the state in a context where state power has become increasingly prevalent and state structures have been penetrating to an increasingly localized level. *Iddirs* therefore

---

10   The 1995 profile suggests that an *iddir* was established prior to 1940, though it also mentions the *yejoka* customary institution in the next sentence as being prior to 1941. In the 2010 Situation report, it was claimed that the oldest *iddir* was 50 years old, which would suggest it was established around 1960.

represent an uncaptured form of social organization and provide a legitimate context for people to meet for funerary purposes where they can discuss political issues and mobilization. Although there has not been the scope and space to address this adequately here.

Finally, I have tried to show that *iddirs* have, at times, taken on additional roles in development issues when state institutions have been weakened, particularly during periods of transition, and in conducive environments when state institutions have reached out to involve them. However, the state's tendency towards co-option and control risks tarnishing the legitimacy of *iddirs* and has meant that they have tended to retract into their primary functions whenever this threat becomes apparent.

Bibliography

Alemayehu Seifu (1968): "Eder in Addis Ababa: A Sociological Study." *Ethiopia Observer* 12/1, pp. 8–33.

Ardener, Shirley (1964): "The Comparative Study of Rotating Credit Associations." *Man* 94/2, pp. 201–229.

Ardener, Shirley (2014): "Credit Unions and Money Clubs (ROSCAs)." *Anthropology Today* 30/4, pp. 3–6.

Ardener, Shirley/Burman, Sandra (1995): *Money-Go-Round: The Importance of ROSCAs for Women*, Oxford: Berg.

Areba Abdella/Berhanu Amenew (2008): "Customary Dispute Resolution Institutions in Oromia: The Case of Jaarsa Biyyaa." In: Alula Pankhurst/Getachew Assefa (eds.), *Grass-Roots Justice: The Contribution of Customary Dispute Resolution*, Addis Ababa: French Centre of Ethiopian Studies.

Bustorf, Dirk/Schaefer, Charles (2005): "Edder." In: S. Uhlig (ed.), *Encyclopaedia Aethiopica* vol. 2., Wiesbaden: Harrassowitz, pp. 225–227.

Chabot, Jarl/Boal, Manuel/Da Silva, Augusto (1991): "National Community Health Insurance at Village Level: The Case from Guinea Bissau". *Health Policy and Planning* 6/ 1, pp. 46–54.

Damen Haile Mariam (2001): "Traditional Insurance Mechanisms and the Choice of Health Care Providers in Ethiopia," In: D. Leonard (ed.), *Africa's Changing Markets for Human and Animal Health Services: The New Institutional Issues*, New York: Macmillan Press, pp. 40–67.

Dejene Aredo (1993): "The Iddir: A Study of an Indigenous Informal Financial Institution in Ethiopia." *Savings and Development* 17/1, pp. 7–90.

Dercon, Stefan/De Weerdt, Joachim/Bold, Tessa/Pankhurst, Alula (2006): "Group-Based Funeral Insurance in Ethiopia and Tanzania." *World Development* 34/4, pp. 685–703.

Dercon, Stefan/Hoddinott, John/Krishnan, Pramila/Woldehanna, Tassew (2008): *Collective Action and Vulnerability: Burial Societies in Rural Ethiopia. Collective Action and Property Rights (CAPRI)*. Working Paper no. 83. International Food Policy Research Institute.

Fecadu Gadamu (1972): *Ethnic Associations in Ethiopia and the Maintenance of Urban/ Rural Relationships, with Special Reference to the Alemgana-Walamo Road Construction Association*. Ph.D. thesis, University of London.

Fekadu Gadamu (1974): "Urbanization, Polyethnic Group Voluntary Associations and National Integration in Ethiopia." *Ethiopian Journal of Development Research* 1, pp. 71–80

Feleke Tadele (1998): *Iddirs in Urban Areas: Retrospect and Prospects*. Paper Presented at the Workshop on the Role of Indigenous Associations and Institutions in Development. Ethiopian Society of Sociologists, Social Workers and Anthropologists, Addis Ababa 25–26 June 1998.

Getinet Assefa (2000): *Report of Research on CBO's Umbrella Organization*, ACORD – Ethiopia, Addis Ababa CBO's Support Programme.

Koehn, Eftychia/Koehn, Peter (1975): "Eder as a Vehicle for Urban Development in Addis Ababa." In H. Marcus (ed.), *Proceedings of the First United States Conference of Ethiopian Studies*, East Lansing: African Studies Center, Michigan State University, pp. 399–426.

Koehn, Peter (1976): "Edir and Community Development." In: Marina Ottaway (ed.), *Urbanization in Ethiopia. A Text with Integrated Readings, Department of Sociology and Anthropology*, Addis Ababa University.

Korten, David (1972): *Planned Change in a Traditional Society: Psychological Problems of Modernization in Ethiopia*, New York: Praeger.

Little, Kenneth (1965): *West African Urbanization: A Study of Voluntary Associations in Change*, Cambridge: Cambridge University Press.

McNulty, M./Lawrence, M. (1996): "Hometown Associations: Balancing Local and Extra Local Interests in Nigerian Communities." In: M. Blunt/P. Warren (eds.), *Indigenous Organizations and Development*, London: Intermediate Technology, pp. 21–42.

Meillassoux, Claude (1968): *Urbanization of an African Community: Voluntary Associations in Bamako*, Seattle: University of Washington Press.

Mekuria Bulcha (1973): *Eder: Its Role in Development and Social Change in Addis Ababa*, Senior Essay in Sociology and Anthropology, Addis Ababa University.

Mekuria Bulcha (1976): "The Social and Historical Background of Edir." In: Marina Ottaway (ed.), *Urbanization in Ethiopia. A Text with Integrated Readings*, Department of Sociology and Anthropology, Addis Ababa University.

Mesfin Bantayehu/Social Beyene (2000): *A Preliminary Study on Iddir Institution in Addis Ababa, Final Report*, City Government of Addis Ababa, Addis Ababa.

Mulunesh Tenagashaw (1973): *A Study of the Changing Role of Entoto Woreda Eddir Associations*, Senior Essay in Applied Sociology, Addis Ababa University.

Ottaway, Marina (ed.) (1976): *Urbanization in Ethiopia: A Text with Integrated Readings*, Department of Sociology and Anthropology, Addis Ababa University.

Pankhurst, Alula (2004): *Building Civil Society Capacity: A Review of Care's Partnership with Tesfa Social and Development Association in the Light of Past Experiences and Current Initiatives*, Addis Ababa.

Pankhurst, Alula (2010): "The Emergence, Evolution and Transformations of *Iddir* Funeral Associations in Urban Ethiopia." *Journal of Ethiopian Studies* 41/1–2, pp. 143–186.

Pankhurst, Alula/Andargatchew Tesfaye/Ayalew Gebre/Bethlehem Tekola/Habtamu Demille (2008): "Social Responses to HIV/ADIS in Addis Ababa, Ethiopia, with Reference to Commercial Sex Workers, People Living with HIV/AIDS and Community-Based Funeral Associations in Addis Ababa." In: *The HIV/AIDS Challenge in Africa, An Impact and Response Assessment: The Case of Ethiopia*, Addis Ababa: Organisation for Social Science Research in Eastern and Southern Africa.

Pankhurst, Richard/Endreas Eshete (1958): "Self-Help in Ethiopia." *Ethiopia Observer* 2/2, pp. 354–364.

Shiferaw Tesfaye (2002): *Civil Society Organizations in Poverty Alleviation, Change and Development: The Role of Iddirs in Collaboration with Government Organizations: The Cases of Akaki, Nazareth and Kolfe Area of Addis Ababa (1996–2002)*, MA Thesis, Addis Ababa University.

Sime Tadele (1986): *The Origin and Development of Iddir in Nazareth Town*, Senior Essay in Sociology, Addis Ababa University.

Tenagne Tadesse (2003): *Summary Notes on the Census and Sample Study of Iddirs in Addis Ababa*: Workshop Background Material, City Government of Addis Ababa Social and NGO Affairs Office.

Tesfa Social and Development Association (2008): Yätäsfa Demts 1st Year, no. 1 Ginbot 1994. Addis Ababa: Lesan Printing Press.

Tilahun Gamta (1989): *Oromo–English Dictionary*, Addis Ababa: Addis Ababa University Printing Press.

Walford, V./Olikira, B. (1997): *Review of the Kisiizi Hospital Society*, Ministry of Health, Uganda.

Informal savings and insurance associations
Advancing solidarity and key for a 'good life'

Abraham Asnake

Abstract *The project is interested in comprehensively scrutinizing what rotating saving and mutual self-help associations in Hawassa City have to do with the everyday lives of individuals, their future aspirations, and ideas of 'good life', how they ease migration. It also explores developments in the associations due to the interface of formal and informal savings and insurance associations. In doing so, focal weight is given to how the informal savings and insuring systems pave the way for the 'good life' and migration, and an investigation of how future aspirations are channelled with informal savings and insurance institutions. These informal associations are indigenous and known in local terminologies as equbs (rotating savings groups) and iddirs (traditional insurance associations). Both equbs and iddirs provide their members with material (money, assets, and investments) and non-material (emotionally priceless solidarity, affiliation, and support) benefits that cannot be accessed easily through formal financial and insurance institutions. Thus, they are great alternatives for individuals and communities seeking to achieve an aspired 'good life' in the future.*

Introduction

Informal associations are present in large numbers in low-income countries such as Ethiopia. A significant amount of economic and social activities are channelled through them (Anderson et al. 2003, cited in Bisrat Agegnehu 2012). In their study of the development of the Ethiopian financial sector, Aderaw Gashayie and Singh (2016) provide a definition of the term 'informal' that characterizes it as the provision of services that are not, or are only partially, regulated by law but are based on self-regulatory mechanisms. Moreover, due to the weakness of existing formal saving schemes and the prevalence of traditional support mechanisms in developing countries, informal organizations are among the most important financial institutions (Kedir/Ibrahim 2011). Rotating savings and insurance associations are widely known as informal saving and credit institutions in which individuals form a coalition for a definite period to save and loan money (Kedir Abbi/Ibrahim Gamal 2011). They are indigenous financial institutions in Africa and known by many names globally, for example, *ajo/isusu* in Nigeria, *tontines* in Francophone West African countries such as Senegal and Cameroon, *hui* in China, *muzikis* or *likelambas* in the Democratic Republic of Congo, *equb/iddir* in Ethiopia, *stokvel* in South Africa, *mukando* in Zimbabwe, *susu* in Ghana, *chama* in Kenya, *tandas* in Mexico, and *chits/kuries* in India (Lukwa et al. 2022).

In Ethiopia, rotating savings groups (*equbs*) and insurance associations (*iddirs*) are among the informal financial institutions that serve as sources of savings alongside formal financial bodies such as banks and insurance. *Iddirs* and *equbs* play a pivotal role in the people's lives though the forms and types of these institutions greatly vary across societies. *Equbs* are Rotating Savings and Credit Associations (ROSCAs) whose members make regular contributions to a revolving loan fund. They are a form of traditional cooperative in Ethiopia and are formed voluntarily (Lidetu Alemu Anjulo/Ewun Markos Madda 2019). Addisu Karafo (2017) mentions that *equb* associations display both saving and credit features, as they make loans to members at different times and are established for various purposes, such as starting or expanding business ventures, making purchases, or simply for saving.

Iddirs are another widely known type of informal financial institution and provide the means to socially insure oneself. *Iddirs* in Ethiopia are socially formed associations that were traditionally designed primarily to facilitate funeral ceremonies. They thus provide a way of showing solidarity to an individual who has lost a relative. However, over time, the purpose of *iddirs* has extended beyond burial issues (cf. Pankhurst et al. 2009; Pankhurst this volume). Dejene Aredo (2010:57) defines such associations as "a ubiquitous indigenous insurance institution (found in Ethiopia) that covers different risks such as funeral ceremonies, death of major productive assets (such as draft oxen), medical expenses, and food shortages". Hence, indigenous insurance activities constitute one of the response mechanisms, developed over time through network-based collective action arrangements, to cover individuals' specific shocks. Consequently, this study deals with the most widely known and practised financial means of ensuring survival in society, with particular emphasis on *equbs* and *iddirs*.

These financial institutions and their participants have received growing attention over the last two decades. For example, Kedir/Ibrahim (2011) have studied ROSCAs in urban Ethiopia. Their study is more concerned with the importance of *equb* as an informal saving institution mainly in urban areas and examines members' participation and volume of saving. Addisu Karafo (2017) scrutinizes the role of *equb* in financing micro and small business enterprises, and his study is confined to the Konso people from the southern part of Ethiopia. His work shows that informal financial institutions like *equbs* surpass other financial establishments and significantly back micro and small business enterprises. Similarly, Worku Zeleke (2011) considers the role of *equbs* in promoting small and medium-sized enterprises in Ethiopia. The study shows how enterprises are partially filling the gaps left by formal money lending institutions through *equb*. A Master's thesis by Bisrat Agegnehu, published in 2012, explores why people join informal financial institutions, and gives emphasis to *equbs*. A study by Lidetu Alemu Anjulo and Ewun Markos Madda (2019) reveals the various factors driving household saving participants in *equbs* by providing empirical evidence from Areka, Boditi, and Sodo, major towns in the Wolayita Zone, southern Ethiopia.

There are similar studies of *iddir* associations. A report by Léonard (2013) on agricultural projects of support to familial farming describes the characteristics and types of *iddirs* among the Kambatta and Wolayita people. A study conducted by Dejene Aredo (2010) scrutinizes the practice of *iddir* as social insurance and describes how it serves as an indigenous social security arrangement. Arega Bazezew and Wubliker Chanie's (2015) study sheds light on *iddir* and social capital in the Gende Woin town of East Gojjam in the Amhara region of Ethiopia. The study reveals the role of *iddir* associations in creating strong networks among the communities. To sum up, most of the studies on *equbs* and *iddirs* are focused on the role of these associations in individual households, their structure, members' proclivity to indigenous financial institutions, and their function in terms of funding business enterprises. However, with my research, I want to offer a new perspective on informal saving and insurance associations, presenting them as the means to design future aspirations, lead a 'good life', and ease migration from rural areas to cities. Moreover, the study scrutinizes the developments in the associations evolving from the interface between formal and informal savings and insuring associations.

Equb and *iddir* are seen as practices that not only raise money or provide security but also preserve cultural values and build social capital that can be used for advancement (Bourdieu/Wacquant 1992:119; Nida this volume). Above all, they are future-making practices. Such cultural arrangements empower individuals and societies to work towards their future goals and desired well-being by providing coping mechanisms for unpredictable and stressful life events. While doing so, they reverence both the tangible external traits and intangible internal features necessary for overall well-being and fulfilment. Therefore, informal associations such as *equbs* and *iddirs* serve as equipoise between the material (external) and non-material (internal) aspects in the pursuit of a 'good life' (i.e., a well-rounded and fulfilling life). Material well-being (incorporating necessities such as food and shelter, income, health, and security) provides the indispensable foundation for a comfortable life, whereas the non-material traits that define the 'good life' hinge heavily on aspiration and opportunity, self-respect and fairness (Fischer 2014), meaningful relationships, and belonging to a community. This perspective, which is in line with the Aristotelian ideal of a fulfilled life (*eudaimonia*), suggests that ethically virtuous actions shaped by culturally specific belief systems and values as well as robust relationships in all their forms with colleagues and the broader community contribute to the richness and depth of the human experience; in other words, they contribute to a 'good life' (Waldinger/Schulz 2023). Thus, it is seminal to recognize the interconnectedness of different life domains in comprehending greater overall well-being. Giving exclusive weight to material wealth may not guarantee fulfilment, and attention to non-material traits is indispensable for a more comprehensive and persistent sense of well-being and 'good life'. Alongside this line, this research investigates future aspirations and ideas of a 'good life' as channelled through informal savings and insurance associations.

Under the umbrella of social construction, a qualitative research design was employed and empirical evidence was collected through in-depth interviews, focus group discussions, and observations. In-depth interviews were conducted with association members, key individuals from the associations, as well as elders in Hawassa city. Focus group discussions with local community members were carried out to collect more primary data. Participant observation on the other hand was used to gather detailed data on the *equb* and *iddir* activities of the study society.

Informal savings and insurance associations

Ethiopia has rich historical traditions that reflect the unique and egalitarian nature of the society (Dobler 2011). Among these traditions, the most notable are the indigenous institutions such as *iddirs* (insurance associations) and *equbs* (saving associations), and mutual customary organizations such as *mahibers/tsïwwas* (a religious association organized by lay people), *sänbätes* (religious associations celebrated within the church compound), and *afooshas* (the insurance cooperatives of the Oromo people). These cultural heritages are available across socio-cultural contexts and function for the well-being, stability, and security of the communities. Close relationships that include family and friends are essential for individual and community resilience. Successfully overcoming challenges often depends on having supportive relationships to fall back on during difficult times. As Beardslee (1989) points out, these relationships serve as an important catalyst for personal change and form the core of a person's ability to thrive in familiar communities. They can also be understood as a notion of cultural resilience. Individuals and communities can deal with and bounce back from harsh conditions not just through personal characteristics alone, but through the support of bigger socio-cultural traits (such as institutions, values, customs, and norms) (Clauss-Ehlers 2010). Hence, in vulnerable situations, those cultural values, customs, and indigenous knowledge systems are crucial for reinforcing resilience, as they adapt and cope through the use of traditional skills and knowledge passed from generation to generation, which is also vital to the sustainability of livelihood systems (Ledesma 2014).

Iddir: indigenous life insurance

An *iddir*, which is characterized as offering group life insurance, is a large self-helping association often established among residents of the same neighbourhood, friends, and family, or workers at the same organization to raise funds that will be utilized in times of misfortune, sickness, and/or death within the group and their families. The study also revealed that *iddirs* occasionally can be embedded in religious institutions and structured as church-based self-help organizations.

Death is an inevitable but difficult part of life. The death of a loved one, whether they be an intimate friend, spouse, sibling, parent, or other kinsman, is painful. The ritual of burial bears witness to the life of the deceased or the family. The more people who attend a funeral, the more it says about the social relations and the righteous nature of the deceased or their family. Hence, *iddirs* deal with death as an integral part of life; by organizing a eulogistic funeral ceremony, they keep the memory of the deceased alive (Solomon Dejene 2007).

When members lose family members or loved ones, *iddirs* provide them with condolence money and everything necessary for the funeral service. The family or associate of the deceased is given a set amount of money from members' monthly contributions to help them cope with their grief. The amount given depends on the degree of relation or intimacy of the deceased to the family or person that is a member of the *iddir*. *Iddir* members are required to attend the funerals of those connected to members and must always be ready to offer support. The traditional association also extends its help through the provision of money and material capital at other times of emergency or major life events such as sickness, weddings, and student graduations. The structures of these traditional insurance institutions include a chairperson, secretary, moderator, treasurer, and auditor. The members of the *iddir* have the power to define the position of authority held by those leaders. The amount of each member's contribution, the number of members, and the frequency of meetings are decided at a meeting at which all members are present. The same set-up is also common in *equbs*, in which the fixed amount of money contributed regularly and the timing of meetings is decided mutually. Sometimes, when the number of deaths in a month becomes high, these five committee members will call for a general members' meeting to propose an additional contribution for the next month. At the meeting, they decide on the new increment after evaluating various scenarios.

In this informal socio-economic tradition, the responsibilities of the men and women are well defined regarding the arrangements after a death. The men are in charge of setting up tents or rooms to accommodate people, organizing chairs and related materials, looking after the arriving guests, digging burial sites, and arranging the casket. The women help with preparing food and drinks for the grieving family and arriving guests. Thus, the *iddir* guarantees that everyone is taken care of in times of need through participatory and enabling means. When there is a death, the community is kept intact and the grieving family instantly gets financial and social support (Ayele Bekerie 2003).

As far as membership is concerned, married individuals are more likely to engage in traditional financial arrangements than youths. To be regarded as fully matured people, the married members of a society are required to join an *iddir* association in their neighbourhood or surrounding area. Even if they are living in a certain locality temporarily, they must join the neighbourhood *iddir* to raise funds to be used during emergencies. As one informant, who is a member of three different *iddir* associations and treasurer in one of them, explained:

> "A person who is usually married and established in a family is eligible to be a member of a certain *iddir*. Hence, he has both the right and obligation to participate in the association. It is not dependent on age as long as one is married. An individual who is not married is indirectly thought to be a member of a certain *iddir* as his/her family is directly involved in one." (treasurer of *iddir*, Hitata Kebele, September 21, 2022: Interview)

Therefore, marriage leaves a person no option but to be included in an *iddir*. One informant, who was a teacher but is now a merchant, also outlined that, *iddir* members are often economically poor and know the value of a person in times of sorrow: "In our church, a woman who is not married and whose family is in a remote area is encouraged to join the iddir. It is not supposed for her to get married or have a child to be a member" (businesswoman, Dume Kebele, November 22, 2022: Interview). Thus, people with low financial capacity and those who are married are the ones who usually join an *iddir*. It gives them social security. During the tough times that accompany a death, it is the *iddir* members who will be there first, attending the funeral and paying a visit to the grieving family to offer condolences.

Furthermore, it was asserted by the main study participants that *iddirs* do not consider potential members on the basis of their ethnicity, belief system, class, age, or sex. Every resident of a certain community has the right to be associated with these traditional socio-economic organizations. At times, most or all of the members of an *iddir* may belong to one ethnic assembly, but it is not justifiable to label them as identity-based *iddirs*. In particular, people from minority ethnic groups might be part of an *iddir* whose members are exclusively from their ethnic group. However, this is mainly because most of the minority ethnic groups like the Kambatta, Wolayita, and Dorzes come from an area that is relatively small and homogenous. It is also common for people who move to towns from the countryside to settle in one neighbourhood and form an *iddir* (Solomon Dejene 2007).

In the study area, however, there are *iddirs* for men (*yabawora*) and for women (*yegwada*), both with their own responsibilities. As mentioned, the men facilitate the installation of the big white tent at the residence of the bereaved family, while the women prepare and endow it with household materials sufficient to provide accommodation for the *iddir* associates. Nevertheless, there is no cleavage between the men's and women's *iddirs*, and sporadically, a woman who has lost her husband can be part of the men's *iddir* and no one can remove her from this group.

Equb: indigenous saving institution

An *equb* is an association often established by individuals such as businessmen, government employees, and people who know each other in the vicinity to contribute a certain amount of money from their income to obtain funding for such things as holding a wedding, building a house, starting a micro-business, or buying furniture for one's home. Depending on the income and amount of money contributed by members of the *equb*, this informal savings institution can be practised on a small or large scale. Street retailers and market traders often form the smaller *equbs*, in which members allot 10 or 20 birrs per week. Neighbours and staff of an organization who earn a monthly income may also join and practise this type of *equb*. However, larger *equbs* are widespread among business owners who prefer this traditional means of saving money to accumulate funds through daily, weekly, or monthly deposits to the conventional financial system. Occasionally individuals with urgent emergencies are given priority when the lump-sum pay-out for members is rotated.

Equbs are not embedded in categories such as ethnic identity, religion, or other forms of boundary. However, the nature of these associations – which, according to some of the study's interlocutors, are based on trust, social obligation, and the commitment of the members, and which have various purposes, such as starting a business, saving, and purchasing expensive assets – means that they are often formed by homogenous groups. Most are structured with members that are selected from the same ethnic background, income level, occupation, or neighbourhood, usually in retail business[1] *equbs*. According to the study's informants, the identity-based nature of many *equbs* results from the issue of trust. As one study participant in Tabor sub-city stated: "The basic thing in *equb* is the issue of trust. There should be a person whom you know very well. More essentially, it is all about who is the chairperson and is that person trustworthy." Nevertheless, the selection criteria are poles apart from one *equb* to another, and most of the study's informants assumed that what matters is the grade of worthiness to be a member, which, according to Bisrat Agegnehu (2012) is assessed by the *equb* administrators. One member of an *equb* that has 12 members, each contributing 1,500 birr every week, clarified that religious, ethnic, class, and/or other social stratifications don't matter but that the capacity and willingness to take part do:

---

1   Retail business *equbs* are financial associations of individuals who own boutiques, electronics shops, shoe shops, bookshops, supermarkets, butchers, laundries, etc.

> "Participation is possible for all as long as one has the capacity and willingness to make a regular saving contribution. Therefore, issues like religion and ethnic affiliation don't matter. For instance, I have a weekly *equb* based on my capacity and income, which determines the type of saving I choose to participate in. Though we are from the same area, we don't belong to identical religions, ethnic affiliations, income, sex, or age." (businesswoman, Hawassa, September 24, 2022: Interview)

A statement from the focus group discussion (FGD) participants confirms the egalitarian nature of *equb*: "Everyone is allowed to participate in those indigenous institutions of the society; male, female, old, young, the poor, or the rich. They are all-inclusive and people from different backgrounds participate in them" (FGD with *equb* members, Mehal Sub-city, Hawassa, September 20, 2022). Accordingly, Ayele Bekerie (2003) claims that both *equb* and *iddir* associations are national phenomena that are embraced by society across linguistic, religious, and ethnic lines. For example, Muslims can participate in *iddir* or *equb*, although Christians form the majority of members. In summary, the fundamental requirements when a person asks to join an *iddir* or *equb* as a new member are trust and their capacity to save.

In terms of the gender of members who participate in *equbs*, male participation is higher. Membership of *equb* groups is not a way for men to hide money or assets from their wives. Rather, they inform their partners and consult with them before joining an *equb* group. The money saved by the husband via *equb* is not spent for personal purposes, but for the joint household. Furthermore, several research participants maintained that women up to the age of 30 are highly involved in *equb* savings, but when they get married, their participation usually declines as they take on the responsibility of caring for children.

Membership of *equbs* is also not determined by age as it is determined by economic status and capacity. There are some merchants who have saved via *equbs* from a young age, for example. Retired people often do not have *equbs*/savings. Yet the study suggests that there is a significant difference in the level of participation in *iddirs* between old and young household heads. Membership in *iddirs* upsurges with the increasing age of household heads (Arega Bazezew/Wubliker Chanie 2015; Pankhurst et al. 2009).

Informal institutions: future-making and dreams of migration

In a context of anxiety about the unknowable future, the identity of self (individual or communal based) is to a significant degree future-oriented, shaped by a desire to understand or give meaning to the future. This meaningful future equates to a conception of a 'good life' that is rational and worth living (Korosteleva/Petrova

2022). People in different cultures have diverse notions about what constitutes a 'good life' (Wilk 1999), but social expectations, values, and norms regarding well-being, relationships, and personal fulfilment play a seminal role. Thus, people's views of well-being across cultures cannot simply be reduced to material conditions (Fischer 2014).

The imagined meaningful future is persistent manifested in peoples' lives when they plan, dream, and aspire for an affluent livelihood or a 'good life.' Furthermore, anticipation, preparation, and hope are also key to turning complexity from a liability into an asset. Yet few have thought about the anticipatory systems and processes that not only surround us but are also critical ingredients of actions everyone takes constantly (Miller et al. 2018). Anticipatory actions signify the proceedings activated before emergencies to mitigate the impending effects of crises, prevent them altogether, and build communal resilience (Levine et al. 2020).

Participation in the indigenous voluntary self-help associations of *iddir* and *equb* is a future-oriented anticipatory action that seeks to activate and restore the competence of community pliability and foster hope and security in the face of uncertainty. The practice of *equb*, which provides a group savings structure for households, empowers members of society to utilize financial resources efficiently and intelligently for the construction of rational visions and dreams of the future, and to attain long-term economic stability/sustainability. Cooperation in such indigenous financial institutions is voluntary, but it is sustained by reciprocal altruism, trust, congruence between benefit allocations, and collective and adaptive rules (rule-making processes are participatory and responsive to changing contexts and needs) (Arana/Wittek 2016). The study found that people do not lose if they have *equb* savings, and that this is a key mechanism in encouraging and motivating them to work hard and have attainable dreams. Those who refuse to join an *equb*, on the contrary, become sluggish in their occupation and lack the ingredient needed to bounce back from setbacks. One female informant, who owns a coffee shop, asserted that "*equb* is a means of meeting future aspirations leading one to achieve well-being in life. For example, if I plan to purchase a Bajaj taxi, there is a weekly *equb* I know in which members' contributions are around 3000 birr; the final pot is 200,000 birr. Thus, thinking of buying that Bajaj and saving for that purpose is a huge step forward for a successful outcome" (businessperson, Hawassa, September 19, 2022: Interview). Therefore, *equb* is a stimulating cultural practice that is characterized by trust and solidarity; it enhances saving traditions and encourages people to use their time and money wisely. This contributes to the realization of a 'good life' and affluence.

Ideas about a stabilized future operate on a collective level, and communities possess features like those of individual human beings such as collective consciousness' as well as cognitive and emotional desires (Wendt 1999, 2003 cited in Berenskoetter 2011). Correspondingly, *equb* and *iddir* associations have mutual future aspirations (such as offering all-inclusive medical benefit funds and creating employment opportunities or income-generating activities for poorer members), which martial and motivate the group toward a better tomorrow. For this purpose, many indigenous saving and insurance institutions are shifting a certain amount of their monthly contributions into other forms of investment, such as buying share-holds and securing assets such as land to fund and enhance sustainable individual, neighbourhood, and communal resilience.

Beyond the material benefits they extract from being a member of an *iddir* or *equb*, members are also entitled to emotionally priceless, non-material benefits and values. Aspiring for the future 'good life' envisioned through these two informal as-sociations provides individuals with hope for future investments and secure assets that are hard to attain through individual effort. In addition, the solidarity offered by members 'in times of adversity is considered as a support system, preventing one from feeling alone through life's unhappy moments. Similarly, in joyful times – a wedding, a baby's birth, graduation, and other traditional events – members can be counted on to share in the celebrations. The non-material gains are thus deep and meaningful, and at the heart of individuals and communities. This was observable in the interviews when, at various times, informants showed their delight in their faces as they explained, expressing their motivation, what their tomorrow holds and what awaits them. This shows how the material benefits and the non-material gains complement each another.

Income, wealth, and material resources are imperative to one's ability to achieve a 'good life', but alone they are not enough. The idea of a 'good life' is something very individual (Fischer 2014). A person may live in an affluent community and still ex-press an experience of abject poverty. Likewise, a person may express a high quality of life despite living in profound poverty. It is therefore important to understand in-dividual's and communities' internal ideas of 'good life' rather than to deduce what it might be based on what society defines objectively as a good quality of life (Gbiri/ Akinpelu 2010).

Future-making and migration are two sides of the same coin, and the latter involves not merely physical relocation but often a movement from one framework of knowledge to another. The decision to migrate is often based on the recognition of imminent threats at the present location or better opportunities elsewhere. Hence, migrants do not leave their regions or countries with blank slates, nor do they flow in certain directions without some knowledge to guide their journeys (Taa 2003). Members of the household who prefer to migrate are responsible for supporting families and friends at home as well as improving their future lives (McLeman/Gemenne 2018). To help fulfil these commitments, migrants regularly form self-help associations such as *equbs* and *iddirs* with fellow migrants. Feleke Tadele et al. (2006) have also shown that internal migrants often form *iddir* and *equb* institutions with fellow migrants in the urban areas where they live. If a relative living in the countryside encounters adversity, the expatriated friends and/or family affiliates are expected to send money and material support back home. While the expressed purpose of *equbs* and *iddirs* is to provide financial and mutual assistance to members in times of adversity, they also serve to maintain links between migrants and the rural communities from which they come. Furthermore, success in gaining employment for most migrants lies in the support that they obtain from their networks of *iddir* and *equb* members, kin, and ethnic affiliates already established in the host country (ibid.).

As well as promoting migration to relatives back home, friends/ethnic affiliates and/or members of *iddir* and *equb* networks may also serve to deter migration. As the study findings demonstrate, this is oftentimes done by transporting destitute migrants back to their families and by enhancing the transfer of funds and material benefits to the natal homes. Hence, there are times in which the customary associations play a role in combating rural–urban and urban–urban migration by showing solidarity to members and directing money to poorer households. Solidarity involves mutual support within a group. Therefore, support measures such as the transfer of money to poorer households are essential to reduce internal migration. FGD participants from Wukro Kebele *iddir* affirmed this: "In 2021 their insurance association was able to help a couple of individuals to repatriate to their homeland by providing them money for transportation and other essential expenses" (FGD with *iddir* members, Mehal Sub-city, Hawassa, September 20, 2020).

Informal vis-à-vis formal savings institutions

Informal financial institutions play a complementary role to the formal financial system by serving the lower end of the market (people with lower income levels or budget constraints) (Ayyagari et al. 2008:2). Hence, regardless of the increasing numbers of banks, bank branches, and insurance companies, especially in urban areas, the informal (*iddir* and *equb*) mutual cooperatives are still functioning simultaneously with the formal financial institutions of the country (Lidetu Alemu Anjulo/Ewun Markos Madda 2019). The reasons why these mutual cooperatives survive are, in part, because they have developed, operating in new ways and offering new options beyond their conventional purpose. For example, many now offer the flexibility[2] of a payment from the pot if a member encounters an urgent issue and can present a witness; many have modernized to take advantage of mobile

---

2   This complements the more rigid structures of the formal institutions.

56 Saving and being safe in Ethiopia

banking[3], to make payments easier for their members; and some are planning to provide medical benefit funds and employment opportunities.

Moreover, contemporary *iddir*[4] and *equb* associations have become progressive and are acclimatizing to the banking industry and its comprehensive procedures such as deposit facilities, loans and advances, and transfers. For example, earlier participants of the customary insurance and saving organizations used to save cash collected from members in a traditional box at home. But, following the emergence of private banks, which have enhanced the convenience and outreach of the formal banking system, these organizations now keep their money in bank accounts and have the facility to make payments by cheque. This has given these traditional associations access to special interest benefits (with a rate from 7–10 per cent) and ensures their money is in a safe place. Banks also benefit from such arrangements: an informant from NIB bank told me, they mobilize part of the deposits for loan purposes (i.e., offering short- and long-term loans to importers, wholesale traders, and regional governments) and to create multiple accounts. In addition, *equbs* and *iddirs* linked to the banking system are viewed as more formal and thus trustworthy as banks have mechanisms in place to prevent or mitigate any problems. There is thus mutually productive and interdependent collaboration between traditional self-help institutions and formal financial agencies.[5] They work together in a coordinated and symbiotic manner to maintain the essentials of individuals and the broader society. Bank accounts opened in *iddirs*' and *equbs*' names are common in the

---

3   The same informant claimed: "I have a fear that introducing mobile banking has a chance of minimizing the social interaction and strong social bonds we brought this far. This could be one of the drawbacks of mobile banking and adopting modern platforms like Telegram [a messaging app]. Similarly, members who lack smart phones are not able to access information shared through Telegram. Physical interaction and gathering are grounds for information exchange, societal discussion, and conversations" (public relation officer of an *iddir*, Mehal Sub-city: Hawassa, November 22, 2022: Interview).

4   According to Léonard's (2013) report on rural *iddir* cooperatives of the Kambatta and Wolaita, the majority of community-based *iddirs* he observed do not have a bank account in their names. Bank accounts per se are seen as a burden (they are far from villages, taking time and money to reach). It seems also that *iddir* members in rural areas do not completely trust the bank system (Léonard 2013).

5   Banks optimise their income by working directly with the *equb* and *iddir* associations. Authorised bank representatives attend *equb* and *iddir* meetings. This practice encourages the establishment of multiple savings accounts with increased liquidity. For example, in an *equb* where 3 million birr is collected weekly with each member depositing 25,000 birr, the person receiving the *equb* kitty is expected to deposit a portion of it (usually between 20,000 and 30,000 birr) into their bank account. This strategy allows banks to capitalise on the increase in savings deposits and liquidity. Given these links to *equbs* and *iddirs*, banks are strategically positioning themselves in places where they can capitalise on these financial transactions. By capitalising on profitable relationships with these associations, banks facilitate various forms of lending.

study area. This integration, when done correctly and with proper oversight, helps bridge the gap between the underserved population and the formal sector, offering broader financial opportunities, inclusion, and security to participants and the community (Temesgen Teshome 2008:63).

Continuity and changing trends among *iddirs* and *equbs*

The indigenous institutions of saving and insurance continue to exist within a societal context of disruptive politics, alarming inflation, unemployment, and lack of income among the society. Indeed, according to members, both *equbs* and *iddirs* have received growing attention (growing number of members) over the years, and they believe this will persist in the future. Nothing can affect the good reputation of these two indigenous socio-economic institutions. The practice of *iddir* in particular is vital for the order and cohesiveness of the society, as it strengthens social interaction and solidarity among members regardless of any differences.

The secretary and chairperson of Wukro and the surrounding area's cooperative *iddir* outlined that their association was established in 1973 by between five and seven individuals with a contribution amount of 0.50 cents. Over time, the service, trustworthiness, and capacity (both in terms of money and assets) of the *iddir* attracted more people to join; currently, the *iddir* has about 1200 members, including females. In a context of inflation increasing the cost of living, and in a developing country, in which funeral expenditure represents a high proportion of households' monthly income (Dercon et al. 2007), it is economically wise to be a member of such indigenous insurance associations. Moreover, as we have seen, membership of an *iddir* provides comfort and support during difficult times.

Iddirs also provide opportunities for members to meet and discuss non-financial issues, such as crime prevention, village-level security issues, community sanitation (cf. Yasmin Abdu Bushra this volume), development, and combating harmful traditional practices, such as *selist* (third-day mourning), *hawilt sera* (tomb or monument building), *yehazen cherk* (wearing of black cloth), *yehazen mels digis* (feast after burial) and *teskar* (commemoration feast) (Arega Bazezew/Wubliker Chanie 2015). Members also help protect their surrounding locality from various security threats by involving themselves as community guards in consultation with *kebele* administrators. There are even times when meetings are arranged with *iddir* members to discuss political matters and development activities with local government administrative bodies (*kebele* officials). Governmental institutions may communicate with *iddir* members when they require their cooperation on national issues. In relation to this, participants at the FGDs and key informants noted that during the Derg and EPRDF (which came to power after the fall of the Derg in 1991) regimes, *iddirs* were involved in the political affairs of the government and played a substantial role during the country's civil war, fought between the Ethiopian military dictatorship (Derg) and the northern anti-government rebels (TPLF and EPLF) as well as in the war between the EPRDF and the current state of Eritrea (1998–2000). They supplied materials such as tents to the national military and provided a portion of their capital to the regimes as a form of subsidy. Though most *iddirs* later retreated to focus only on burial activities, the Derg period witnessed the spread of *iddirs* throughout rural Ethiopia, while the size of some urban-based *iddirs* increased significantly. The EPRDF government has also been interested in working with *iddir* associations, most notably on anti-HIV/AIDS campaigns and spreading modern agricultural activities (Dercon et al. 2007). The research participants explained that the prominence of *iddir* in society's well-being will persist despite several contemporary challenges.

As mentioned, today's *iddirs* are extending their scope beyond their conventional purposes by organizing a mobile banking system[6] and planning, though it is not yet practical, to provide medical benefits funds and create employment opportunities and income-generating activities. Thus, associates of the Tabor and Wukro neighbourhood *iddirs* assert that these transformations meant that their associations are a different form than the traditionally known concept of *iddir* and that this is reflected in both the increasing provision of multiple services and the involvement of *iddirs* in community development programs. For instance, the Wukro neighbourhood *iddir* has developed a project proposal in consultation with government officials to create container shops in front of Hawassa University. It is hoped that these containers will provide a place where those members without an income can launch small enterprises. The *iddir* will also provide them with start-up loans from its capital. A limited number of insurance associations have also been able to buy restaurants and run them as a side business to provide extra income. This affirms the evolution of the practice of *iddir* as a cooperative means to reach the future-aspired 'good life'. Though the practice was initially created as an indigenous insurance system to cover after-death expenses and provide solidarity, these days, it is helping living members and their families attain their desires in life.

Traditionally, *equb* associations were very important in helping businesses develop and grow, as the savings one earned was a substantial amount of money. However, this is not the case currently. Given the contemporary socio-economic situation of the country and the extended saving cycle, coupled with the purchasing power of Ethiopian birr dropping over time, saving through *equb* associations is becoming

---

6   The same informant claims, "I have a fear that introducing mobile banking has a chance of minimizing the social interaction and strong social bonds we brought this far. This could be one of the drawbacks of mobile banking and adopting modern platforms akin to telegram. Similarly, members who lack smart phone are not able to access information shared through telegram. Physical interaction and gathering are grounds for information exchange, societal discussion and conversations."

worthless, at least, according to one merchant and member of the Haike Dar sub-city *equb*. The duration of the savings cycle is decided depending on the number of members and what they decide on the frequency of contributions. As the cycle duration gets longer, the chance that the money is affected by inflation and the increasing cost of living increases (Bisrat Agegnehu 2012). This in turn results in the loss of a golden investment opportunity, valuable time, resources, and money (Worku Zeleke 2011:6). Thus, being the last person to collect the savings is a disadvantage, as the value of the money reduces over time.[7] This is one of the reasons why interest in *equbs* is declining. Several tradespeople reinforced this and asserted that, since 2019, *equbs* have been given less consideration because of the fragile economic and political state of Ethiopia and have been turning to banks and micro-financial institutions instead. However, this is not always the case and despite all this, the practice of *equb* persists. This persistence appears to be the result of the tiny but effective tricks that members employ to forge benefits out of their savings. This includes but is not limited to (as things are changing and unpredictable) increasing the number of shares a person has in a single *equb* association, making in-kind *equb* arrangements to cope with inflation, and reducing the number of participants in a single *equb* cycle. Hence, *equb* remains part of the work culture and is deeply entwined with the everyday lives of people. It was there in the past and persists in the present for those who are financially weak or wish to start a business and for petty traders and retailers.

Conclusion

The indigenous institutions of *iddir* and *equb* are among a variety of voluntary traditional heritages and self-support systems that are available across socio-cultural contexts and function for the well-being and stability of society in Ethiopia. Notions of well-being/'good life' are encumbered with deeply held moral valuations – the various standards behind a 'meaningful life'. Such conceptions are culturally specific and even idiosyncratic, but they share a common concern with values (what is important in life) and an orientation toward the future that is not necessarily, or at least not easily, quantifiable. The practices of *iddir* and *equb* are future-oriented and anticipatory; they seek to activate and restore the competence of community resilience and foster hope and security in the face of uncertainty. The study revealed that *iddir* and *equb* associations are also working on migration-related issues, and there are even times when they have taken part in combating internal migration by returning

---

7   The reasons members join ROSCAs are diverse and may include wanting to purchase durable goods or secure insurance (in which case, members do not necessarily want to take the pot early), and/or to avoid the question of income divisibility among relatives.

destitute migrants to their families and enhancing the transfer of funds and material benefits to the natal homes. The associations have also created a mutually productive collaboration with formal financial organizations, and they continue to persist within contemporary social, political, and economic scenarios. Compatible with these modern financial institutions and their mounting accessibility, *equbs* continue serving many to attain future careers and goals, and sustain business. Furthermore, these associations tighten interaction, affirm solidarity, and are vital for social cohesion.

Bibliography

Addisu Karafo (2017): "Role of Equb in Financing Micro and Small Business Enterprises in Konso." *Universal Journal of Accounting and Finance* 5/1, pp. 1–8.

Aderaw Gashayie/Singh, Manjit (2016): "Development of Financial Sector in Ethiopia. Literature Review." *Journal of Economics and Sustainable Development* 7/7, pp. 9–20.

Arana, Marina Montelongo/Wittek, Rafael (2016): "Community Resilience: Sustained Cooperation and Space Usage in Collective Housing." *Building Research & Information* 44/7, pp. 764–774.

Arega Bazezew/Wubliker Chanie (2015): "Iddirs as Community-Based Social Capital in the Amhara Region of Ethiopia: Case Study in Gende Woin Town of East Gojjam." *The Ethiopian Journal of Social Sciences* 1/1, pp. 1–11.

Ayele Bekerie (2003): "Iquib and Idir: Socio-Economic Traditions of the Ethiopians." *Tadias Online*. Accessed January 23, 2024, (http://www.tadias.com/v1n6/OP_2_2 003-1.html).

Ayyagari, Meghana/Demirgüç-Kunt, Asli/Maksimovic, Vojislav (2008): "Formal versus Informal Finance: Evidence from China." *The World Bank Policy Research Working Paper* 4465, pp. 1–75.

Beardslee, W. R. (1989): "The Role of Self-Understanding in Resilient Individuals: The Development of a Perspective." *American Journal of Orthopsychiatry* 59/2, pp. 266–278.

Berenskoetter, Felix (2011): "Reclaiming the Vision Thing: Constructivists as Students of the Future." *International Studies Quarterly* 55/3, pp. 647–668.

Bisrat Agegnehu (2012): "Why Do Members Join Indigenous Informal Financial Institutions – RoSCAs? Empirical Evidence from Equbs in Ethiopia." Master Thesis, Environmental Economics and Management, Uppsala: Epsilon Archive for Student Projects.

Bourdieu, Pierre/Wacquant, Loic. J. D. (1992): *An Invitation to Reflexive Sociology*, Chicago: University of Chicago Press.

Clauss-Ehlers, Caroline S. (2010): "Cultural Resilience." In: Caroline Clauss-Ehlers, *Encyclopedia of Cross-Cultural School Psychology*, Boston: Springer, pp. 324–326.

Dejene Aredo (2010): "The IDDIR: An Informal Insurance Arrangement in Ethiopia." *Savings and Development* 34, pp. 53–72.

Dercon, Stefan/De Weerdt, Joachim/Bold, Tessa/Pankhurst, Alula (2007): "Membership Based Indigenous Insurance Associations in Ethiopia and Tanzania." *QEH Working Paper Series* 126, pp. 1–21.

Dobler, Constanze (2011): *The Impact of Formal and Informal Institutions on Economic Growth: A Case Study on the MENA Region*, Frankfurt a. M.: Peter Lang International Academic Publishers.

Feleke Tadele/Pankhurst, Alula/Bevan, Philippa/Laver, Tom (2006): *Migration and Rural–Urban Linkages in Ethiopia: Cases Studies of Five Rural and Two Urban Sites*, United Kingdom: University of Bath.

Fischer, Edward (2014): *The Good Life: Aspiration, Dignity, and the Anthropology of Wellbeing*, Stanford, California: Stanford University Press.

Gbiri, Caleb/Akinpelu, Aderonke Omobonike (2010): "Relationship between Objective and Subjective Quality of Life Measures." *The Journal of Community and Health Sciences* 5/1, pp. 41–47.

Kedir, Abbi/Ibrahim, Gamal (2011): "ROSCAs in Urban Ethiopia: Are the Characteristics of the Institutions More Important than those of Members?" *Journal of Development Studies* 47/7, pp. 998–1016.

Korosteleva, Elena A./Petrova, Irina (2022): "What Makes Communities Resilient in Times of Complexity and Change?" *Cambridge Review of International Affairs* 35/2, pp. 137–157.

Ledesma, Janet (2014): "Conceptual Frameworks and Research Models on Resilience in Leadership." *SAGE Journals Home* 4/3, pp. 1–8.

Léonard, Thomas (2013): "Ethiopian Iddir Mechanisms: A Case Study in Pastoral Communities of Wolayta and Kembatta-Tembaro". Accessed March 8, 2024, (https://reseau-pratiques.org/en/ethiopian-iddir-mechanisms-case-study-pastoral-communities-wolayta-and-kembatta-tembaro/).

Levine, Simon/Wilkinson, Emily/Weingärtner Lena/ Mall, Pooja (2020): *Anticipatory Action for Livelihood Protection: A Collective Endeavor*, London: ODI.

Lidetu Alemu Anjulo/Ewun Markos Madda (2019): "Factors Affecting the Household Saving Participations on 'Equb': A Study on the Three Major Towns of Wolaita Zone, Southern Ethiopia." *Journal of Poverty, Investment and Development* 48, pp. 1–10.

Lukwa, Akim/Odunitan-Wayas, Feyisayo/Lambert, Estelle/Alaba, Funke (2022): "Can Informal Savings Groups Promote Food Security and Social, Economic and Health Transformations, Especially Among Women in Urban Sub-Saharan Africa: A Narrative Systematic Review." *Sustainability* 14, pp. 1–26.

McLeman, Robert/Gemenne, François (2018): *Routledge Handbook of Environmental Displacement and Migration*, New York: Routledge.

Miller, Riel/Poli, Roberto/Rossel, Pierre/Tuomi, Ilkka (2018): *Transforming the Future: Anticipation in the 21st Century*, New York: Routledge – UNESCO Co-Publication.

Pankhurst, Alula/Dercon, Stefan /Bold, Teresa /De Weerdt, Joachim (2009): *Group-Based Funeral Insurance in Ethiopia and Tanzania*, Oxford: University of Oxford.

Solomon Dejene (2007): "Exploring Iddir toward Developing a Contextual Theology of Ethiopia." *Selected Papers of the 16th International Conference of Ethiopian Studies*. Trondheim: Harrassowitz Verlag, Wiesbaden, 535–547.

Taa, Busha (2003): *The Role of Knowledge in the Integration Experience of Ethiopian Immigrants to Toronto*, Toronto, Canada: University of Toronto.

Temesgen Teshome (2008): *Role and Potential of 'Equb' in Ethiopia*, Addis Ababa: UNICEF Ethiopia Country Office, 63.

Waldinger, Robert/Schulz, Marc (2023): *The Good Life. Lessons from the World's Longest Scientific Study of Happiness*, London: Rider.

Wilk, Richard (1999): *Quality of Life and the Anthropological Perspective*, Bloomington, IN: Indiana University.

Worku Zeleke (2011): *The Role of the Informal Financial Sector in Promoting Small and Medium Sized Enterprises in Ethiopia*, Pretoria: Tshwane University of Technology Business School.

Wijjo and *kochoo*
Indigenous rotating saving and cooperation institutions among Mareko and Arsi-Oromo

Yohannes Tesfaye Getachew and Zelalem Mulatu Demu

Abstract *In Ethiopia, there are several types of indigenous rotating savings and cooperative associations. These indigenous associations help members to save fundamental resources like money, labour, and time. Among the inhabitants of central Ethiopia, the Mareko and the Arsi-Oromo have indigenous rotating savings and cooperative institutions known as wijjo and kochoo. Wijjo is a type of indigenous rotating savings association established by neighbouring village women, with the aim of saving milk their cattle produced daily. Kochoo is a type of men's savings and cooperation association. Farmers set up this type of association so its members can take turns taking care of the cattle. For the Mareko and the Arsi-Oromo in Adami-Tulu Gido-Kombolcha, wijjo and kochoo associations are guardians of their resources. This paper assesses the role that both institutions play in the social and economic development of the study area.*

Introduction

In the middle of the 20th century, an increasing number of reports called attention to the worldwide existence of indigenous rotating savings and credit associations (ROSCAs). In 1977 Bouman suggested that comparative analyses by several scholars revealed that rotating credit association were a worldwide phenomenon, appearing in many parts of Africa, Asia, both Americas, the Caribbean, the Middle East, and even in Early Europe.

Since the advent of urbanization and monetization in Africa, most African ROSCAs save their deposits in cash. However, ROSCAs, that save their deposits in kind and time may have been the forerunners to these cash ROSCAs and they still exist today. Among the Mareko and the Arsi-Oromo in Adami-Tulu Gido-Kombolcha in Central Ethiopia Regional State for example, there exist unique forms of indigenous rotating savings and cooperative association – *wijjo* and *kochoo* – whose members deposit their resources in kind, in time, and in labour.

Like other ROSCAs, *wijjo* and *kochoo* associations have members, coordinators, an objective, a goal, and rules and regulations. They differ in what is saved: *wijjo* concerns milk and *kochoo* manpower for herding. There is also a sex division in these associations: *wijjo* is an association of women (Jemila Adem 2014; Dinkessa Deressa Layo 2017), and *kochoo* is an association of men (according to my interlocutor F.). Similar to other groups in rural and urban Ethiopia, the Mareko and the Arsi-Oromo practise the establishment of several types of local association to serve as instruments to organize socio-economic collaborations and mutual assistance. These associations are run by the local people themselves and differ in some aspects.

Among the Mareko and the Arsi-Oromo in Adami-Tulu Gido-Kombolcha, *jigi* is the most extensive and time-consuming cooperation institution. A *jigi* is a cooperative group or work party that is called by someone who needs the help of friends and relatives with some extensive work for example, house building. Work parties are common all over Ethiopia and have been well-described in literature (cf. Donham 1979:105ff and 1985:265ff for the Maale; Gebre Yntiso 1991, 1994, 1995:78ff for the Aari; and Epple 2007:253ff for the Bashada). An important aspect of work parties is that no service in return is required. Thus, they do not have the rotating element that the associations below described have. The number of participants in a *jigi* is not constant because there is no obligation, and every one participates only to give assistance when needed. The one who summons the *jigi* prepares good food for his working guests. The main tasks of a *jigi* are harvesting, preparing arable land for cultivation, and cutting grass (for covering the roofs of traditional, conical houses) (Jemila Adem 2014; Dinkassa Deressa Layo 2017). Participants are usually between 20 and 40 years old. Even though only men participate in the field work, women play a major role by preparing food and different kinds of liquor at home (according to my interlocutors F., and G.). Thus, the institution of *jigi* plays a great role in strengthening people's cooperation and economic activity.

Among the different types of ROSCAs among the Mareko and Arsi-Oromo *wijjo* and *kochoo* are the most important and define their daily activities. Yet, the academic community has made only a few attempts to explore *wijjo* as an indigenous cooperative organization. Jemila (2014), in her MA thesis "Women and Indigenous Conflict Resolution Institutions in Oromia: Experience from Siinqee of the Wayyu Shanan Arsi Oromo in Adami Tullu Jiddu Kombolcha District of The Oromia National Regional State", has given an insight into the fundamentals of the social and economic of women in the region under the study. In his book "Ye Gedebano, Gutazer ena Welene Hezeb bahe-l" (Culture of the Gedebano, Gutazer and Welene People) Abdulfeta Abdela (2009) mentions *wijjo* under the term "*agee*" and gives a very brief description on the culture of working together among the women of the people of Gedebano, Gutazer, and Welene. Generally, both studies do not mention the existence of *kochoo* in the region where they conducted their research.

This paper presents the socio-economic importance of *wijjo* and *kochoo* and explains the elements and organization of the two kinds of ROSCA. Additionally, it addresses the objectives, goals, and rule and regulations of *wijjo* and *kochoo* associations. Data was primarily collected through personal interviews with organizers of *wijjo* and *kochoo* associations at Koshe and Batu over two weeks from 15 July to 5 August 2022. Observations were made on these two associations in the town of Koshe and the village of Werja around Batu. Secondary data sources were also explored and used to gain some information on the global and national experience of indigenous rotating savings and cooperative associations. Numerous research projects have been carried out in this area of research, some of which are related to our field of study and therefore represent an additional source of information (cf. Abdulfeta Abdela 2009; Brink/Chavas 1997; Dejene Aredo 1993, 2004; Epple 2007; Gebre Yntiso 1994; Jemila Adem 2014; Pankhurst/Endrias Eshete 1958).

Description of the study area

The people of Mareko are one of the ethnic groups living in central Ethiopia. They live in Mareko *woreda* (district) (Yohannes Tesfaye Getachew 2020), and their ethnic group consists of 66 clans and hundreds of sub-clans. Among Mareko's 66 clans, 49 now live permanently in the administrative division of Mareko district; the remainder live in the neighbouring Meskan district and in the Lanfaro district of Silite Zone. At present, Mareko district is one of the thirteen districts that makeup of Mareko Special *woreda* in central Ethiopia. Economically, the Mareko are agrarian; they practise both plough agriculture and cattle keeping. Mareko is well known for its production of both wheat and red pepper, and the area's red pepper is nationally branded as *ye Mareko berbere* (Mareko's pepper).

The administrative centre of the permanent habitat of the Wayyu-Shanan of Arsi Oromo is Adami-Tulu Jiddo-Kombolcha *woreda*. It belongs to Eastern Oromia zone in the Great Rift Valley. The capital city of eastern Shawa zone is Adama, formerly called Nazreth. The Adami-Tullu Jiddo-Kombolcha *woreda* is found around 116km from the administrative city of Eastern Shawa zone Adama (Sub-province) (Jemila 2014). The livelihoods of the people under study here primarily depend on agriculture, and farming and cattle more or less equally support the Arsi-Oromo economy.

Wijjo: Women's ROSCAs

The word *wijjo* is an Oromo word that means cooperation. A *wijjo* is a ROSCA set up and run by the women from a particular village. All members of this rotating savings association are female. According to my interlocutors in Batu town (F., G., and F.),

Saving and being safe in Ethiopia

among the Arsi-Oromo, the coordinator of the *wijjo* is called *sooreti* an Oromo word that means leader and wealthy. The objective of *wijjo* associations is to save sufficient milk to be able to produce butter and other dairy products, such as cheese.

Most members of *wijjo* associations are farmers who have a small number of cattle. It is difficult to get a good supply of milk in the area as the climate and the absence of hybrid herds affect the yield. The area is semi-dry, so there is a shortage of grass, and it is very costly for farmers to feed their livestock during the dry season. Some farmers still buy animal fodder to get a better amount of milk. It is impossible for a household to store milk at home individually because the heat during the long days sours the milk. Milk made with soured, acidic milk does not make good butter and cheese, and there is no demand for such produce as it is no good for consuming (according to F., G., and F.). This is why the Mareko and the Arsi-Oromo women pool their resources through *wijjo* and use their small amount of produce for the market, holidays, weddings, and other occasions.

At Koshe town and Wereja village around Batu town in Adami-Tulu Gido-Kombolcha a *wijjo* has 20 participants. Each contributes four cups (around a litre) of milk a day and will thus eventually collect 20 litres of milk each. After 20 days, the cycle is closed and the rotation restarted. When preserving milk, it is important that the milk does not sour prematurely. Every day, all participants deliver their milk to a specific woman, creating a pool of around 20 litres. This consolidated quantity is then used immediately for the production of butter, cheese and other dairy products. The timing of the conversion of milk into yoghurt, a precursor to the production of butter, depends on local weather conditions. In regions with high temperatures, such as Mareko and Adami-Tulu Gido Kombolcha, the transformation of milk takes 3–4 days on average. Such climatic conditions are considered favourable for the rapid processing of butter. A woman producing one litre of milk a day would have to accumulate milk over a period of at least 20 days to obtain the quantity required for butter and cheese production. However, the long waiting time would lead to premature acidification of the milk. Through their *wijjo* practice women among the Mareko and Adami-Tulu Gido-Kombolcha preserve and protect their milk both from souring and dissipation.

All traditional institutions like *equb* and *iddir* have rules and regulations, which play a major role in maintaining the efficiency of an institution. Among the Mareko and the Arsi-Oromo, all *wijjo* associations have rules and regulations. Violating these rules and regulations leads to possible punishment. According to my interlocutors (R., F., and T.), the major rules and regulations of *wijjo* are as follows:

- **Rule one**: all members should present pure milk.
- **Rule two**: all members should present the milk in a clean vessel.
- **Rule three**: all members should present the milk on time.

In every *wijjo* association, members are accountable to the rules and regulations that they set up. Most of the time, punishment is concluded by the withdrawal of the offender's membership. However, this happens very rarely, because it is very shameful for a woman to lose her membership for committing such violations (R., F., and T.).

Kochoo: Men's ROSCAs

Kochoo is another ROSCA among the Mareko and the Arsi-Oromo in Adami-Tulu Gido- Kombolcha. The word *kochoo* is an Oromo word meaning shift. According to my interlocutors (F., G., and F.), members of a particular *kochoo* association pool their labour for managing grazing. The closing rotation cycle of the *kochoo* varies depending on the number of its members. *Kochoo* is setup by farmers in towns and urban dwellers who engage in a mixed farming economy. Among the Arsi-Oromo, the coordinator of a *kochoo* is called *abba qabba*, which is an Oromo world that means collector (F., G., and F.).

The Mareko and Arsi-Oromo in Adami-Tulu Gido-Kombolcha most commonly own cows, oxen, goats, and sheep. The number of animals varies from household to household between three and five. It is exhausting to find sufficient fodder and water for animals, because of climatic conditions in the area. Even worse, it is time consuming and boring work for herdsmen with only a few animals. According to my interlocutors (F., G., and F.), people invented the rotating savings and cooperative institution known as *kochoo* to escape this routine and time-consuming work. In the case of my interlocutors, this means that a different member of the *kochoo* looks after the animals every day and searches for grazing areas and water sources. My interlocutors' *kochoo* group consists of 20 members, and each member only has to look after the grazing of the animals every 20 days.

Most *kochoo* associations have been set up by residents of particular villages. The primary aim of limiting the scope of membership to a specific village is to easily and effectively manage the institution. As a member of a *kochoo* association each household has responsibilities and accountability determined by the four major rules of their institution. However, the member is only responsible for any violations of the rule or problems that happen on his shift day (F., G., and F.). The following are the four rules seen in most *kochoo* associations in the study area:

- **Rule one**: on his shift day, the herdsman should feed the herds sufficiently and give them access to sufficient amounts of water.
- **Rule two**: the herdsman should prevent the herds from damaging the property of a third party, for instance their farmland, fences, etc.

68 Saving and being safe in Ethiopia

- **Rule three:** the herdsman should take off and bring back the herds on time. Most of the time he takes off the herds at 8 am and returns them at 6 pm.
- **Rule four:** the herdsman should protect the herds from thieves.

Any member who misses or violates the above rules is held accountable and has to compensate for any damage. Punishment will be implemented based on *kochoo*'s rules. According to F., G., and F., the following penalties may be imposed on a shepherd who has broken the rules or caused a problem:

- **Rule one:** any herdsman, who brings back the herds without sufficient fodder and water, will be punished by herding again the following day.
- **Rule two:** if the herds enter a third party's farmland or house and damage property, the herdsman must account on behalf of the owner of the herd. Such punishment is known as *afelama*, which means 'compensation for damage'.
- **Rule three:** the herdsman who is late in taking off the herds or who brings them back early will be punished by herding again the following day.
- **Rule four:** the herdsman who loses animals or has them stolen through his negligence will be punished by paying the value of the herd.

Based on the rules of most *kochoo* associations as stated above, the simplest punishment is being made to keep the herds for an additional day and the most heavy punishment is paying the value of any missing livestock. If a member frequently violates the rules, the *abba qabba* and the other members meet, and if they consider this behavior is negligence, will withdraw the offender's membership. However, this is unusual, because the Arsi-Oromo and Mareko consider such disregard for the rules to be indicative of low status, so every member is generally punctual and follows the rules and regulations of his *kochoo* in order to maintain their dignity (F., G., and F.).

According to my interlocutors (F., G., and F.) and my field work observation, most of the time it is the *dabalee* among the Arsi-Oromo and the *lodissa* among the Mareko who take care of herds. The term *dabalee* relates to an age structure of the Oromo that means young; *lodissa* is its equivalent term among the Mareko. Even though *dabalee* and *lodissa* are responsible for taking care of the herds, any damage is the responsibility of the household.

The Socio-economic significance of *wijjo* and *kochoo*

Writing in 1997, Brink and Chavas suggested that indigenous ROSCAs provided accessible options for Africans hoping to finance a major purchase. Every village, hamlet, farm, or family compound can form its own association, bringing saving and credit facilities right down to the most basic level. This is in contrast to formal financial instruments, to which large segments of the rural population have no ready access due, in part, to geographical isolation.

My interlocutors who are members of ROSCAs believe that they can survive socially and economically only when they build a community. Therefore, they create different indigenous rotating savings and cooperative institutions. Among the factors that force the Mareko and Arsi-Oromo in Adami-Tulu Gido-Kombolcha to work in groups and organize such associations are the paucity of daily incomes, the time intensive labour, required by herding, and the short-term need for additional labour for work such as harvesting and house construction. Moreover, my interlocutors who are members of these institutions consider their indigenous institutions as social security that contributes to their socio-economic safety. These indigenous institutions have a moral dimension in that everybody has a moral obligation to belong to them.

Conclusion

Globally ROSCAs play a vital role in strengthening the financial capability of economically weak societies. In Ethiopia, *equb, iddir,* and *jigi* have a significant role in supporting the economic and social life of the people. While most ROSCAs have a common feature, which is that make their deposits in cash, in Central Ethiopia Regional State, the Mareko and the Arsi-Oromo have established ROSCAs known as *wijjo* and *kochoo* that they make their deposits in kind, time, and labour. These help them cope with the arid and semi-arid climatic conditions in the region, which result in shortages of food and water for their small numbers of cattle. Generally, my interlocutors who are members of these institutions believe that they can survive socially and economically only when they actively participate in these *wijjo* and *kochoo* associations.

Bibliography

Abdulfeta Abdela (2009): *Ye Gedebano, Gutazer ena Welene Hezeb bahel* "Culture of the Gedebano, Gutazer and Welene People", Dire printing S.C.

Bouman, F.J.A. (1977): "Indigenous Saving and Credit Societies in the Third World. A Message." *Savings and Development* 1/4, pp. 181–219.

Brink, Rogier/Chavas, Jean-Paul (1997): "The Microeconomics of an Indigenous African Institution: The Rotating Saving and Credit Associations." *Economic Development and Cultural Change* 45/4, pp. 745–772.

Dejene Aredo (1993): *Financial Sectors in Ethiopia: A Study of the Iqqub, Iddir, and Savings and Credit Co-Operatives, Report Presented at the African Economic Research Consortium, Nairobi.*

Dejene Aredo (2004): "The Iqqub: Towards the Qualification of the Economic Importance of an Ethiopian Saving and Credit Association (ROSCA)." *Ethiopian Journal of Development Research*, 26/1, pp. 33–76.

Dinkessa Deressa Layo (2017): *Documentation and Description of Libido People Traditional Ceremonies: Marriage and Conflict Resolution*, PhD dissertation, Addis Ababa University.

Donham, Donald (1979): *Work and Power in Maale, Ethiopia.* New York: Cambridge University Press.

Donham, Donald (1985): "History at One Point in Time: 'Working Together' in Maale, 1975." *American Ethnologist* 12/2, pp. 262–284.

Epple, Susanne (2007): *The Bashada of Southern Ethiopia: A Study of Age, Gender and Social Discourse.* PhD thesis, Johannes Gutenberg-Universität, Mainz.

Gebre Yntiso (1991): "A Nominal Marriage Among the Aari Youth in the Context of Sociology and Anthropology." *Sociology Ethnology Bulletin* 1/1, pp. 35–36.

Gebre Yntiso (1994): "Indigenous Work Parties Among the Aari of Southwest Ethiopia." *New Trends in Ethiopian Studies*, pp. 816–833.

Gebre Yntiso (1995): *The Ari of Southwestern Ethiopia: An Explanatory Study of Production Practices.* Addis Ababa: Department of Sociology, Anthropology and Social Administration.

Jemila Adem (2014): *Women and Indigenous Conflict Resolution Institutions in Oromia: Experience from Siinqee of the Wayyu Shanan Arsi Oromo in Adami Tullu Jiddu Kombolcha District of the Oromia National Regional State.* MA thesis, Department of Anthropology, Addis Ababa University.

Pankhurst, Richard/Endrias Eshete (1958): "Self-help in Ethiopia." *Ethiopia Observer* 2/1, pp. 354–364.

Yohannes Tesfaye Getachew (2020): "A History of Koshe Town in South-Central Ethiopia from 1941 to 1991." *Ethnologia Actualis* 20/1, pp. 119–137.

The activities, benefits, and challenges of Awada women's self-help groups in empowering women in Sidama region, southern Ethiopia

Dagne Shibru Abate and Hanna Getachew Amare

Abstract *The aim of this contribution is to assess the activities, benefits, and challenges of Awada women self-help groups (SHGs) in empowering women in the Sidama region of southern Ethiopia. SHGs target resource-constrained women and make a tremendous contribution to concerted efforts to reduce poverty and empower women. They are important to both for women's empowerment and development, and can be found in various countries of the world – USA, UK, India, etc. In Ethiopia, SHGs were introduced in 2002. The findings of the study reveal that SHGs enable members to increase their savings and to access loans. They also serve as a platform from which group members become active participants in the affairs of their respective localities. The study also shows that SHGs contribute toward reducing women's dependence on men, building their self-confidence, enabling them to think and act independently and to value their dignity and participate in decision making at family and community levels.*

Introduction

In Ethiopia, as in many of African countries, women are the backbone of the food production system. Women have been proved to be a valuable resource and an asset for the country, with the ability to handling multiple tasks simultaneously in a way that may be not so easy for men (Afroz 2010; Chalchissa Amentie/Emnet Negash 2013). As women make up more than half of the total population in most developing countries, it is important to utilize them effectively so that the talent of the whole population is optimally used (Afroz 2010). Consequently, the sustainability of a country's economy depends on the extent to which women participate in public decision making and the inclusion of their needs and interests in policy, which ultimately helps to ensure good governance (Abebayehu Chama Didana 2019:30).

Studies on rural women in Ethiopia reveal that women account for 70 per cent of the household food production. Their share in the total agricultural labour force is considerable: about 48 per cent of the agricultural labour force derives from female family members (Ministry of Agriculture 2011). Thus, any political, economic and social activity that does not incorporate and benefit women cannot be fruitful because it would be based on less than half of the country's labour force, half the knowledge, and half the effort that is available in the country (Abebayehu Chama Didana 2019).

Despite the contribution made by women, they are a poorer and less educated section of the Ethiopian population and are to a large extent financially dependent on their husbands or relatives (Dejene Mamo Bekana 2020). To change this scenario, the federal government of Ethiopia made an explicit commitment to the development of women, announcing the creation of a Women's Affairs Office at the Prime Minister Office in 1992 (Karunakaran/Huka 2018). This was followed by the enacting of the National Policy on Women (referred to as the Women's Policy) in 1993. Moreover, Article 25 of the 1994 Constitution guarantees all people equality before the law and prohibits any discrimination on the grounds of gender. Article 35 states the principles of equality of access to economic opportunities, including the right to equality in employment and land ownership (Schonard/Socea 2022). In addition, key government programs and strategies, including the Plan for Accelerated and Sustained Development to End Poverty (PASDEP: 20052010 (Federal Democratic Republic of Ethiopia 2005)) and the Growth and Transformation Plan (GTP: 2010/11-2014/15 (Growth and Transformation Program 2011)) pay special attention to women and their legitimate claim for social, economic, and political inclusion (Nigatu Regassa/Tesfaye Semela 2015).

While these developments reflect an improving broader legal and policy context for women and the poor of both sexes, at the grassroots level, barriers to economic development still remain.

For a long time, local associations such as *equbs*[1], a form of rotating savings and credit association (ROSCA), have played an important role in this regard. To be able to participate in, and benefit from, practices such as *equb* – the weekly, biweekly, or monthly pooling of money – however, requires a sustainable source of money. This means that many rural and urban poor are excluded. More recently, credit and savings cooperatives from which beneficiaries take loans to invest in different kinds of small-scale business or income generating activities have also become important sources of funds (Fekadu Negusie 2014:28). However, experience shows that women who take loans from these credit and savings associations can barely save the small

---

1   *Equb* is a traditional savings and credit institution with a rotating fund system of saving, whereby people form groups and pay periodically a fixed amount of money. This is collected in a common pool, so that, in rotation, each member of the group can receive one large sum (Yonas Bessir 2017). "*Equb* is an informal institution established voluntarily to collect a specific amount of money from the members on a specific date to be paid on round and lottery basis to the members. The members know each other and thus trust each other to make the *equb* function smoothly" (Kiros Habtu 2012).

profit they make. Most of them even find it hard to repay their loans at the designated time. As a result, many of them face legal measures by the credit associations. Development scholars agree that this is because the loan beneficiaries do not have a part in the process of pooling the financial resources. Since the beneficiaries do not contribute to the fund, they do not have the sense of ownership that would make them loyal to the bylaws formulated by the organizations from which such loans come.

In the context of the challenges associated with *equb* associations, self-help groups (SHGs) have emerged as an alternative source of loans for the rural and urban poor. Indeed, a number of NGOs are now encouraging a move away toward an SHG approach (Fekadu Negusie 2014:28). SHGs have some elements of *equbs*. Like *equbs*, they are based on money pooled by members. However, in the *equbs* money moves or rotates among the members on the basis of a lottery until the last member receives his/her turn; in an SHG, money moves around in the form of loan that involves interest,[2] albeit a nominal amount compared to the interest charged by other sources of finance, such as savings and credit associations. Membership in SHGs leads to being active in *equb* groups and vice versa. Most SHG members in our study area, after saving for some months (usually 6–12 months), got the chance to obtain a loan and begin a business, and were thereby able to join an *equb* to boost their earnings. This would eventually help change livelihoods at family and community levels. Thus, SHGs can be used as a gateway for participation in an *equb* association.

Table 1: Summary of the major differences between equbs and SHGs

	features	differences	
		equbs	SHGs
1	type	As ROSCAs, money moves or rotates among members based on the lottery system until the last member receives his/her turn.	Money moves among members in the form of a loan that involves interest, though nominal compared to other sources of finance, such as savings and credit association.
2	initiated by	Members	Usually by NGOs
3	size of members	The number of members varies, as does the amount of capital they have.	The number of members usually does not exceed 13–20.

---

2   In the study area, SHGs lend out money with an interest rate of only 5 per cent.

	features	differences	
		equbs	SHGs
4	member-ship	People with various socioeconomic statuses.	People with similar socioeconomic status, often the poor.
5	duration	It terminates after each member has received the collected /saved money pot once.	Permanent, unless it is dispersed due to various reasons.
6	loanable fund[3]	Not available in the hands of treasurer or in banks.	Available in the hands of the treasurer/or in the bank.
7	orienta-tion	Often economic	Economic, social, and political
8	motive	Individual drive for financial change /growth or a mechanism for saving money.	Serve as a development strategy to empower and enable poor people.
9	interest payment	They do not charge interest on the money they distribute.	They charge interest on the money they distribute.

An SHG is an informal association of small, economically homogeneous group of people in a village or urban neighbourhood that has the principal objective of empowering poor women (and men) economically, socially, politically, institutionally, and spiritually. SHGs can serve as a development strategy to empower and enable poor people to utilize the existing assets and bring real change in their life and among the community (Yohannes Mindaye 2014). Usually, the number of members in an SHG does not exceed 20 and comprises very poor people who do not have access to formal financial institutions. SHGs act as the forum for the members to provide space and support to each other. In SHGs, the rural poor voluntarily come together to save small amounts regularly, which are deposited in a common fund to meet members' emergency needs and for establishing businesses (Pandey 2014). The SHG approach encourages poor women to lift themselves out of poverty through making regular (weekly or biweekly) savings, and giving them access to internal and external loans and intensive capacity-building training to begin and expand small business and income-generating activities. It is founded on the principle that women can realize their potential and work towards their own development. A focus on attitudinal change is central to the approach, and the outcome is material well-being along with

---

3   A loanable fund is the sum total of all the money people and entities in an economy have decided to save and lend out to borrowers as an investment rather than use for personal consumption.

social and political development and empowerment (Lawson-McDowall et al. 2016). Whether called saving groups (SGs) or self-help groups SHGs, these NGO-promoted organizations are ROSCAs and use similar modalities to accomplish the same goals. However, the five NGOs that work on these groups in Ethiopia (CARE, CST,[4] Tearfund,[5] CoSAP,[6] and Oxfam) have slightly different philosophical approaches to their work. Those that prefer the label 'savings group' (CARE and CST) view their work in more instrumental terms and provide members with services that facilitate market access. Those that prefer the label 'self-help group' (Tearfund, CoSAP and Oxfam) take a more rights-based approach and focus on empowering their members to solve their own problems (Lawson-McDowall et al. 2016).

According to the report of Kindernothilfe,[7] between the introduction of SHGs in Ethiopia in 2002 and 2008, about 25 local NGOs implemented more than 40 SHG-based projects. Over these six years, 2,958 SHGs were established. Some 49,910 women, with a total of 192,117 children, had actively participated in the SHGs, which had proven to be successful in changing the lives of their members and their families for the better (Kindernothilfe 2008). In 2014, the number of SHGs in Ethiopia rose to 20,000, with a total of about 400,000 members (Gebre Yntiso et al. 2014:5).

So far, the SHGs have made significant progress in creating opportunities for powerless and voiceless people, particularly women, to unleash their potential and alleviate poverty. However, the approach has not yet been given enough attention by academics, NGOs, and the government looking at development policies, strategies, and activities. There are a few NGOs (noted above) working on the approach especially in urban areas of Ethiopia (Yohannes Mindaye 2014). To list some of the few studies on the topic, Gebre Yntiso et al. (2014) conducted a rapid assessment of SHGs in Ethiopia. This study was not detailed enough to show what these groups look like at grassroots level. Bezabih Tolosa (2007) investigated the socio-economic

---

4   CST represents the overseas development and humanitarian agencies of the Catholic Church from England and Wales (CAFOD), Scotland (SCIAF), and Ireland (Trócaire).

5   Tearfund is a UK-based, Christian INGO working in over 45 of the poorest countries around the world to lift people out of poverty using local partners and churches wherever possible. The Ethiopian Kalehiwot Church (EKHC) is an implementing partner of Tearfund. Tearfund's major objective is tackling economic empowerment and social norm change, that is, the social and economic empowerment of poor and vulnerable communities to move them out of poverty (Lawson-McDowall et al. 2016).

6   CoSAP is a consortium of self-help group approach promoters.

7   Kindernothilfe (KNH) is a charity organization and was founded in 1959 by a group of Christians in Duisburg, Germany, in order to help needy children in India. Over time, it has become one of the largest Christian organizations in Europe for children's aid (https://www.devex.co m/organizations/kindernothilfe-40000).

impacts of SHGs in five *kebeles*[8] of Adama city. His study appreciates the positive contributions SHGs make to enhancing the life of members; it also points to challenges such as loose group integration and the absence of accountability on the part of office holders in such groups.

The overall aim of the current study is to assess the activities, benefits, and challenges of Awada women SHGs in empowering women of Dale *woreda*[9] in Sidama region, southern Ethiopia. The study specifically attempts to describe what SHGs means to them and how they benefit them; to explore SHGs' roles in promoting grassroots-level participation and democratization; to examine the changes occurring in the lives of the SHG members; and to identify the challenges encountered by the groups. The study will help disseminate the positive experiences of SHG members to other rural areas in the region and beyond, and could broaden the existing literature and knowledge on women's empowerment and development through SHGs, initiating further research interest in the topic.

Our study focuses on six women's SHGs in Awada *kebele* of Dale *woreda* (which amounts to 25 per cent of the women's SHGs in the *woreda*). Dale is one of 37 *woredas* in Sidama region; it is also one of the four *woredas* (the others being Shebedino, Boricha, and Loka Abaya) in which SHGs have been established in the region. In Dale *woreda*, there are 36 rural *kebeles* and three rural towns. SHGs have been introduced in eight rural *kebeles*. The approach was introduced by the Kalehiwot Church Development Program (KHCDP) in 2002 to empower and develop the rural poor. Since then, it has been actively functioning in the *woreda*. There are 24 women's, 22 men's, and 33 mixed SHGs in these eight *kebeles*. In each *kebele*, one SHG facilitator is assigned by Kalehiwot church. The total number of members in the 79 SHGs is 1359.

In addition to the SHG members, *kebele* officials, Kalehiwot Church development program leaders, micro- and small- enterprise development agencies, and a *kebele* agricultural development agent also took part in the study. Purposive sampling was used as a technique to draw informants from the total population of the *kebele*. As this was qualitative research, ongoing thematic organization, analysis and interpretation was carried out as of the very first day of the fieldwork. To enrich the findings of primary sources and triangulate them, secondary sources were also used. The most important primary data collection instruments employed included structured observation, in-depth interviews, focus group discissions (FGD), and case studies. The SHGs' bylaws, bookkeeping, document management, small-business materials, and members' day-to-day relationships were examined through structured observation, which involved participation in their weekly meetings.

---

8   *Kebele* is the smallest unit of administration below *woreda*.

9   *Woreda* is an administrative unit above *kebele*.

The nexus between empowerment and SHGs

Empowerment can be defined as the process of multiplying power or creating autonomy in a social system to help an individual take charge of their efforts; it promotes the ability to act collectively to solve problems, influence important issues, and contribute to the achievement of main objectives. The fundamentals of empowerment have been defined as agency (the ability to define one's goals and act upon them), awareness of gendered power structures, self-esteem, and self-confidence (Kabeer 2001).

Empowerment is related more directly with power, as "a multidimensional and interlinked process of change in power relations" (Mayoux 2000). It helps people to realize and recognize their internal power and exercise it for the benefit of themselves and others. Two points are worth noting in this regard. First, the core of the empowerment process is the individual. Therefore, each individual must take charge of empowering herself/himself. Second, empowerment is both a process and an outcome and, hence, must be visualized in this perspective. All the tools of empowerment can be categorized into two groups: structural and process interventions. In the former we mainly include political action and policy commitment, while the latter involves social commitment and action on the part of the disempowered themselves. The SHG approach falls into the second category (Pandey 2014).

SHGs are formed in response to a particular issue, such as limited income-generating opportunities, or a common goal, based on members' felt needs. Some of the major characteristic features of SHGs include regular meetings among members, voluntary membership, regular saving, active participation, democratic decision making, rotational leadership, and having bylaws by which members' behaviour is governed.

The SHG approach promotes complex aspects of development that contribute to members' capacity and well-being, such as training programs in accounting and bookkeeping, leadership, self-realization, confidence, decision making, and dealing with banks and government officials (Nagarajan/Ponnusamy 2019). Accordingly, a SHG is a community-based finance and self-governing, domestic institution that acts as a mechanism to strengthen the community through collective action and enable women to acquire power (Quiroz-Niño/Murga-Menoyo 2017).

Throughout history and across nations today, men on average have greater access to power (cf. Brown 1991). The gender power model (Pratto/Walker 2004; Pratto et al. 2011) suggests that power is gendered. Specifically, relative to women, men have greater access to the use of force and have greater access to resource control. This gender inequality can be observed in several aspects of daily life, such as access to education, job opportunities, and economic resources (UNDP 2015).

SHG help bridge this gap, both meeting women's financial needs and strengthening their capacity, leading to their empowerment (Arockiasamy 2012). For example, a survey by Rajeev et al. has shown that women participating in SHGs are aware of the non-economic benefits of the program, such as building self-confidence and improving their social status. Active participation and the rotation of responsibilities, which are compulsory under the SHG approach, result in improvements to women's ability to express their views both in the home and broader community and facilitate their mobility (Rajeev et al. 2020).

In summary, investing in building women's capabilities and empowering them to exercise their choices is valuable in itself but is also the unquestionable way to contribute to economic growth and overall development in society. Eradicating poverty and achieving sustainable development cannot be separated from achieving gender equality and the empowerment of women.

Figure 1: Conceptual framework: The relationship between SHGs and women's empowerment

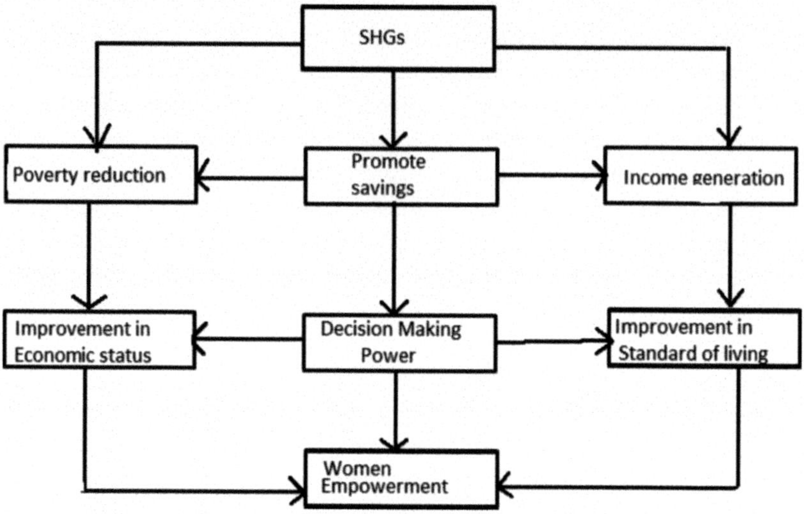

Source: Reshi (2023:83)

Awada women's SHG activities, benefits, and challenges

The Ethiopian Kalehiwot Church Development Program (EKHCDP) facilitator for Awada *kebele* has stated that the participants of a SHG range from 13–20 people in Awada, and these are comprised predominantly of women from similar socioeconomic backgrounds and neighbourhoods. Each of the SHGs has its own bylaws. The SHGs are funded entirely through members saving an agreed amount each week.

The EKHCDP facilitators assist in establishing SHGs and provide a range of training, on financial management, bookkeeping, environmental cleanups, and the importance of mutual support, social development, and a collective capacity to solve problems encountered by members. After a fixed period, members gain access to small loans at low interest rates from the accumulated funds and agree on the terms of repayment. Initial loans are used to set up individual and collective income-generating activities (IGA). These IGAs include selling maize flour, butter, dairy products, and purchasing, fattening, and selling livestock (e.g., sheep, goats, and bulls), and selling local drinks.

Generally, SHGs gather together a total of 15–20 individuals from the same neighborhood and the same socio-economic level, who develop their own bylaws. Some 8–12 similar SHGs operating in close proximity then establish a Cluster Level Association (CLA), which represents its members to lower levels of local government (e.g., *kebele* and *woreda*) and undertakes numerous other activities. Certain CLAs in each area form Federation Level Associations (FLAs) to represent their members to higher levels of local government (e.g., city, zone, and region). The federations have higher bargaining power and become the main supporters of the SHGs instead of the NGOs after three to five years. Federations also make the whole SHG program sustainable by linking it with banks.

Awada Womens' SHGs act as a forum for the members to provide space and support to each other. In line with this, Pandey states that the most vibrant argument for the group approach is in the form of "synergy effect". Simply stated, it refers to the phenomenon in which the whole is greater than the sum of individual parts. Mathematically it is represented as $2 + 2 > 4$. Thus, the output always exceeds the input. It has one important implication: it indicates great leverage of team effort. This leverage effect improves the performance of SHGs in every arena, whether income generation or environmental protection; community participation is better compared to the combined individual performances. This leverage effect can be further strengthened and employed as, for instance, a social commitment to produce a change in the status of women in the society. This synergy effect is of utmost importance and lies at the heart of SHG theory, which is why SHGs have the capacity to alter the lives of women and have already greatly altered the lives of millions of women in various countries of the world, including Ethiopia (Pandey 2014:92–93).

In Awada, SHGs are not only instrumental in improving the economic status of women. They also enhance the status of women as participants, decision makers, and beneficiaries in the economic, political, and social spheres of their lives. SHGs enable their members to learn to cooperate and work in a group environment. Collective wisdom and peer pressure are used to ensure proper end-use of credit and timely repayment.

In the traditional arrangement of *equbs*, the members knew each other from the village, work, or from other fields of life. This was in itself assurance enough that

80 Saving and being safe in Ethiopia

everyone would get what he/she was entitled to. In fact, one advantage of these institutions has been that they help uphold the societal values of honesty and integrity. However, today's diversity of members and the amount of money held by the *equbs*, these values may not give adequate security. Although many *equbs* claim that such values still work, the course have provided judicial recognition for *equbs* and can enforce defaulters to pay back *equb*, suggesting the need for additional security measures.

Social benefits

Most successful functioning organizations, whether at micro or macro level, reinforce the significance of the group approach to problem solving (Pandey 2014), and in SHGs this approach has huge social benefits. For example, in Awada, SHG women organized yearly environmental cleaning and sanitation campaigns within their communities. They constructed pit latrines in the compound of every member, constructed a big bridge on Woyima river (at the cost of about 8,000 birr). The bridge enabled rural people in four *kebeles* (Awada, Beramera, Wicho, and Bedeye) to access Yirgalem town.

Groups with a rotating leadership system ensured that the most capable did not dominate, leaving space for the more marginalized to develop capacity to lead. As a result, husbands began to consult their wives and allow them access to decision making; this had a cascading impact on children, who had better access to school supplies when their mothers were able to plan and save to purchase them. For example, with the bridge and their improved financial and social status, some women SHG members in Awada are now able to send their children to schools at Yirgalem by covering all the necessary expenses, which include stationary, house rents, food, and uniform. The training offered by NGOs also emerged as an important catalyst for empowerment and development (Lawson-McDowall et al. 2016).

Similarly, SHG members in Awada stated that participation in groups considerably improved their health and social well-being. They noted that groups are places where one can share experiences and learn different ways to live with individual conditions or overcome any challenges one might face. But more than that, groups are places where one can establish lasting friendships. Groups mean help, support, and safe places to talk to one another.

Case 1

TD is a young woman of 30 and mother of four who was born and grew up in Awada. TD's husband is a library attendant at Yirgalem comprehensive secondary school. His meagre income could not sustain the family. To supplement her husband's income, TD joined Jiro (literally 'wealth') SHG in her *kebele* and started saving 1 birr every week. After saving for about six months, she borrowed 100 birr (about US$2) and started a banana business. She borrowed a further 200 birr soon after returning the first loan. Then she became involved in selling butter from her home. After returning the second loan, she borrowed another 300 birr.

With the profit TD made, she sent her children to school in Yirgalem town. Apart from covering meals and clothing for her children, TD pays 250 birr monthly for house rent in Yirgalem. TD told me that, in the past, they could not afford to send their children to school in Yirgalem, but now they can.

TD also has money saved in 2 *equb* associations in Yirgalem. She pays 50 birr (with 22 women) every Monday, and 100 birr (with 21 women) every Thursday. The total sum of Monday's *equb* is 1100 birr, while Thursday's *equb* is 2,100 birr. TD put her 2,100 birr into the bank at Yirgalem when she received her turn. After some time, she withdrew 2,000 birr from the bank and repaired the hut in which she lives with her family.

Before joining the SHG, TD and her family were living in a small old hut. After receiving her *equb* money, and with a 6,300 birr loan from her business colleagues at Yirgalem market, TD recently constructed a new house with a corrugated iron roof. Lending money for house construction is a norm among TD's business friends in Yirgalem.

TD has furnished her house and bought kitchen utensils. TD said that in the past, for every 50 birr loan from village money lenders, they paid 100 per cent interest. Thanks to the SHG, they now pay only 2.5 birr interest for every 50 birr. In the past, some village moneylenders did not trust them enough to lend them money. Now they do not knock on the doors of the village moneylenders. TD has a vision to open a big shop in Yirgalem. TD confidently says that now she is a rich woman. Her family has no food problems. She has sent all her kids to school. In the past, she could not even imagine that saving one birr could have value. Now she understands that richness begins from saving a single coin. She remembers that there was a time when her family ate sugarcane for dinner and slept.

Economic benefits

Women's economic empowerment includes women's ability to participate equally in existing markets. It means giving them access to and control over productive resources, access to decent work, control over their own time, lives, and bodies, as well as greater voice, agency, and meaningful participation in economic decision making. When women are economically empowered, they participate in decision making. Saving in SHGs, in particular, has played a significant role not only in terms of creating access to credit facilities but also in ensuring women have control over resources.

Most of the informants in Awada described how they had learned to save a small amount of money regularly and manage their expenditure. Every group reported that they had come to understand and appreciate the value of having a 'savings culture'. Informants further stated that their saving culture saved them from the unreasonable interest charged by money lenders and helped them gain economic independence, recognition by their community, and assets, and to meet their family's basic needs, which include education, health care, and social recognition.

Case 2

"My name is AB. I am 26. I have two kids of 6 years and 4 years old. My husband is a daily labourer in one of the private garages at Yirgalem. His meagre income as a temporary employee in the garage could not sufficiently sustain the livelihood of our family. Besides, my husband is an alcoholic, and he spends his income by drinking alcohol and chewing *khat* [a stimulant leaf]. One lucky morning, in the month of June some years back, I was approached by the SHG facilitator in our *kebele*, and he told me about SHGs and invited me to participate in the group. At the beginning, I rejected his invitation, due to the mere fact that I had no money to save, and squarely told him that I will not come to the meeting, which in my eyes was futile. But the facilitator insisted that I had to come to the SHG meeting whatever my position was. With so much resistance, I then accepted the invitation and attended the meeting. The SHG members told me about their group and the advantages of joining them. Besides, the community facilitator also told me what SHG meant, its benefits, and how to make savings.

As I normally dislike dependency and handouts, I immediately started saving 0.50 per week, all from the small amount of money I usually obtain from my husband for purchasing daily food items/consumer goods. After saving for over six months, I got a loan of 200 birr and started a petty business of selling butter in our village. After four months, I made enough money to repay the first loan and borrowed another 400 birr, which helped me to expand my business and get a good sum of money within a couple of years.

The *equb* I joined a year ago with 20 persons by contributing 50 birr on a weekly basis allowed me to get 1000 birr after the settlement of the previous loan. With the collected *equb* money, I bought timber wood to repair our old hut, which was about to fall down. So, encouraged by the SHG initiative and the *equb*, I have a plan to organize another new *equb*, and thereby to change our Tukul for a new corrugated iron-roofed house. In the past, I had been jobless, fully dependent on my husband's meagre income, but now I am so grateful to God for the strength he has given me. So, capacitated to assist my husband, now I cover the lion's share of our family's expenses. I have bought several household items, such as chairs, bed, and kitchen furniture, which made our house a relatively ideal place to live. Nowadays we have no problem with food or clothes for our kids and ourselves. My problem is a lack of money to expand and diversify the business I am running and to get an area/place to run my business." (AB, 2022: Interview)

In Awada, because of their group saving, every SHG member has the opportunity to access credit services where loan conditions are decided by themselves in a participatory way. Furthermore, the loan conditions are flexible and based on a member's ability and capacity and the purpose of the loan.

Between 2002 and 2008, the Awada women SHG members saved over 33,000 birr, which is in the hands of treasurers. As a principle, every member of an SHG in Awada saves 0.5–5 birr weekly. To maintain proper accounts and records, every SHG we visited has a ledger held by the secretary of the group, and every member of the SHGs has their own passbook. The initial challenge for most members was to accept the idea that such a small saving would become a big sum to make a difference in their lives. However, the savings steadily increased, allowing them to take loans on low interest rate (5 per cent) to cover household expenses and engage in small business. Over 90 per cent of the informants saved amounts that they had never had before.

In Awada, members of the visited SHGs borrow money to cover household expenses (e.g., consumer goods, education, construction, etc.) and their involvement in petty businesses. Over 80 per cent of members received loans from their respective SHG, and all, except one woman, returned the money. Defaulters face being ignored by fellow members and not being allowed to participated in similar social matters in their localities. Key informants in Awada disclosed that loans from SHGs have multiple benefits: as opposed to commercial banks, microfinance, and village moneylenders, SHGs lend out money with low interest rates (5 per cent), require no collateral, and do not involve bureaucratic bottlenecks. Peer pressure is the methods for enforcing repayment. Across all visited SHGs, the loan repayment period is based on negotiations, which may range from three to twelve months. Repayment is in installments, which may be weekly, fortnightly, monthly, or as agreed upon at the time of taking the loan. The SHG committee members stated that the members of the SHGs developed faithfulness. They work hard and pay loans on time.

The implementation of SHG has also generated self-employment opportunities for the rural poor. Access to credit has enabled the women (25 per cent of the women in SHGs) to undertake gainful/productive employment/activities (IGAs).

In summary, access to loan can help expand the material base available to women by enabling them to start and expand small businesses, often accompanied by market access. The women also experience 'power within': feelings of freedom, strength, self-identity, and increased levels of confidence and self-esteem (Pandey 2014).

Political benefits

Members in all visited SHGs are able to conduct their meetings by themselves. It is reported by the *kebele* officials that women SHG members are active participants in most *kebele*-level community matters. They attend meetings, save, and participate in all activities of their respective groups voluntarily. Each SHG develops its own bylaws through the direct involvement of its members: the group frames the rules and regulations that are required for the SHG's effective functioning. All the SHGs are impartial in nature, and the procedure of decision making is democratic. All the SHGs visited also practised rotational leadership, which provides fertile ground for the women to learn democracy and the rule of law. Women have begun to explicitly discuss their problems by themselves. Matters relating to savings, loans, interest, repayments, social issues, women's rights, etc. are deliberated democratically.

Case 3

BB and DG are in their early 20s. BB (educated to 6th grade level) and DG (educated to 9th grade) are chairperson and secretary of Beleto (*beleto* literally means 'first') SHG. BB and DG state the following:

> "SHGs are places where poor women become well off. It is a place where there is no discrimination on the basis of religion, clan, ethnicity, or gender. It is a place where you can learn how to live and help each other. It is a place where members share their problems. SHGs are places where members learn democracy and the rule of law. The experience and self-esteem we develop in the SHG enable us to be active participants in every public meeting in our locality and we have developed the courage to express our ideas without any fear, which formerly had been hardly possible to us to do. Our involvement and activities in the SHG have added to our family an understanding of the value of self-determination, social life, and above all the endless love of the almighty God."

BB and DG further state that these days they no longer only have money from their husbands for household expenditure, as they are also able to contribute. They take part in making decisions on important social and economic issues of their respective families. Relationships with their husbands have improved. They disclosed that their relationships with their respective husbands are smooth, warm, and sweet, as conflicts that may arise due to critical resource shortages have been lessened. They say that their husbands are happy and have no objections to their involvement in SHGs.

Some women members of SHGs have convinced their husbands that they can make changes in their family. Thus, their husbands have started considering their wives views whenever they make decisions on important economic, social, and political matters.

The case studies show that women were not only able to increase their income by participating in group memberships, but also developed self-confidence, self-esteem, and an optimistic outlook for the future. This development reflects a proactive engagement in the present and is consistent with Rebecca Bryant's view that our daily life and actions are influenced by our expectations for the future (Bryant 2020:16; see also introduction to this volume). These women have taken encouraging and visible steps in the direction of democratization and grassroots level womens' empowerment. Similarly, Brody et al. (2017) conducted a systematic review on SHGs between 1980 and 2014 that concluded that they are positively related to economic, social, and political empowerment.

Challenges encountered

There are several challenges that the women involved in SHGs still face:

- Financial risk: In all the visited SHGs, savings are held in the hands of treasurers and are not audited. This is risky, and due attention should be given to this issue by concerned bodies.
- A lack of access to capital and a place to work: Women do not generally have property in their names to use as collateral for obtaining additional funds from external sources with which to expand their businesses or start a new one. Informants complain that they could not secure workplace/area from their *kebele* administration, even though they regularly ask for one.
- Insufficiency of funds: Informants complain that the internal savings and loans they get do not cover their needs. The money remains insufficient to meet the growing loan demands, which can only be covered through external loan provision.
- Insufficiency of training: There is no adequate training on bookkeeping, entrepreneurship, small-scale vegetable and fruit farming, a balanced diet, family planning, etc.
- Poor education: In the study area, almost all (over 95 per cent) of the women are still illiterate. Due to the lack of education, the majority of the rural women in Awada do not have an awareness of business, technology, and market knowledge. Though most of the members of the SHGs are committed and have strong ambitions to make changes in their lives, they are engaged only in one type of business: most have small businesses selling butter, and a very few sell maize flour. This will create market saturation.

- Household inequality: In Awada, it is mainly the women's duty to look after the children and other members of the family. Men play a secondary role only. Married women have to strike a fine balance between their business and family. Their total involvement in family leaves little or no energy and time to devote to business. Some non-members of SHGs in Awada state that the support and approval of their husbands seems a necessary condition for women's entry into business. In other words, if a man does not want his wife to be involved in activities that would make her work outside her home, he will simply not allow her to engaging in IGAs.

Conclusion and recommendations

The major achievements of Awada's SHGs are the economic, social, and political benefits they have brought to members. In economic terms, members of SHG have access to saving and credit facilities and receive training from the Kalehiwot Church Development program in the business skills they need to run a small business of their own. SHG members also benefit socially from increased social interactions among members and by developing self-esteem, winning respect from the surrounding community, and actively participating in community services. This can be considered an important aspect of women's social empowerment. Members of the SHG also gain a political voice, developing the skills to express their opinions in the household and at public meetings.

Joining a SHG is a transformative process that leads to women's economic, social, and political empowerment and enables them to actively shape their present and future lives. In Awada, women's empowerment is reflected in increased self-esteem, greater self-confidence, and a change in decision making within the family. Overall, SHGs are playing a significant role in empowering and developing their members in Awada *kebele* of Dale *woreda*.

However, all SHGs raised the lack of access to a workplace as a major problem. Thus, it is imperative that local-level governments respond positively to their requests, and also support them through training on such topics such as bookkeeping, entrepreneurship, small-scale vegetable and fruit farming, diet, family planning, and dispute settlement.

The existing SHGs' money is held by members/treasurers and not in a bank. This is risky, being open to both theft and wastage. Finally, internal loans alone cannot satisfy the needs of SHG members, especially those who run businesses and IGAs. This is a serious issue among Awada women, and needs a practical response in terms of increased access to financial support.

Tables

Table 1: Summary of the major differences between equbs and SHGs

Figures

Figure 1: Conceptual framework: The relationship between SHGs and women's empowerment

Bibliography

Abebayehu Chama Didana (2019): "Determinants of Rural Women Economic Empowerment in Agricultural Activities: The Case of Damot Gale Woreda of Wolaita Zone, SNNPRS of Ethiopia." *Journal of Economics and Sustainable Development* 10/3, pp. 30–49.

Afroz, Maksuda (2010): *Effect of Organizational Governance on Women's Participation in Decision Making*, MA thesis, Public Policy and Governance Program, Department of General and Continuing Education, Bangladesh: North South University.

Arockiasamy, Sundaram (2012): "Impact of Self-Help Group in Socio-Economic Development of India." *Journal of Humanities and Social Science* 5/1, pp. 20–27.

Bezabih Tolosa (2007): *Socio-Economic Impact Of Self-Help Groups*, MA thesis, School of Social Work, Addis Ababa.

Brody, Carinne/Hoop, Thomas de/Vojtkova, Martina/Warnock, Ruby/Dunbar, Megan/Murthy, Padmini/Dworkin, Shari L. (2017): "Can Self-Help Group Programs Improve Women's Empowerment? A Systematic Review." *Journal of Development Effectiveness* 9/1, pp. 15–40.

Brown, Donald E. (1991): *Human Universals*, Philadelphia: Temple University Press.

Bryant, Rebecca (2020): "The Anthropology of the Future." *Ethnofoor* 32/1, pp. 11–22.

Chalchissa Amentie/Emnet Negash (2013): *Women's Involvement as an Effective Management Tool in Decision Making in Oromia Region's Public Organizations*, Jimma: Jimma University.

Dejene Mamo Bekana (2020): "Policies of Gender Equality in Ethiopia: The Transformative Perspective." *International Journal of Public Administration* 43/4, pp. 312–325.

Federal Democratic Republic of Ethiopia (FDRE) (2005): *A Plan for Accelerated and Sustained Development to End Poverty (PASDEP)*, Addis Ababa.

Fekadu Negusie (2014): "The Impact of Self-Help Group Approach in the Lives of Beneficiaries at Household Level: The Case of Children's Home Society and Family Services Hosanna Family Empowerment Program." *Journal of Social and Development Sciences* 5/1, pp. 26–33.

Gebre Yntiso/Dagne Shibru/Temesgen Chibsa (2014): *Self-Help Groups in Ethiopia: Activities, Opportunities and Constraints. Tracking Trends in Ethiopia's Civil Society (TECS)*, Report 11, Addis Ababa.

Growth and Transformation Program (GTP) (2011): *The Five-Year Growth and Transformation Plan of Ethiopia (2010/2011 – 2014/2015)*, Addis Ababa.

Kabeer, Naila (2001): "Reflections on the Measurement of Women's Empowerment." In: Sisask, Anne, (ed.), *Discussing Women's Empowerment: Theory and Practice*. SIDA Studies 3. Swedish International Development Cooperation Agency, Stockholm, Sweden, pp. 17–57.

Karunakaran, R./Huka, Roba (2018): "Leadership Skills in Primary Multipurpose C ooperative Societies in Ethiopia." *Agricultural Economics Research Review* 31/1, pp. 131–139.

Kindernothilfe (2008): *The Self-Help Approach Annual Report. The Self-Help Approach – Ethiopia*, Addis Ababa: Central Printing Press.

Kiros Habtu (2012): *Classifying Informal Institutions in Ethiopia*, Wageningen: Wageningen University.

Lawson-McDowall, Julie/Bekele Tefera/Presler-Marshall, Elizabeth/Kiros Berhanu/ Bethelihem Gebre/ Pereznieto, Paola/Jones, Nicola (2016): "Savings and Self-Help Groups in Ethiopia: A Review of Programming by Five NGOs". Accessed March 8, 2024, (https://learn.tearfund.org/-/media/learn/resources/reports/2016-odi-savings-and-self-help-groups-in-ethiopia-en.pdf).

Mayoux, Lida (2000): *Microfinance and the Empowerment of Women: A Review of the Key Issues*. Social Finance Unit Working Paper 23, Geneva: ILO.

Ministry of Agriculture (2011): *Guidelines for Gender Mainstreaming in Agricultural Sector*. Addis Ababa, Ethiopia.

Nagarajan, Sivakami/Ponnusamy, Ilango (2019): "Mainstreaming Women Self-help Groups to Promote Social and Solidarity Economy Lessons from Rural Areas of Tamil Nadu, India." UNTFSSE Knowledge Hub Draft Paper Series. Geneva: UN Inter-Agency Task Force on Social and Solidarity Economy (UNTFSSE). Accessed March 8, 2024, (https://knowledgehub.unsse.org/wp-content/uploads/2019/07/163_Sivakami_Mainstreaming-Women-Self-help-groups_En.pdf).

Nigatu Regassa/Tesfaye Semela (2015): "Regional Context and Research Framework." In Tesfaye Semela et al. (eds.), *Impacts of Women Development and Change Packages on the Socioeconomic and Political Status of Women in SNNPR: Promise, Success and Challenges*, Hawassa: Center for Policy and Development Research (CPDR), Hawassa University.

Pandey, Jaya Kumari (2014): *Women Empowerment through Self Help Group: A Theoretical Perspective*, Varanasi: Department of Economics, FSS, Banaras Hindu University.

Pratto, Felicia/Lee I-Ching/Tan, Judy Y./Pitpitan, Eileen V. (2011): "Power Basis Theory: A Psycho-Ecological Approach to Power." In: D. Dunning (ed.), *Social Motivation*, New York: Psychology Press, pp. 191–222.

Pratto, Felicia/Walker, Angela (2004): "The Bases of Gendered Power." In: Alice H. Eagly/Anne E. Beall/Robert J. Sternberg (eds.), *The Psychology of Gender* (2nd edition), New York and London: The Guilford Press, pp. 242–268.

Quiroz-Niño, Catalina/Murga-Menoyo, María Ángeles (2017): "Social and Solidarity Economy, Sustainable Development Goals, and Community Development: The Mission of Adult Education and Training." *Sustainability* 9/12, p. 2164.

Rajeev, Meenakshi/Vani, Balasubramanian/ Veerashekharappa (2020): "Group Lending Through an SHG Bank Linkage Programme in India: Transaction Costs and Social Benefits." *Development in Practice* 30/2, pp. 168–181.

Reshi, Irshad Ahmad (2023): "Women Self-Help Groups Role in Poverty Nexus and Empowerment." *International Journal of Economic, Business, Accounting, Agriculture Management and Sharia Administration* 3/1.

Schonard, Martina/ Socea, Alice (2022): "Briefing on Elimination of Female Genital Mutilation/Cutting (FGM/C) in Ethiopia". Accessed March 8, 2024, (https://data.unicef.org/wp-content/uploads/2020/02/A-Profile-of-FGM-in-Ethiopia_2020.pdf).

United Nations Development Program (UNDP) (2015): "Human Development Report 2015. Work for Human Development". Accessed March 8, 2024, (https://hdr.undp.org/content/human-development-report-2015).

Yohannes Mindaye (2014): *Challenges and Contributions of Self-Help Groups in Empowering Poor Women: The Case of Ethiopian Kale-Heywet Church*, Addis Ababa Integrated Urban Development Project. MA Thesis, AAU.

Yonas Bessir (2017): *Salient Features Behind Informal Financial Institutions: The Case of Edget Behibret Equb and Ras ZeSilasse Former Students Iddir*, Addis Ababa: School of Graduate Studies, St. Mary's University.

Saving and being safe in the Ethiopian diaspora

'Wealth in people'
Equbs as forms of investment among Ethiopian immigrants in the US

Worku Nida

Abstract *Rotating saving and credit associations (ROSCAs) are ubiquitous in world cultures. Drawing on a case study of local-turned-transnational equbs (Ethiopian ROSCAs) in Los Angeles (L.A.) and Seattle in the USA, in this contribution, I examine how equb (and ROSCAs in other communities cross-culturally) work as forms of investment in 'good lives' and futures, the success of which depends on participants' 'wealth in people' values. By extending the 'wealth in people' framework into the discourses of ROSCAs, I show how intersubjectively assessing equb actors' 'wealth in people' values is vital to the success and workings of equbs, through which investment capital is created by and for the participants. In doing so, I offer three fresh insights. First, equb actors (leaders and members) are repositories of 'wealth in people' that consists of embodied and embedded relationships and personal characters. Second, equbs (ROSCAs broadly) are key resources with which marginalized immigrant and local groups fight against financial, social, and racial exclusion, and create diasporic communities. Third, I show how actors perform both as investors and borrowers in the creative practices and processes of equbs, through which they actively mobilize and create various forms of capital and deploy 'wealth in people' to create 'wealth in things' (money, properties, and businesses) and diaspora communities such as Little Ethiopia in L.A. In doing so, I juxtapose Little Ethiopia with ROSCA-mediated formation of other immigrants enclaves (namely, Chinatown and Koreatown) and 'racial enclaves' (such as the African-American communities in Tulsa and Durham).*

Introduction

"We created our own banking system." (*equb* leader in L.A. June 12, 2022: Interview)
"Excluded by banks, minorities in California became their own lenders." (*L.A. Times* journalist, Shyong 2019)

Studies on rotating savings and credit associations (ROSCAs) have long established that ROSCAs are omnipresent traditional financial institutions that play a major role in providing alternative saving and lending services to people who lack access to 'formal' financial and credit markets (Geertz 1962; Ardener 1964). Both Geertz and Ardener, arguably two of the most influential classical theorists on ROSCAs, characterized ROSCAs as practices of capital formation. In his analysis of a local Javanese traditional financial institution in Indonesia, Geertz coined the phrase "rotating credit association" (RCA), which he defined as offering "rotating access to a continually reconstituted capital fund" (1962:243). Similarly, based on her extensive research on ROSCAs in Nigeria and Cameroon, Ardener dubbed ROSCAs "capital-forming institutions" (1964:223). She redefined ROSCAs as: "An association formed upon a core of participants who agree to make *regular* [emphasis added] contributions to a fund which is given, in whole or in part, to each contributor in rotation" (1964:201). These early theoretical perspectives shaped subsequent generations of scholars who conducted a vast range of studies on ROSCAs in multiple cultural contexts.

Started as local, traditional banking institutions, *equbs*, like other ROSCAs, have confounded scholars' predictions that modernity and globalization would eliminate them (Geertz 1962). Instead, they have refused to remain local and have become global, transnational informal financial institutions through migratory processes. Ethiopian immigrants (and other immigrant communities) use *equbs* and other ROSCAs to advance their well-being and create new communities and identities in the USA and elsewhere. By transnational, I refer to the fact that ROSCAs have been brought by migrants to their destination countries, for example, *equbs* in the USA. The term also refers to how ROSCAs are created by people who live and work transnationally and use them to achieve diverse life aspirations both in the diaspora and countries of origin.[1]

In this article, I extend Guyer's (1993) and Guyer and Belinga's (1995) perspectives on 'wealth in people' into the world of ROSCAs, with a focus on *equbs*. By reworking anthropological perspectives on 'transactions' from two regions – Equatorial Africa and Melanesia (with a focus on New Guinea) – comparatively and examining the processes of "valuing people's qualitatively different dimensions", anthropologist Jane Guyer developed a 'wealth in people' framework (1993:246). Guyer's relational constitution of values as 'wealth in people' strongly resonates with Bourdieu's "forms of capital" (1986), in which he expanded the definitions from economics' narrow and abstract idea of financial capital to include cultural, social, symbolic, and, of course, economic capital, the formations of which he relocated in relationships. This underpins the interpretation of capital as socially valued resources (Neveu 2018:348)

---

1   I would like to thank Lisa Bohmer, my wife, Sophia Thubauville and Kim Glück for reading drafts of my manuscript and providing me with valuable critical suggestions and editorial assistance that helped me improve my article.

used here. Similarly, Hossein's (2023:188) apt conceptualization of black Caribbean women's lived experiences with ROSCAs as "the Black social economy" or "co-op economies" echoes perspectives of 'wealth in people'. Through her body of work, Hossein (2023, 2018, 2013; Hossein/Austin/Edmonds 2023; Hossein/Christabell 2022) has analyzed ROSCAs that are organized and led by black women, whom she calls "Banker Ladies", in five Caribbean countries and their diasporic communities. Hossein's "Black social economy" is relevant to our discussion of *equbs* in that it highlights the self-help and cooperative aspects of ROSCAs, i.e., the relationships or 'social solidarity', which are foundational to the success of ROSCAs and come in various forms in different contexts.

Following these three lines of thoughts, as the epithets at the top hint, I argue that *equbs* function as types of investment and *equb* actors perform as both investors and borrowers in the creative practices and processes of *equbs*, through which they actively mobilize and create various forms of capital. The concept of 'wealth in people' emphasizes the cyclical process of using *equb* to create both tangible wealth (wealth in things) by saving money and intangible wealth (social networks, and relationships) by investing in social capital. By analyzing the valuation process and interrelationships among *equb* actors, I analyze participation in *equbs* as acts of investment in and by people who embody and are embedded in relationships that are generative of various transferable forms of capital (Bourdieu 1986) and wealth (Guyer 1993). In doing so, I provide insights into how relationships play both foundational and constitutive roles in the life of ROSCAs.

This article is based on ethnographic research, including observation of the dynamics of *equb* meetings in L.A. and in-depth interviews in L.A. and Seattle. I conducted a total of 14 interviews with individuals (two *equb* leaders and 12 *equb* participants, of which four were female and ten were male) both in-person and via Zoom during 2021–2022 (supplemented by digital research). In doing so, I generated data on aspects of two *equbs* in L.A. and Seattle, which I use as examples of a number of *equbs* that exist not just there but also in other cities with a concentration of diasporic Ethiopians across the USA.[2] In the following, I present brief backgrounds of the *equbs*, the evaluation process of their participants, their manifestations as 'wealth in people' and forms of capital while working as forms of investment, and their role in building diasporic communities such as Little Ethiopia (juxtaposed with other ROSCAs-mediated immigrant communities), before offering a conclusion.

---

2   This study on *equbs* in L.A. and Seattle is part of a multisided research on informal banking and insurance associations among diasporic Ethiopian communities funded by the German Research Foundation (DFG). Elsewhere, I have analyzed aspects of this research in an article (Nida 2024), where I examine how Ethiopian immigrants use *equb* associations to craft their 'good lives' and futures.

Equbs in Ethiopia, L.A., and Seattle

Equbs are common in Ethiopia as reported by various scholarly studies that have provided motivational, historical, economic, and ethnohistorical accounts of these associations (Dejene Aredo 1993; Engdawork Desta 1995; Nida 2022; Mamo Tirfe 1999). *Equbs* are the Gurage-turned-Ethiopian version of ROSCAs and have played crucial roles in Gurage entrepreneurial success. They are widely found both in Ethiopia and its diasporas (Nida 2006; cf. Abraham Asnake; Dagne Shibru Abate/ Hanna Getachew; Glück; Sebhatleab Tewolde Kelati; Kelemework Tafere, this volume).

Elsewhere, I have examined how the Gurage emerged as the quintessential entrepreneurial class of Ethiopia over the last seven decades (Nida 2006, 2022). In those studies, I demonstrated that *equbs* were one of the three key intersecting elements of what I call the three-legged scaffolding of entrepreneurial success: individual initiative, ethnocultural resources (mainly via *equbs*), and political opportunity structures. The Gurage used the practice of *equb* as shorthand for solidarity, and the associations generated otherwise scarce capital. They provided an organizational structure and ideology for building and expanding business enterprises. Gurage migratory experiences transformed *equb*, a village institution, into a capitalist enterprise and helped the Gurage achieve demographic and leadership superiority within the national entrepreneurial landscape of Ethiopia. The Gurage data reveals that, historically, *equbs* were an innovation by Gurage village women, who used them to mobilize scarce resources such as milk, butter, and money for annual festivities and weddings in village contexts (Nida 2006). Later, these institutions proved their flexibility when Gurage migrants begin using them in new ways in urban and migratory contexts. Thus, in the context of Ethiopia, I argue that the practice of *equb* was a Gurage innovation,[3] one that was subsequently adapted by non-Gurage Ethiopians living in Ethiopia and in the country's diasporas.

Some have argued that *equbs* originated in urban contexts (Pankhurst/Endrias Eshete 1958). However, based on my research, the Gurage data show that *equbs* were village institutions that were transplanted into urban settings through migratory and entrepreneurial processes, and, at least in the case of the Gurage, were pre-urban, pre-capitalist, and traditional institutions that served social, cultural, and economic purposes, with their own operational and organizational structures that did

---

3   Cf. Nida (2022). Similarly, contributions in kind were commonly used in various ROSCAs, see Bascom (1952) for how Yoruba people in Nigeria contributed in cowries to *esusu*, their ROSCAs, in pre-colonial times. Parallel stories of the evolution of ROSCAs from women's activities are reported elsewhere (see Ardener/Burman 1995). In their edited volume, Ardener and Burman provide comprehensive accounts of women's ROSCAs in a variety of sociocultural contexts around the world.

not necessarily involve the use of writing. However, once they were transplanted to cities, they evolved operationally and organizationally, and were reorganized to support people's commercial economic lives (Guyer 1993:250), which involved monetary and writing systems. They did however, continue to perform their social and cultural functions even in urban, capitalist market economies. In a similar vein, *equbs* were (and are) practised in rural and urban contexts among other communities in Ethiopia (cf. Abraham Asnake; Dagne Shibru Abate/Hanna Getachew this volume). As anthropologists, we should value and respect the local people's stories of their indigenous institutions and inventions as told by themselves.

Further, the cultural idea of *equb* has been transplanted from Ethiopia to some of the world's most advanced capitalist societies, including the USA (cf. Glück, Kelemework Tafere, and Sebhatleab Tewolde Kelati this volume, for diasporic case studies in Israel, Dubai, and Germany, respectively). This transplantation process via forced or voluntary migration, leading to transnational cultural elements, has been seen in other contexts too. For example, Hossein (2023:188) has recently written about how five local ROSCAs (invented by Black Caribbean women, whom she calls the Banker Ladies) travelled across national boundaries from the Caribbean countries to their diasporas in the USA, Canada, and Europe.

Equbs in L.A. and Seattle

Diasporic Ethiopians have organized many *equbs* of various sizes in cities throughout the USA, including L.A. and Seattle. My study focuses on two examples in L.A. and Seattle. The histories of *equbs* in L.A. and Seattle are related to the history of Ethiopian immigration in the two cities. Ethiopian immigrants in L.A. and Seattle, like many other diasporic groups, live and work transnationally in a global and globalizing world that is characterized by flows of people, ideas, cultures, capital, and labour. Participating in these flows of things and people, Ethiopians brought elements of their cultures, including *equb*, through waves of immigration to L.A., Seattle, and other cities in the USA from the 1950s. Ober (2022) reports that 70,000–80,000 Ethiopians live in Greater L.A.[4] Ethiopian immigrants in L.A. and Seattle come from various ethnic groups in Ethiopia including the Amhara, Oromo, Wolayta, and Gurage, where *equbs* originated.

The practice of *equb* was transplanted to other regions of the world outside Ethiopia through the acts of immigrants such as Mr. S and Ms. W, two of my interlocutors. When Mr. S. came to L.A., there was one Ethiopian restaurant, whose business was not thriving. Mr. S. created an *equb* based at this restaurant in order

---

4   For more on Ethiopian diasporas, cf. introduction, this volume, Chacko (2003), Nida (2007), Kebede Kassahun (2017), Mary Goitom/Indemudia (2022), and Mary Goitom (2019).

to both help the owners improve their business and to provide other Ethiopians with loans in order to advance their well-being. Mr. S. said that *equb* is "a historical process, in our country, in Ethiopia, where people come together, improve their lives, build, and lead their future lives by contributing a specific amount of money. That is what we brought here" (June 12, 2022: Interview). The development of *equbs* in Seattle followed a similar pattern. Ms. W. told me that she created her *equb* in Seattle to improve her own and the *equb* members' life chances. She came from Ethiopia to Kentucky in the 1990s for school and subsequently moved to Washington, D.C., and then to Seattle in 2008. After struggling to survive on low-wage jobs and working multiple shifts, she wanted to work for herself. Ms. W. told me, "I was living from paycheck to paycheck. I was struggling with life, [and] work. One night I just came up with this idea that I have to create an *equb* and start my own business, instead of working for others with little payment" (January 12, 2023: Interview). In response to my question about where she got the idea for starting an *equb* as a means to improve her life, she said, "*equb yemetanibet new, bahilachen new*" in Amharic, i.e., *equb* is part of our history, our culture. Growing up in Ethiopia, I saw my father participating in *equbs* with friends for so many years, and sometimes he would take me to the *equb* meetings with him on Sundays. That is what came to my mind. I know that *equb* is useful" (January 12, 2023: Interview). That is how Ms. W. created her first *equb* ten years ago, and she has been the leader of that *equb* ever since.

These stories reveal how *equb* actors lean into their values and the belief that wealth resides in people to run successful of *equbs*. The value of 'wealth in people' consists of *equb* actors' embodied and embedded cultural and social capital, and specifically in two of Bourdieu's (1986) four forms of capital (social and cultural capital), which Ms. W. and Mr. S. were enculturated into while growing up in Ethiopia.[5] Building on Bourdieu's concept of habitus, Neveu writes, "embodied cultural capital ... [is] embodied in perceptual or interpretive dispositions" (2018:351). This resonates with my interlocutors' dispositions and the cultural views on *equb* that resulted from their enculturation. As repositories of 'wealth in people', these *equb* leaders (like other organizers of ROSCAs) are capable of mobilizing individuals who are also repositories of 'wealth in people' and of (re)producing various forms of capital for investments in activities aimed at building good lives and futures.[6] As such, the leaders (and members) function as investors, "the banker gentlemen and ladies", to borrow Hossein's phrase (2013:423–42). Both leaders and members invest money and other forms of capital that they embody in each other. In addition to this, leaders invest their time, knowledge (cultural capital), and networks (social capital).

---

5   Including, cultural, social, economic, and symbolic capitals.

6   Elsewhere, I have developed a framework, *equbs* as "*technologies* of the good life and future", to examine the transformative work of *equbs* as a social means of fighting poverty and advancing well-being (Worku 2024).

Thus, *equb* actors' 'wealth in people' (that is, the cultural and social capital stored in them through their socialization) translates into their capacities to imagine what a 'good life' might look like and how to realize it. 'Wealth in people' in the form of *equb* becomes a resource with which they envision and build a 'good life'; it becomes a form of investment in a 'good life', as *equb* actors' capacity to envision is shaped by and embedded in the cultures of *equb*. Following Appadurai (2004), I characterize the practice of *equb* as diasporic Ethiopians' socio-cultural capacity to lift themselves out of poverty. As unbanked and marginalized people with no or little access to formal financial services in the USA, *equb* enables diasporic Ethiopians to fight against (social and financial) exclusion and inequity in a racialized US political economy. The success of these efforts depends on effective ways of evaluating *equb* actors' values (trustworthiness, strong work ethics, social/cultural capital) as 'wealth in people'. In discussing how Caribbean Banker Ladies create "equitable economies" both in the home countries in the Caribbean and countries of their diasporic destinations including the USA, Canada, and UK, Hossein underscores that ROSCAs are tools for taking care of collectivity/community and fighting against exclusion, arguing that "ROSCAs are an antidote to racial capitalism" (2023:187); "ROSCAs take care of people's needs through collaboration and mutual aid. In proposing collective banking the women show that they are also addressing financial exclusion" (ibid.:188).

In a similar vein, other immigrant diasporas in the USA, such as the Korean, Chinese, and Japanese have used their versions of ROSCAs to mitigate against their financial and social exclusion. It is worth noting that some *equb* members have access to formal credit systems because they have already established some collateral, and that some individuals join *equbs* for social reasons, not just for economic ones. However, almost all *equb* members without demonstrable have little access to formal bank loans; the same is true among other minority immigrant groups in the USA. For example, in his aptly titled *L.A. Times* column, "Excluded by banks, minorities in California became their own lenders"[7], Shyong offered the following assessment of the role of ROSCAs in immigrants' lives and in creating communities:

"In Los Angeles, diverse neighborhoods probably wouldn't exist today without ROSCAs, which are most often run by women. When banks wouldn't lend to minorities, the kye helped Koreatown business owners cluster in central Los Angeles. The hui helped finance Chinatown, and tanomoshis helped start some of Little Tokyo's early businesses. There are also Latino tandas or cundinas, Filipino paluwagans and Ethiopian ekubs, and in South Los Angeles, family investment teams were formed after the L.A. riots to help black people buy property." (Shyong 2019)

---

7   This affirms that other ROSCAs also work as forms of investment and their participants are both investors and borrowers.

'Wealth in people' – The evaluation process of *equb* actors

These reconstituted *equbs* in the USA can be interpreted as cultures in action (i.e., as putting cultural ideas into practice) (Swidler 1986). In the *equbs'* processes and practices, being able to assess *equb* actors' 'wealth in people' values intersubjectively is vital to the success of *equbs*. According to the *equb* leaders and members that I interviewed, the assessment of who should be a valued member and why is always carried out in reference to whether individuals possess 'wealth in people' values, including embodied cultural and social capital and socially valued personal charactersitics such as trustworthiness, embodied relationships, leadership skills, and knowledge about *equb*, all of which are rooted in relationships.

In a similar vein, Ghosh (2020:195) deployed Guyer's (1993) 'wealth in people' model to examine the relationships between investors (running venture capital companies, VCs) and start-up entrepreneurs in India, providing insights into how prospective investors assess the 'wealth in people' values of entrepreneurs seeking investment capital, and how entrepreneurs actively establish their wealth in person (values) by "performing self through pitching". In the case of India, "investment is made in the specific personhood of the entrepreneur rather than the business plan" (Ghosh 2020:190). By contrast, in *equbs* among diasporic Ethiopians in the USA, investments are made both in the specific personhood and the business plans. According to my interlocutors, the specific personhood consists of both the relationships (ethnic and kin ties, for example) embodied by prospective *equb* members who are seeking investment capital and their personal qualities/characters. For example, one *equb* organizer told me that when individuals approach him about joining his *equb*, they always share their desires, ideas, and plans for improving their lives with him. He said people know that the main aim of an *equb* is to improve lives and that they do not join just for the sake of joining an *equb*. He further reflected on the ways in which he diligently judges the values of prospective *equb* members/borrowers as 'wealth in people' as follows:

> "If you are an *equb* organizer, you cannot allow [just] anyone to join your *equb*. You do not want someone to take the lump sum, which is other people's money, and disappear on you, or not be able to repay. You have to be very careful and selective in order to avoid problems such as default. When someone was proposed who I did not know about, in terms of their *history, background,* and *character,* I did not accept them as a member, unless someone else who I knew *vouched* for him/her [emphasis added]. *Bahiriachewen maweke wesagne new* [i.e., 'knowing their characters is critical']." (June 12, 2022: Interview)

Another *equb* leader echoed the significance of assessing people's 'wealth in people' values (social/cultural capital and socially valued personal characteristics), by highlighting the importance of trust for an *equb*'s success: "Trust is our collateral guarantee. For anyone to join my *equb*, either I must know them well personally or they have to come through my friends or other people who I trust [...]." (November 20, 2022: Interview). It is particularly revealing that this *equb* leader invoked the phrase "collateral guarantee", which is a mechanism through which formal financial institutions ensure that their borrowers will pay back the money that they lend them by linking the loans to other assets, properties, and businesses owned by the borrowers. These testimonies illustrate how *equb* leaders/organizers work like investors, judging prospective borrowers' value and worth. Unlike in formal banking and credit systems, however, what *equb* leaders/organizers look for as a guarantee from a prospective *equb* member/borrower is their 'wealth in people' and personal character rather than material assests, which most individuals seeking *equb* capital do not have. In contrast to formal institutions, *equbs* (and ROSCAs broadly) work as an alternative banking system that is based on trust – itself based on socially valued relationships and specific personhood – which translates into various forms of capital, both 'wealth in people' and 'wealth in things'.

Aside from trustworthiness and 'wealth in people' values, *equb* leaders also look for other qualities in prospective *equb* members. All members are potentially borrowers and lenders, including the leaders, because a member becomes a borrower when it is their turn to receive the lump sum; the other members who contributed to the lump sum are lenders. The organizers/leaders of *equbs* also act as investors, as do the Banker Ladies in the Caribbean cases. In this context, the assessment of a prospective *equb* member's values and relationships is necessary but not sufficient to secure their access to investment (*equb*) capital. In addition to being embedded in and embodying the relationships that are the sources of their 'wealth in people', prospective *equb* members must perform two tasks. First, in approaching the leaders/investors, prospective *equb* members must tell compelling stories as to why they want to join the *equb* and what they intend to use the money for. I interpret this as a form of the pitching that start-up entrepreneurs perform to convince potential investors to support them in places that include India (cf., for example, Ghosh 2020). Many non-leader *equb* actors told me about the critical role pitching/sharing their visions with the *equb* leaders plays in securing investment capital. One of them reflected, "whenever I join an *equb*, *I have a plan to improve things* [emphasis added]. I have *a vision for the future*. When you tell *equb* leaders that you have a plan, they want to help you achieve your goal. They have to view you as a person who plans for the future" (November 22, 2022: Interview). Second, prospective *equb* members are expected to embody the good character that translates into 'wealth in people'. What one leader called *"melkam bahiry yalachew"* ("those who have good characters") are individuals who are trustworthy, creditworthy, visionary, hard-working, and are not drunkards and extravagant with their money. These are the specific elements of personhood that are valued by the investors, that is, *equb* leaders, and this provides a critical insight into the workings of *equbs* as forms of investment.[8] This resonates with Guyer's argument: "The multiple dimensions of the value accorded to persons – manifest in the sheer breadth of techniques for the cultivation of personal beauty, strength, skill, and general worth – are intrinsic to any understanding of the dynamics of the wealth in people model" (1993:258).

This evaluation process is intersubjective in that it is not just *equb* leaders who evaluate prospective *equb* members. *Equb* members, on their part, judge the 'wealth in people' value of the *equb* organizers and leaders while electing them and making *equb* commitments. Both groups evaluate one another based on their being repositories of socioculturally valued relationships and on the personal characteristics of the individual, using what Guyer refers to as the criteria to evaluate "the multidimensional characteristics of people" (Guyer 1993:245). This is because both *equb* leadership and membership depend on people's values as wealth. My interlocutors mentioned that the same criteria are applied to assessing the values and worth of both leaders and members, that is, of all *equb* actors. One member recounts the following:

> "Due to elections, there is always a change in committee members, that is, leaders of *equb*. But everybody knows everybody else. Members would not elect someone who is not trustworthy (*abalate yemiamenute sew eza lie aysekemetum*). The same is true for people who are joining *equb*, and who are taking the *equb*. When you receive *equb*, they have to trust you. Since people's characters are known in the community, members and leaders know the who is who of *equb* community members. If you have a fishy character or a bad reputation in the community, people tell on you. They [*equb* leaders] will make you wait until the end of *equb*, that is when you can have the lump sum." (November 22, 2022: Interview)

These vetting processes are critical to creating *equb* capital for investment.

Equbs/ROSCAs working as forms of investment

The experiences of diasporic Ethiopians show that *equbs* are a social means for fighting poverty, achieving development, and advancing well-being. "*Equb* is a ladder for development" (February 22, 2022: Interview), one *equb* participant told me. "As *equb* leaders, we are lifting people [*equb* members and their families] out of poverty" (November 1, 2022: Interview), one *equb* leader said. These two personal

---

8   I used these examples in my upcoming (Nida 2024) article, but I use them in this piece from the perspective of 'wealth in people', as the interlocutors' own definitions of the values that constitute 'wealth in people'.

testimonies represent the local interpretations of *equb* associations among diasporic Ethiopians in the USA, who see them as tools to achieve development and lift people out of poverty. Such testimonials constitute a story (or stories) about how diasporic Ethiopians use *equbs* to envision and create their 'good lives' and futures. Fischer underscores that it is critically important to value local people's aspirations and agency: "Aspiration, a hope for the future informed by ideas about the 'good life', gives direction to agency – the power to act and the sense of having control over one's own destiny" (2014:207).

Diasporic Ethiopians in L.A. and Seattle join *equbs* with clear ideas about their futures and building well-being and a 'good life'. They imagine/envision better lives and futures for themselves and their (transnational and translocal) families to be achieved through membership of *equbs*, and this constitutes one of their cultural capacities to aspire that is deeply rooted in their 'wealth in people' values. One interlocutor benefitted from his *equb*'s priorities due to his clear vision and plans; he recounted a story of his own lived experiences with *equb* savings as a type of investment:

> "I was working as a taxi driver when I joined [an] *equb* for the first time in my entire life because I wanted to buy a taxi in partnership with my friend, half a taxi each. In *equb*, when you start new work and a new business, you get the first prize [i.e. the lump sum of *equb*]. ... I consulted with the judges, and I shared my goal of purchasing a taxi. They said you can have the first prize, according to our bylaw. That is what the first paragraph of the *equb* bylaw says, especially for people who want to start a new business. *That is one of its primary goals* [emphasis added]. I purchased my first taxi using the first prize of US$20, 000, in partnership with my friend. The taxi cost us about US$53,000, which we split between us. My friend and I agreed that I should drive our new taxi, as my friend already had his own taxi, which he was driving." (November 22, 2022: Interview)

This *equb* story explains how things work from the perspective of the local people, which can translate into what Nader (2011) dubs as "ethnography as a theory". This specific story illustrates how *equbs* function as forms of investment in the 'good life' and a better future. This interviewee's development did not stop with the purchase of his first taxi. Using *equb* as goal-directed saving and investment, he said that he saved money from being a driver-co-owner of his taxi and working long hours, with no vacations and limited sleep. He paid off the first *equb* debt, joined a new *equb*, and purchased another taxi that he fully owned. He also became a full owner of his first taxi, by paying his friend off. Subsequently, he bought a third taxi and employed a fellow Ethiopian as his driver, becoming an owner of three taxis, all by using *equb* money. Further, he told me that the *equb* leaders made him wait his turn to bid for the *equb* payouts that he used to buy his second and third taxis. Similarly, one of the leaders of the *equb* also used his *equb* money to purchase his own taxis. According to the leader in L.A., 45–50 people had become owners of various businesses – mostly taxis, restaurants, grocery stores, and liquor stores – because of the *equb* he established[9]: "We created our own banking system (*yerasachen bahilawi bank fetirene*). First, our people used our bank to buy taxis, then to purchase property, mostly residential houses, then grocery stores, then restaurants, etc. Because of such *equb* benefits, *equb* expanded in L.A. and throughout the US subsequently" (June 12, 2022: Interview). It is interesting to note how the leader used the word 'we', as it suggests that *equbs* are inherently social. The 'we-ness' also signifies the collective agency required to create your own banking system, evidencing my argument that all *equb* actors (leaders and members) are both investors and borrowers, simultaneously creating, seeking, and using investment (*equb*) capital. These stories also illuminate that *equb* actors actively create new 'wealth in people' values – in addition to mobilizing the 'wealth in people' values that people already embodied when/before they joined – through the practices and processes of *equbs* as forms of investment. The collective nature of ROSCAs has been underscored and characterized by other scholars as "community economies" (Hossein/Christabell 2022), "Black solidarity economy" (Hossein 2018; 2013), and "the helping ideology" (Wingfield 2008), to mention just a few.

The Seattle *equb* members followed a similar pattern of using the practice of *equb* as a type of investment in business and wealth creation. Ms. W., the *equb* leader in Seattle, told us: "Many of us in this *equb* are women. Almost all of us now are engaged in businesses in health care (some are nurses running elderly care and daycare centres with licences), and real-estate sectors thanks to my *equb*" (January 20, 2023: Interview). A total of eight out of my 14 interlocutors had acquired homes, businesses, and rental properties, and had amassed considerable wealth with which to create good lives and futures both in the USA and in Ethiopia.

Equb actors thus create assets by investing *equb* capital in various activities, and these newly created assets signify people's ability to produce new capital out of 'wealth in people'. These processes change the *equb* actors' terms of reference (Appadurai 2013), as they make the transition from being people 'without collateral' to individuals 'with collateral' from the perspective of formal financial and credit institutions. This shows how 'wealth in people' translates into 'wealth in things'. Furthermore, the process of creating assets (namely, businesses) has translated into the building of diasporic communities, as I will show below.

---

9 Beyond L.A., taxis constitute a niche for many diasporic Ethiopians in several cities. including San Jose, Seattle, Dallas, and Washington, D.C. where many people have evolved from being employed cab drivers to driver-owners and owners of their own taxis. On taxi driving as a niche among diasporic Ethiopians in Washington, D.C., cf. Chacko (2016).

Making diasporic communities through *equbs*/ROSCAs: Little Ethiopia and other immigrant communities

As forms of community building themselves, *equbs* have been instrumental in starting various businesses, including Ethiopian restaurants and stores, the concentration of which paved the way for the emergence of Little Ethiopia in L.A. (Chacko/Cheung 2011; Chacko 2003). A widely shared version of the story of Little Ethiopia is that an Ethiopian restaurant called Adolis was the first business to be opened on Fairfax, but it did not survive. Then Rosalind's Ethiopian restaurant was opened in the late 1980s. According to their website, the owners of Rosalind's claim that Rosalind's is the "oldest Ethiopian restaurant in L.A.". Subsequently, other Ethiopian businesses moved to the area and several new ones opened on Fairfax in the 1990s. As a result, currently, there are 13 Ethiopian-owned businesses in the area, of which eight are restaurants. This concentration of Ethiopian businesses gave birth to Little Ethiopia on Fairfax Street, between Pico and Olympia. It was officially named in 2002 and is demarcated by colourful Little Ethiopia street banners, positioned at each entrance to the neighbuorhood.

In addition to their entrepreneurial activities in this neighborhood, the political work of some diasporic Ethiopians, especially one group of business owners and political activists, contributed to the emergence of Little Ethiopia. This group of individuals worked hand-in-glove with locally elected African-American city officials and campaigned hard to get the neighbourhood renamed as Little Ethiopia. Today, more than two decades later, with its bustling ethnic restaurants, stores, cafes, and barbershops, Little Ethiopia has evolved into one of Southern California's most attractive destinations for both local Angelenos and tourists. After an in-depth interview, one of my interlocutors in Little Ethiopia walked me out of his restaurant. As we stood in front of the restaurant, he pointed to his restaurant and the Little Ethiopia sign at the northern end of the neighbuorhood and said: "We are here because of *equbs*" (November 12, 2023: Interview). This clearly illustrates the link between the *equbs* and Little Ethiopia. This particular interviewee owns one of the Ethiopian businesses that gave birth to Little Ethiopia in L.A. and played a leadership role in the struggle to receive official recognition for the area. He also served as the president of the Ethiopian Business Association in Little Ethiopia for several years.[10] Thus, by mobilizing their various resources, including 'wealth in people' values, diasporic Ethiopians in L.A. have constructed a new identity and community, reshaping the ethnic landscape of the city. In doing so, they have changed what Appadurai (2004:83) referred to as "the terms of recognition", becoming a (social, economic, and political) force to be reckoned with.

---

10   Ethiopian business owners established the association immediately after the formation of Little Ethiopia in 2002.

Ethiopians are not unique in using ROSCAs as instruments for creating diasporic minority communities and fighting against financial and social exclusions in the diaspora. In a similar way, other diasporic groups in the USA (and across the world) using culturally specific versions of ROSCAs have constructed businesses, identities, wealth, and communities, and have changed their terms of recognition.

Stories of the ROSCA-mediated formation of businesses and communities have become part of public discourse as well. Like Ethiopians, other immigrants lack access to formal loans and, therefore, resort to their cultural capacities (such as ROSCAs) to create 'good lives' and futures. Shyong (2019), a journalist writing on diversity and diaspora for the *L.A. Times*, observed: "In Los Angeles, home to one of the highest unbanked populations of any metropolis, the popularity of ROSCAs is both a product of discrimination and the tool to fight it" (Shyong 2019). Meanwhile, a PBS documentary, *Nailed It*, told the story of how Vietnamese Americans used ROSCAs to create and dominate the multibillion-dollar nail salon industry, which started in 1975, when American actress, Tippi Hedren, hired her manicurist, Dusty Coots, who trained 20 Vietnamese in nail work, laying the foundations for the industry.[11] Similarly, Netflix's 2020 film *The Donut King* followed the entrepreneurial trajectory of Cambodian refugee Ted Ngoy, recounting how Cambodian Americans came to dominate the doughnut business in California, largely by using *tontine*, their ROSCA. As Shyon (2019) notes, "If you've ever been to a Cambodian-owned doughnut shop, fried chicken restaurant, or jewelry store, there's a good chance it was financed by a *tontine*." Thus, the Ethiopian saying "*equbs* make people" appears to apply to the lived experiences of other groups, including Cambodians, Vietnamese, Korean, Chinese, and Japanese, as their own versions of ROSCAs have worked as engines of entrepreneurship and community building. These groups have also built their own ethnic enclaves, including Koreatown, Chinatown, and Little Tokyo in Los Angeles (Shyong 2019).

Scholarly studies have analyzed the entrepreneurial success of these diasporic groups and their neighborhoods (Woodrum/Rhodes/Feagin 1980; Bonacich 1973; Bonacich/Modell 1981; Light 1972; Porters/Back 1985; Light/Kwuon/Zhong 1990). Studies that suggested that African Americans lack entrepreneurially relevant resources to generate businesses overlooked and misrepresented the specific mutual help mechanisms of African Americans. African Americans have been portrayed as groups without the cultural resources needed to build entrepreneurship, and are hence lacking entrepreneurial acumen, in mainstream (dominant) studies on immigrant entrepreneurship in the USA, which Light (1972) spearheaded in sociology. It is interesting to note that journalist Shyong (2019) included African

---

11 NPR's Lulu Garcia-Navarro's interview with the director of the film Adele Free Pham, https://www.npr.org/2019/05/19/724452398/how-vietnamese-americans-took-over-the-nails-business-a-documentary (accessed, June 23, 2023). Cf. Light/Kwuon/Zhong (2009).

Americans in his account of groups with cultures of mobilizing versions of ROSCAs, including family-based resources, for building businesses and property. In contrast, however, some African-American scholars have provided correctives to these stereotyped (mis)representations of African Americans in the entrepreneurship literature. These scholars include Hossein and Christabell (2022; and Hossein 2018; 2013), who have critiqued mainstream topical studies that have excluded Black people's experiences with ROSCAs in both the Global North and South. Although Hossein's treatment of Black people's long-established cultures of ROSCAs focuses on Caribbean women, she rightly and forcefully critiques mainstream scholarship on ROSCAs in general and those created and run by women in particular for leaving out Black people's experiences. In her own work, she traces the long histories of Black Caribbean women who have created ROSCAs in five countries locally and used them in diasporas in various cities in North America and Europe (namely Great Britain and Ireland), and have made these local co-ops transnational, uplifting themselves, their families, and communities. Yet, some important works on the topic by African-American scholars including John Butler (2005) and Aida Harvey Wingfield (2008) are curiously absent from her otherwise significant work.

In his seminal work, Butler (2005) debunked the stereotyped views of African-American entrepreneurial experiences expressed by Light (1972) and others, through his robust archival and historical research. He reconstructed the histories of African-American entrepreneurship, showing that African Americans had long used their own 'wealth in people' values, which largely consisted of family- and faith-based resources, to create thriving business enterprises that gave birth to two famous Black business districts – one in Durham, North Carolina, and another in Tulsa, Oklahoma – which emerged during the last decades of the nineteenth century and the first two decades of the twentieth century, respectively. In Tulsa, Black entrepreneurial activity gave rise to a bustling business district in the Greenwood area, which came to be known as Little Africa and the Negro Wall Street. The area was burned down by white race-rioters in 2021 during the Tulsa race massacre (Butler 2005:215).[12] The Black business district in Durham was also called the Negro Wall Street. African Americans achieved these feats despite racial segregation and discrimination that was uniquely applied to African Americans, an accomplishment that Butler analyzed as "entrepreneurship under an economic detour" (2005:151–237). In a similar vein, Wingfield, drawing on her ethnographic and archival study of Black women's hair salon businesses, has provided powerful perspectives on how Black women used various mutual support mechanisms, which she explored as "the helping ideology" (2008:74–86), to create their businesses. Using insights from feminist scholarship to fill the gender void in Butler's otherwise important work, Wingfield (2008) developed a theory of "gendered racial enclave

---

12   For more on the story of Greenwood in Tulsa, cf. Butler (2005:207-237).

economy" to specify and explain the uniquely gendered racial segregation that Black women face in their entrepreneurial trajectories, which are different from the trajectories of those who worked in an ethnic enclave economy.

No other (non)immigrant groups were subjected to the economic detours and gendered racial enclave economies that have meant that African Americans have not been allowed to do business outside their own communities. For example, data from my own participant observation of businesses and interviews with Ethiopian business owners in Little Ethiopia shows that non-Ethiopian customers constitute a large majority of clientele for four successful restaurants there. In contrast, most, if not all, of the clientele for businesses owned by African Americans and operated under an economic detour and gendered racial enclave economy – in places like Tulsa and Durham which were racially segregated – were African Americans themselves. By banning African Americans from doing business with non-African Americans, the US government denied African Americans access to wider business opportunities as they were forced to do business only among themselves. This did not happen with other ethnic minorities such as Ethiopians, Koreans, and Chinese. Thus, those scholars who portrayed African Americans as non-entrepreneurial in comparison with other immigrant groups did not pay attention to the uniquely racialized sociohistorical realities of African-American experiences in the USA.[13]

Conclusion

Rooted in village Gurage women's practices in Ethiopia, *equbs* have refused to remain local, becoming critically important resources with which diasporic Ethiopians advance their well-being and struggle against financial and social exclusions. In this article, I used Guyer's 'wealth in people' model to rethink ROSCAs/*equbs* as forms of investment in the 'good life' and future. Deploying her framework enables us to shift the focus from discussing ROSCAs as just saving mechanisms to examining how ROSCAs work as forms of investment in which a) actors' 'wealth in people' values are actively assessed and constructed by prospective investors and members seeking investment capital, and b) various "forms of capital" (Bourdieu 1986) and wealth are co-constructed and change from one form to another in and through the practices and processes of *equbs*/ROSCAs. The relationships among *equb* actors (between investors/leaders and members seeking investment money) generate various forms

---

13   Butler (2005:41–68) reclaimed the intellectual history of African American scholars, who researched and wrote about African American business histories and developed concepts such as 'the middleman theory' and 'ethnic enclaves' used by leading scholars of ethnic immigrant entrepreneurship (Light 1972; Bonacich/Modell 1981; Portes/Back 1985) without citing those earlier studies.

of capital and individual/personal characters. I hinted at the broader application of my fresh theoretical perspective: *equbs*/ROSCAs as forms of investment in which social relationships are foundational and constitutive of success, which I dubbed technologies of the 'good life' and future. I demonstrated how *equb* actors participate as depositories of values as 'wealth in people' that are shaped by past relationships and experiences, which in turn are mobilized to create and manage new relationships and to shape future relations. *Equb* narratives reveal that relationships need to be socially valued and are necessary but not sufficient to ensure an *equb's* success. For *equbs* to be successful, *equb* actors must also look for personal characters, including the devotion of personal time and energy to the work of organizing, leading, managing, pooling, and redistributing *equb* resources. I provided comparative perspectives on ROSCAs by comparing the case of *equb* with how other diasporic groups (including Korean, Chinese, Japanese, and Vietnamese Americans) in the USA use ROSCAs to craft their versions of 'good lives' and futures by creating businesses (namely nail salons and doughnut industries), wealth, and communities such as Koreatown, Chinatown, and Little Tokyo. Like Ethiopians, through ROSCA-induced processes and activities, these groups have also shifted their terms of reference at multiple levels and have shaped the ethnic landscape of Southern California.

Further, I juxtaposed the stories of *equb*/ROSCA-users with the uniquely racialized experiences of African Americans, who have used various family and faith-based resources to build their 'good lives' and futures, as well as business districts in Tulsa and Durham. In doing so, I provided comparative perspectives on the cultural capacities to aspire to a 'good life' and future among new African Americans (diasporic Ethiopians included) and historic African Americans by following Butler (2005) and Wingfield (2008) in challenging biased views in the mainstream literature on ethnic (immigrant) entrepreneurship that have falsely claimed that African Americans lacked the cultural resources and entrepreneurial acumen to improve their lot. Thus, my narrative about *equb* and comparative analyses contributes to scholarship on ROSCAs, 'wealth in people', values, capital, well-being, and diasporic experiences more broadly.

Bibliography

Appadurai, Arjun (2004): "The Capacity to Aspire. Culture and the Term of Recognition." In: Vijayendra R./Michael W. (eds.), *Culture and Public Action. A Cross-Disciplinary Dialogue on Development Policy*, Palo Alto: Stanford University Press, pp. 59–83.

Appadurai, Arjun (2013): *The Future as a Cultural Fact. Essays on the Global Condition*, London, New York: Verso.

Ardener, Shirley (1964): "The Comparative Study of Rotating Credit Associations." *The Journal of the Royal Anthropological Institute of Great Britain and Ireland* 94/2, pp. 201–229.

Ardener, Shirley/Burman, Sandra (1995): *Money-Go-Rounds: The Importance of Rotating Savings and Credit Associations for Women*, Oxford: Berg.

Bascom, William (1952): "The Esusu: A Credit Institution of the Yoruba." *The Journal of the Royal Anthropological Institute of Great Britain and Ireland* 82/1, pp. 63–69.

Bonacich, Edna (1973): "A Theory of Middleman Minorities." *American Sociological Review* 38/5, pp. 583–594.

Bonacich, Edna/Modell, John (1981): *The Economic Basis of Ethnic Solidarity: A Study of Japanese Americans*, Berkeley and Los Angeles: University of California Press.

Bourdieu, Pierre (1986) "The Forms of Capital." In: Richardson, J., *Handbook of Theory and Research for the Sociology of Education*, Westport, CT: Greenwood, pp. 241–58, (https://home.iitk.ac.in/~amman/soc748/bourdieu_forms_of_capital.pdf).

Butler, John S. (2005): *Entrepreneurship and Self-Help among Black Americans: A Reconsideration of Race and Economics*, New York, State: University of New York Press.

Chacko, Elizabeth (2003): "Identity and Assimilation Among Young Ethiopian Immigrants in Metropolitan Washington." *Geographical Review* 93/4, pp. 491–506.

Chacko, Elizabeth (2016): "Ethiopian Taxicab Drivers: Forming an Occupational Niche in the US Capital." *African and Black Diaspora: An International Journal* 9/2, pp. 200–213.

Chacko, Elizabeth/Cheung, Ivan (2011): "The Formation of a Contemporary Ethnic Enclave: The Case of 'Little Ethiopia' in Los Angeles, Washington, D.C." In: Frazier J.S./Tettey-Fio E./Henry N.F. (eds.), *Race, Ethnicity and Place in a Changing America*, Binghamton, New York: Global Academic Publishing, pp. 129–141.

Dejene Aredo (1993): "The Informal and Semi-Formal Financial Sectors in Ethiopia: A Case Study of Iqqub, Idder, and Saving and Credit Cooperatives." *African Economic Research Consortium* (AERC), Nairobi, pp. 9–27.

Engdawork Desta (1995): "Agricultural Producer Cooperatives: Some Lessons of Experience from Ethiopia." *GeoJournal* 36/4, pp. 353–360.

Fischer, Edward (2014): *The Good Life: Aspiration, Dignity, and the Anthropology of Wellbeing*, Stanford: Stanford University Press.

Geertz, Clifford (1962): "The Rotating Credit Association: A 'Middle Rung' in Development." *Economic Development and Cultural Change* 10/3, pp. 241 – 263.

Ghosh, Ipshiat (2020): "Investment, Value, and the Making of Entrepreneurship in India." *Economic Anthropology* 7/2, pp.190–202.

Guyer, Jane (1993): "Wealth in People and Self-Realization in Equatorial Africa." *Man* 28/2, pp. 243–265.

Guyer, Jane/Belinga, Samuel M. (1995): "Wealth in People as Wealth in Knowledge: Accumulation and Composition in Equatorial Africa." *The Journal of African History* 36/1, pp. 191–120.

Hossein, Caroline S. (2013): "The Black Social Economy: Perseverance of Banker Ladies in the Slums." *Annals of Public and Cooperative Economics* 84/4, pp. 423–442.

Hossein, Caroline S. (ed.) (2018): *The Black Social Economy in the Americas: Exploring Diverse Community-Based Alternative Markets*, New York: Palgrave Macmillan.

Hossein, Caroline Shenaz (2023): "Caribbean Banker Ladies Making Equitable Economies. An Empirical Study on Jamaica, Haiti, Guyana, Trinidad, and Grenada." In: Hossein, Caroline Shenaz/Wright Austin, Sharon/Edmonds, Kevin (eds.), *Beyond Racial Capitalism*, Oxford: Oxford University Press, pp. 187–210.

Hossein, Caroline Shenaz/Christabell, P.J. (2022): "An Introduction: ROSCAs as Living Proof of Diverse Community Economies." In: Hossein, Caroline S./Christabell, P.J. (eds.), *Community Economies in the Global South: Case Studies of Rotating Savings and Credit Associations and Economic Cooperation*, Oxford: Oxford University Press, pp. 1–25.

Hossein, Caroline Shenaz/Wright Austin, Sharon/Edmonds, Kevin (2023). "Introduction." In: Hossein, Caroline Shenaz/Wright Austin, Sharon/Edmonds, Kevin (eds.), *Beyond Racial Capitalism*, Oxford: Oxford University Press, pp. 1–22.

Kassahun Kebede (2017): "Twice-Hyphenated: Transnational Identity among Second-Generation Ethiopian-American Professionals in the Washington, DC, Metropolitan Area." *African and Black Diaspora: An International Journal*, 10/3, pp. 252–268.

Light, Ivan (1972): *Ethnic Enterprise in America: Business and Welfare among Chinese, Japanese and Blacks*, Berkeley: University of California Press.

Light, Ivan/Kwuon, Im Jung/Zhong, Deng (1990): "Korean Rotating Credit Associations in Los Angeles." *Amerasia Journal*, 16 (2), pp. 5–54.

Mamo Tirfe (1999): *The Paradox of Africa's Poverty: The Role of Indigenous Knowledge, Traditional Practices, and Local Institutions – The Case of Ethiopia*, Asmara, Eritrea: The Red Sea Press, Inc.

Mary Goitom (2019): "The Epistemological Significance of Tizita and Sam-Enna Warq in Understanding the Return-Thinking Processes and Psychological Well-being Among Ethiopian Immigrants in Toronto, Canada." *International Journal of Ethiopian Studies*, 12/2, pp. 145–169.

Mary Goitom/Idemudia, Uwafiokun (2022): "Religion and Post-Migration Aspirations: Ethiopian Migrants in Canada." *Journal of Religion & Spirituality in Social Work: Social Thought*, 41/2, pp. 213–238.

Nader, Laura (2011): "Ethnography as a Theory." *HAU: Journal of Ethnographic Theory*, 1/1, pp. 211–219.

Neveu, Erik (2018): "Bourdieu's Capital (s): Sociologizing an Economic Concept." In: Medvetz, Thomas/Sallaz, Jeffrey J., (eds.), *The Oxford Handbook of Pierre Bourdieu*, Oxford: Oxford University Press, pp. 347–374.

Nida, Worku (2006): *Entrepreneurialism as a Social Movement: How the Gurage Became Successful Entrepreneurs and What It Says About Identity in Ethiopia*, Ph.D. dissertation, University of California, Los Angeles.

Nida, Worku (2007): "African Religious Beliefs and Practices in Diaspora: An Ethnographic Observation of Activities at an Ethiopian Orthodox Church in Los Angeles." In: Olupona, J./Gemignani, R. (eds.), *African Immigrant Religions in America*, New York: New York University Press, pp. 207–228.

Nida, Worku (2022): "African Entrepreneurialism: The Emergence of Ethiopian Gurage Entrepreneurs as a National Capitalist Class." In: Liebow, Edward/McKenna, Janine (eds.), *Anthropology and Entrepreneurship: The Current State of Research and Practice*, published by the American Anthropological Association, pp. 1–12.

Nida, Worku (2024): "*Equbs* as Technologies of "the Good Life" and Future among Diasporic Ethiopians in the US." Annals of Ethiopia, French Center for Ethiopian Studies, Addis Ababa, Ethiopia. Thubauville, Sophia/Glück, Kim (eds.) (forthcoming 2024): *Home and Future Making in the Ethiopian Diaspora*, Addis Ababa: Centre français des étdues éthiopiennes.

Ober, Holly (2022): "Living 'the Good Life' in Little Ethiopia. How an Informal Banking System is Helping a Los Angeles Community of Ethiopian Immigrants Thrive." *UCR Magazine*, Accessed March 8, 2024, (https://news.ucr.edu/ucr-magazine/winter-2022/living-the-good-life-in-little-ethiopia).

Pankhurst, Richard/ Endrias Eshete (1958): "Self-Help in Ethiopia." *Ethiopia Observer*, 2/1, pp. 358.

Porters, Alejandro/Back, Robert (1985): *Latin Journey: Cuban and Mexican Immigrants in the United States*, Berkeley: University of California Press.

Shyong, Frank (2019): "Excluded by Banks, Minorities in California Became Their Own Lenders." Accessed March 8, 2024, (https://www.latimes.com/local/lanow/la-me-tontines-ethnic-financing-20190318-story.html).

Swidler, Ann (1986): "Culture in Action: Symbols and Strategies." *American Sociological Review*, 51/2, 273–286.

Wingfield, Adia H (2008): *Doing Business With Beauty: Black Women, Hair Salons, and the Racial Enclave Economy*, Lanham, Maryland: The Rowman & Littlefield Publishing Group, Inc.

Woodrum, Eric/Rhodes, Colbert/Feagin, Joe R. (1980): "Japanese American Economic Behavior." *Social Forum*, 58/4, pp. 1235–1254.

Solidarity until the end
Insurance associations (*iddir*) of Ethiopians
in southern California

Sophia Thubauville

Abstract *Southern California has an Ethiopian diaspora population that goes back to the exodus from Ethiopia caused by the socialist revolution in the early 1970s. This diaspora increased immensely in number because of political and economic reasons around the turn of the millennium. With around 80,000 members, the Ethiopian population in southern California forms one of the largest immigrant communities in the USA, a country that hosts the largest Ethiopian diaspora in the world, of 500,000 people. One of the central and most widely attended life rituals in Ethiopia is the funeral service. For most members of the community in the USA, it is important to hold this event according to cultural norms or to repatriate the deceased to their home country. Both options are very expensive and require the help of others, whether that be in the preparation of Ethiopian food or knowledge of American laws. Around ten years ago, once many members of the Ethiopian diaspora were more settled in the USA, they established many insurance associations to help give culturally appropriate farewells to deceased members of the community. The following article discusses these groups as a form of "solidarity from below" (Featherstone 2012) and describes the imaginative power and ideas that lie at the foundation of these association as well as their limits.*

Introduction

Southern California has an Ethiopian diaspora population that goes back to the exodus from Ethiopia caused by the socialist revolution in the early 1970s. This diaspora increased immensely because of political and economic reasons around the turn of the millennium. With around 80,000 members, the southern Californian Ethiopian population constitutes one of the largest immigrant communities in the USA – the country with the largest Ethiopian diaspora in the world, with 500,000 people.

One of the central and most widely attended life rituals in Ethiopia is the funeral service. For most members of the community, it is important to hold this important event in the USA according to cultural norms, giving the deceased a religious burial accompanied by a feast with Ethiopian food and hundreds of guests, or to repatriate the deceased to their home country. Both options are very expensive and require the help of others, whether that be in the preparation of Ethiopian food or knowledge of American laws.

Around ten years ago, when many members of the Ethiopian diaspora had become more settled in the USA, they established many new insurance associations to help give culturally appropriate farewells to deceased members of the community. The following article discusses these groups as a form of "solidarity from below" (Featherstone 2012) and describes the imaginative power and ideas that lie at the foundation of these associations, as well as exploring their limits.

In the following, I will first provide an overview of the Ethiopian diaspora population in the USA at large and specifically in southern California, where my research took place. I will then explain the centrality of Ethiopian funerals as a creator of social relationships within the society. Following this, I will come to my main topic: insurance associations in Ethiopia itself and its diaspora. I would like to show how the environment of southern California has shaped these associations and how they help people of Ethiopian origin there to navigate their way, have a 'good life', and make a future as recent immigrants in southern California. Finally, I will explain that the basis for these associations is the "solidarity from below" (Featherstone 2012) among the community members. While I will give several examples of how this solidarity is expressed, I will end with some cases that also show its limits.

Since 2003 I have carried out various research projects within Ethiopia and have been able to observe burials and *iddir* associations within the country. My research in the US diaspora took place within the DFG funded project "On the saf(v)e side: Informal economic associations and future aspirations in the Ethiopian diaspora" in the summers of 2021 and 2022. I spent four months in Los Angeles and San Diego in southern California, where I led qualitative interviews with various members of the Ethiopian diaspora as well as with key figures of the associations studied.[1]

Ethiopians in southern California

Before and during the reign of Emperor Haile Selassie, emigration of Ethiopians to the USA was nearly non-existent. Only a few sons of the ruling class were sent to America for education, and after graduation, they mostly returned to their home country (Solomon Addis Getahun 2007:41).

---

1   The majority of my interlocutors were first generation immigrants to the USA. Also back in Ethiopia, people become members of insurance associations once they start their own families. Most second-generation Ethiopians in the USA have therefore not reached this stage of life yet.

The Ethiopian diaspora in the USA began to form out of the first Ethiopian intellectuals who were on scholarships in the country when the 'Red Terror' began. At that time an estimated 5,000 Ethiopian students, but also diplomats, tourists, and businessmen did not return to their homeland (Chacko/Gebre 2017:220). With the Refugee Act of the 1980s, the USA decided to grant asylum to an even larger number of Ethiopians. Between 1980 and 1999 an average of 1,500 refugees from Ethiopia were admitted to the USA annually. The refugees that arrived during the 'Red Terror' mainly came from Gondar, Tigray, Wollo, and urban centres like Addis Ababa, which had been hit hardest by the 'Red Terror' and the famine in 1984 (Solomon Addis Getahun 2007:135). The end of the socialist regime in 1991, however, did not bring an end to the political turmoil in Ethiopia. From 1998 to 2000 another major refugee flow entered the USA because of the Ethiopia–Eritrea war. From then on, and as immigrants changed their status to become US citizens, a process of chain migration emerged that still continues today (Chacko/Cheung 2011). Another factor – one not linked to Ethiopian politics – driving recent migration was the introduction of the Diversity Program in the USA, known in Ethiopia as 'lottery'. This program provided work permits for professionals and further stimulated the flow of immigrants from Ethiopia between 2003 and 2013.Within the framework of this program, 36,000 Ethiopians arrived in the USA and became legal residents (Chacko/Gebre 2017:221).

It is hard to estimate the total number of Ethiopians in the USA today. Statistics give a number that is too small, as they only include 'foreign-born' citizens. According to the Migration Policy Institute, in 2014 there were about 251,000 immigrants born in Ethiopia and their children living in the USA. The number of people of Ethiopian origin is believed to be about twice as high, that is, 500,000. This makes Ethiopians the second largest African diaspora in the USA after Nigerians. As 60 per cent of the Ethiopian immigrants arrived after 2000 (Migration Policy Institute 2014), they are one of the diasporas that has formed and settled more recently in the USA.

The Ethiopian diaspora in North America is extremely diverse in terms of religion (Nida 2007), ethnic and regional origin, and educational and economic background (Chacko 2011; Solomon Addis Getahun 2007). People are highly politicized and devote enormous monetary resources to their country of origin (Chacko 2011:173; Kaplan 2010:83; Lyons 2007:531). Because of the large number of the Ethiopian diaspora population in the USA, diverse political movements can form (Asafa Jalata 2002) and even influence politics in Ethiopia from afar (Lyons 2006). The Ethiopian diaspora in the USA is comparatively well educated, with 29.5 per cent of the people holding at least a Bachelor's degree (Terrazas 2007).

People of Ethiopian origin are concentrated mainly in large cities. Washington, D.C., with its good infrastructure and job opportunities, not only hosts the largest community, but also serves as an important point of entry to the USA. Another area with a strong Ethiopian diaspora is southern California, where I conducted my research. The larger Los Angeles area is home to an estimated 70,000–80,000 people of Ethiopian origin; San Diego has a community of about 10,000. Los Angeles not only has a high number of residents of Ethiopian origin, central Los Angeles even has the first ethnic designated enclave of Ethiopians in the USA, called "Little Ethiopia" (Chacko/Cheung 2011). This enclave consists of two blocks where Ethiopian restaurants and businesses are lined up next to each other and street signs, flags, and paintings on power boxes remind passers-by which district they are currently in. Little Ethiopia was an important starting point for my research, a place where I could make contact with individuals. The shops located there and their owners play an important role in the social and cultural life of the Ethiopian diaspora and in associations such as the insurance associations.

Bereavement as creator of social relationships

One of the central and most widely attended life rituals in Ethiopia is burial. It is a large-scale event carrying large obligations for the participants. Attendance at a burial of a relative or neighbour and the contribution of money toward its costs are musts. Therefore, burials are central in forming and expressing a relationship between the individual and its community (Kaplan 2003:645). Burials all over Ethiopia have in common that the deceased has to be buried a few hours after death, followed by a church service. Although the burial has to be done quickly, the performance of rites is prolonged and will take several days. The catering thus imposes large costs on the bereaved family.

To be able to cover the costs associated with the mourning period, informal insurance associations (Amharic: *iddir*, Oromifa: *afoosha*) are popular. Mutual support networks, which provide assistance in labour and kind at the time of death, can be considered as the forerunners of *iddirs* (Dejene Aredo 2010:58). *Iddirs*, however, are distinguished by the fact that they function on the basis of regular advance payments in cash, which is why Pankhurst dates their emergence to the beginning of the 20th century in urban centres, where it resulted from the modernization and monetization of the economy as well as urban migration (Pankhurst 2008:144). The regular payments in cash that accumulate in a pool of savings and the pay-out of a fixed amount of money in the case of a death are the *iddir*'s distinct features. In addition to these monetary benefits, *iddir* associations also provide utensils for the funeral service as well as services (cooking, catering, etc.). Outside these basic rules and functions, some associations today own offices or conference halls or even employ salaried staff, such as guards (Pankhurst 2008:166). However, most *iddirs* function only with volunteers. The following positions are usually awarded at regular meetings and are held by volunteers: chair/vice chair, secretary/vice secretary, and treasurer. More recently, *iddirs* have extended their offering into providing money for health expenditures or loans. Today, they are also recognized as effective tools in development activities or in assisting the health sector, for example, in the campaign against HIV/AIDS (Pankhurst 2008:143).

Iddirs are only useful if they function effectively and on a continuing basis. Therefore, compared to mutual support networks in the rural areas, *iddirs* are highly formalized: they keep lists of members, have written by-laws, regular meetings, fines for non-attendance or payment arrears, differentiated rules about pay-outs to the bereaved, and periodically elected executive committee members (Pankhurst 2008:148).

Iddirs are known for their inclusiveness, which is aimed at and accommodates all income levels. The prevalence of *iddirs* is the best sign of this inclusiveness. In Addis Ababa, for example, at least 85 per cent are members of an *iddir;* in some parts of the city, the number is more than 90 per cent. Some 40 per cent of households belong to more than one *iddir* (Pankhurst 2008:176). Most *iddirs* are organized by neighbourhoods and are therefore interreligious and interethnic.

My explanations so far have shown that even within Ethiopia, *iddirs* are highly dynamic associations that have evolved and changed in a period of about a century and constantly take on new forms and functions (Pankhurst 2008:177; Pankhurst this volume).[2] In the following, I show how the environment in southern California has shaped *iddirs*, and how they help people of Ethiopian origin to navigate their way, have a 'good life', and make a future as recent immigrants in southern California.

The rise of Ethiopian insurance associations in the USA

For most members of the Ethiopian community in the USA it is important to organize funerals in their host country as well as possible according to their cultural norms. In some cases, the body will be repatriated if the deceased was visiting family from Ethiopia or if they expressed a wish during their lifetime to be buried in their home country,[3] often going along with another mourning ceremony in Ethiopia.

According to my interlocutors, organizing burials was especially hard in the early days of the diaspora, when the community was smaller, although deaths did not happen so often back then as the new immigrants were usually of young age. At that time, if someone died in the host country, far away from home and in the absence of extended family, the owners of Ethiopian shops and restaurants were put in charge

---

2   For a broad overview of the history, spread, and diversity of the *iddirs* in Ethiopia, see the annotated bibliography by Desalegn Amsalu et al. (2020).

3   According to the numbers I received from the *iddirs* in Los Angeles in 2021, 15 per cent of deceased Ethiopians buried by them were repatriated to Ethiopia.

Saving and being safe in the Ethiopian diaspora

of the burial, since the funeral had to take place quickly and only such business people could provide large amounts of cash fast enough. The money was then returned to the businessmen via notices posted in their shops and restaurants that gave information about the person who had died alongside a box for collecting money. If the deceased had family members, they also collected contributions from the Ethiopian community at appropriate locations. A.[4] described it as follows:

> "They put a box in the house where the people lived, or people had to go all over Ethiopian markets and restaurants and go to the airports and hotels asking the taxi drivers[5] to help, also asking the grocery customers to help out." (A., July 26, 2021: Interview)

This approach seemed to work in most cases, attracting enough people from the Ethiopian community to pay a share of the costs out of solidarity.

Only a few *iddirs*, which were small in membership and pay-outs existed prior to 2010 in the USA and in southern California. Los Angeles, for example, then had only one *iddir*, which had been founded in 1992 with only 44 members, who were all close friends. Then, the Ethiopian population increased in size and became more established in their host country as the early migrants aged. With more professionals among them who could deal easily with US bureaucracy, it became possible to establish *iddirs* according to the Ethiopian model and register them as associations according to US law. Today both Los Angeles and San Diego, have five *iddirs* each. About half of them are organized by churches[6] and at least one of them in each town has more than 1000 members. Ethiopian churches were founded in the USA much earlier than the *iddirs*; Los Angeles has, for example, five Ethiopian Orthodox churches and four Protestant churches.

The services provided by these *iddirs* are extensive and precisely tailored to the needs of the Ethiopian community in the USA. As G. explained:

> "[...] you take care of your mourning and we take care of the other business. Inviting people, feeding them, collecting money, death certificate, sending the body in a cargo to Ethiopia or Eritrea. Have you ever heard of a life insurance company who would do all of that? [...] This is a lot more than insurance." (G., July 23, 2021: Interview)

Several interlocutors made this comparison with formal life insurance. Still, just as many people are members of several *iddirs* in the USA, as well as back in Ethiopia,

---

4   Interlocutors are anonymized in the following by using only the initials of their given names.

5   Ethiopian taxi drivers form an occupational niche in many large US cities (Chacko 2016), also in Los Angeles. At the airport, Ethiopian cab drivers can be found in large numbers.

6   For Orthodox churches in Los Angeles, see Nida (2007).

many members of *iddirs* who can afford to pay or are covered by their employers also have formal life insurance.

In addition to the above-mentioned services they provide to their members, some *iddirs* have even purchased their own burial plots. Burial plots are one of the major costs of a burial, and interlocutors also mentioned the importance of people being buried in the vicinity of other Ethiopians and not just in any random graveyard.

Members of the Ethiopian community in southern California mentioned the issue of time when comparing *iddir* burial services in Ethiopia and the USA. While people in Ethiopia will mourn together for days and weeks accompanied by the members of their *iddir*, solidarity with mourning Ethiopians in the USA is expressed more through sharing in the financial costs of the loss: "But the place where we live in the Western society, you know, it is busy. We don't have time. So, the only means we have is we give them [the mourning family] financial assistance" (F., July 22, 2021: Interview). Of course, the *iddir* provides food and a place where people can come together, but as people still have to continue doing their jobs, the social part of mourning was very reduced in southern California compared to in Ethiopia, where people spend a lot of time at mourning ceremonies. Members have adapted this socializing aspect to their new environment, where people are very busy at work and sometimes live far away from each other; this is very different to Ethiopia, where *iddirs* are neighbourhood associations. The following example from the website of one *iddir* illustrates this:

> "We aren't looking to run this association as it runs back home in Ethiopia, instead we can utilize the internet (e-mail) for communication, the banking system for paying our contributions, and conference meeting as needed to make collective decisions. Information can pass by e-mail between members or to all members, contributions can be paid to the association account by each individual member at his/her convenience, and most meetings can be done without members leaving their living room." (website of Hibret *iddir*)

The *iddir* that has changed most in comparison to *iddirs* back in Ethiopia and has adapted the most to the circumstances that Ethiopians face in their new home in the USA is the Dir Biyabir *iddir*. Founded in Los Angeles in 2014, this *iddir* had 1369 active members by mid-2021. This means that, including dependents, it covers 10,000 Ethiopian individuals in Los Angeles and its surroundings. After an admission fee of US$100, members are asked to contribute US$25 when a member dies. The deceased person's family then receives US$20,000. The payment per loss rather than on a regular basis is one big difference to *iddirs* back in Ethiopia, where people contribute a small fee monthly. The chairperson of the Dir Biyabir *iddir* emphasized that members, unlike in Ethiopia, do not have many obligations apart from the ad hoc payments, which are regarded as very affordable and are often compared to prices for coffee at Starbucks or food in fast food chains. Because of the large number of members, this *iddir* also has the advantage that it can extend its solidarity to non-members very easily. This was described by the chairperson as "we leave no one behind", meaning the *iddir* feels responsible for the whole Ethiopian community in Los Angeles, not only those who are members of the *iddir* before their death. From the 136 people that the *iddir* had buried so far, nine were non-members. The burial of non-members is an obvious difference to *iddirs* back in Ethiopia, which provide services only for their members.

Such large *iddirs* have been established in many US towns recently, but smaller *iddirs* are at the same time still being established and thriving. While large *iddirs*, also have large pay-outs, smaller *iddirs* are preferred for their more intimate atmosphere and for socializing. Most people I have talked to belong to more than one *iddir*, and some members of the first *iddir* in Los Angeles were also founding members of the large Dir Biyabir *iddir*. While they wanted to keep their own *iddir* small and intimate, they wished to extend the solidarity offered through an *iddir* to their whole community. This is something that can only be achieved through larger *iddirs*.

The above-mentioned details on the formation and adaption of Ethiopian *iddirs* in their new environment in southern California shows that these associations are flexible enough to adapt to new social and economic realities within Ethiopia and within Ethiopian communities outside the motherland. This flexibility among the *iddirs* in southern California was particularly obvious during the Covid-19 pandemic that emerged in 2019. About 50 per cent of the associations I interviewed reported a higher death rate among their members during the pandemic. Nevertheless, all associations survived the pandemic and were able to make the required payments to the relatives of members who died. The *iddirs* only had to stop services such as repatriations and large, catered events, because of pandemic regulations.

The power of solidarity

Above, I have explored the growing community of Ethiopians in the USA, the importance of burials as life-cycle rituals and creators of social relations in the Ethiopian community, and how informal insurance associations that provide the financial and social means to bury people have been adapted to circumstances in the USA. In this section, I describe what I see as the foundation of these associations: the solidarity that individuals show for their community. As my interlocutor A. aptly put it: "In Ethiopia love comes when you die."

Understanding the solidarity shown in establishing *iddirs* as representative of equals supporting each other to better their lot is too short-sighted. Yet, in thinking about solidarity, I do not want to draw on a certain nostalgia that often accompanies descriptions of alternative economies based on solidarity that try to regain human dignity (Bähre 2020:11). Rather, what I do is to present the solidarity shown by establishing or engaging in Ethiopian *iddirs* in the USA as an adapted form of solidarity, one that has its limits and is very much oriented towards the new environment of the Ethiopian community, dominated as it is by ideas of capitalism and the importance of the individual and privacy.

But let me start with the imaginative power and ideas that are so central to the transformative force of solidarity or, as Featherstone calls such new connections of assistance and care, "solidarity from below" (2012:6). The best insight into the ideas and images that underlie the *iddirs* is provided by some of their names. Here are two examples:

ድር ቢያብር እንበሳ ያስር = When spiderwebs unite, they can tie up a lion.
ሃምሳ ሎሚ ላንዱ ሰው ሽክሙ ለሃምሳ ሰው ጌጡ ነው = Fifty lemons are a load to one person, to fifty people they are a decoration.

The underlined beginnings of these Amharic proverbs provide the names of two *iddirs* in the USA. The Amharic names of the associations, of course, already create a sense of belonging for members. Moreover, the proverbs on which their names are based clearly call people to work together, to help each other, and to be in solidarity. Their message is "together we are strong" and "what is difficult for one, is easy when you stick together".

While the names and proverbs give a good idea of the imaginative power of the associations, the reasons for the emergence of such solidarity can be found in the new home of the Ethiopian community. Ethiopian funerals differ in many ways from ordinary funerals in the USA, but two points in particular stand out here. First, in Ethiopia, bodies have to be buried quickly and cremation is not an option.[7] Second, the funerals are attended by a very large group of people and last for several days. Then, of course, religious rites in Ethiopian languages and cultural food for the catering add to make hosts and guests feel comfortable even during those sad circumstances. The cultural differences the diaspora community encounters in their new home country creates the solidarity that encourages them to establish or join *iddirs*.[8] On the one hand, group solidarity is necessary to carry out funerals according to Ethiopian cultural norms in a new, culturally very different environment. *Iddirs*,

---

7   Compare Balkan (2023) who describes how Muslim undertakers and representatives of Islamic civil society associations in Berlin see it as their religious duty to 'save' deceased Muslim from cremation.

8   Compare Eckert (2019) who explains how the solidarity among refugees in Germany arose because of improper treatment.

for example, deal with funeral homes and authorities and are therefore cultural brokers between the two worlds. On the other hand, funeral ceremonies and the cultural normative burial of community members are so central to the community that most members are willing to help through their monetary contribution or even through voluntary work for their *iddir*.

The limits of solidarity

However, solidarity and every community have their boundaries. Help cannot be extended to everyone, even if it is desired or if an *iddir* claims to be inclusive. Smaller *iddirs* are often exclusive; some are organized by churches and membership of the church is a prerequisite to membership of the *iddir*. Larger *iddirs* have detailed bylaws that mark their 'boundaries'. While some are, according to their bylaws, open to anyone who resides within a given radius, other associations restrict their membership to Ethiopians and people of Ethiopian origin. This is, of course, a major issue, as many Eritreans or people of Eritrean origin also live in the USA and, sharing the same cultural background as the Ethiopians, might want to be members of an *iddir*. Moreover, the past and present political situation in Ethiopia can be a major stumbling block for Ethiopians in their new host society (Getahun 2007:112). Political discord among the Ethiopian community's members, many of whom are politically very active, constantly challenges many of the community's initiatives. Dissonance is mostly caused by Ethiopia's ethnic federalism, and political events in Ethiopia are reflected in the diaspora. This is one of the biggest points of friction and repeatedly found as a reason why *iddirs* disband or new ones are founded.

Another point that is hotly debated in many *iddir* is the admission of elderly, and especially sick, people. Views diverge on the issue. The headperson of one *iddir* presented the new registration of older and sick people as a central part of group solidarity and as giving the *iddir* a clear advantage over formal insurance options: "If we considered ourselves as a profit organization, we would not take risk persons" (A., August 20, 2022: Interview). As can be seen from his statement, he welcomes the inclusion of old and sick people, who are included in most *iddirs* under exactly the same conditions as healthy, young people, unlike with formal insurance, where the older and sicker one is, the more costly it becomes. However, in another *iddir*, the admission of several elderly and sick people within a short time of their deaths, which led to high costs for the members, was seen by some as exploitative.

Some *iddirs* regulate the admission of elderly people through their bylaws to ensure a healthy age structure in the association, as B. explains: "Even if we have enough members joining, but they are all 60 years and above, we will get a problem soon" (August 18, 2022: Interview). Therefore, to attract more young people, the registration fee for his *iddir* is waived for people below 30 years of age. The same *iddir* recently added two new conditions for new members to their bylaws: relatives of new members aged over 70 years have to wait one year instead of six months to receive a pay-out in case of death; if new members have children aged 30 years and above, these children also have to become members of the *iddir* at the same time. Asked to clarify this second condition, B. explained:

> "It is also about the responsibility of the kids towards their parents. What we are saying is: We are bringing 500 people [the members of the *iddir*] to help you, if you don't join, it [covering and organizing the burial] is your responsibility. [...] If you do not wanna be a member, you are going to outsource your responsibility to the members. That is not fair!" (B. August 18, 2022: Interview)

Such boundaries to solidarity are constantly discussed and renegotiated in the *iddirs'* board meetings. The above examples show that solidarity can become a burden (Bähre 2007:112), thus defining boundaries is necessary.

Another strategy employed by *iddirs* in order to maintain their social and financial health is to minimize the burden of solidarity. The large Dir Biyabir *iddir* has done this successfully, as having many members reduces the financial burden of each individual. The large size of such *iddirs* also makes them nearly as anonymous as formal insurance organizations. People do not know all the other members and are therefore not expected to attend every funeral. In addition, as described above quoting the website of one *iddir*, banking and communication can be done most comfortably electronic so that people do not have to leave their homes and are not burdened with socializing activities. Reducing these burdens of solidarity, especially socializing, might not be in the interests of everybody in the Ethiopian community. However, it might be a compromise that makes an *iddir* attractive to second generation members, who have socialized partly according to US norms, as H. describes:

> "For the younger generation it will be hard for them [joining an *iddir*], because they do not understand it. They can buy an insurance. That is just the money part. The younger kids don't understand how it keeps the village together when you do things like that … as a community as a group. Because each time somebody dies, 300/400 people show up. Just to bury them. That is like an honour thing [...]." (H., July 23, 2021: Interview)

However, large *iddirs* also have their limits, as I heard during my research in 2022. The number of members of the Dir Biyabir *iddir* in Los Angeles had become so high that the volunteers could barely manage it anymore and were thinking about splitting the association into two smaller groups. For the time being, they decided to have a waiting list for new members. As one of the major board members explained:

"Since we do this voluntarily [...] we have to know our limit" (F., August 16, 2022: Interview).

Conclusion

Funerals are very central life-cycle events in Ethiopia. The expense and organization of these big events are covered by informal insurance associations, which have been also adopted and adapted by the growing Ethiopian population in the USA. These informal arrangements attempt to bridge the gap left by the formal insurance sector and, apart from the obvious function of financial assistance, enable people to be buried according to their cultural norms. Here, the flexibility of the *iddirs* and their potential to be adapted to the new life worlds of migrants is proved once again.

I have tried to show that these informal associations or *iddirs* can be seen as an example of solidarity from below that has the imaginative power to invent new institutions of care and support (Featherstone 2012:6). The solidarity, rhetorically expressed by the Amharic proverbs often used for naming those associations, arises among other reason from cultural differences regarding burial practices in migrants' new surroundings.

However, to avoid the burdens of solidarity, associations constantly have to renegotiate the boundaries of their membership, be this for ethnic and political reasons or reasons of elderly applicants. Moreover, I have shown that some Ethiopian *iddirs* in the USA have found a creative and new way to extend solidarity to the whole Ethiopian community with very little effort by enlarging the association to a level where it is nearly anonymous and involves very low monetary and no social obligations. This new version of an *iddir* seems contradictory at first: on the one hand, *iddirs* and their members aim to extend solidarity to the whole Ethiopian community; on the other hand, participants should be spared financial expense and social commitment as far as possible. However, this association, which offers the financial coverage and cultural appropriate burial in return for a minimal monetary and social expenditure, may be successful in catering for young and second-generation Ethiopians in the future.

Bibliography

Asafa Jalata (2002): "The Place of the Oromo Diaspora in the Oromo National Movement. Lessons from the Agency of the 'Old' African Diaspora in the United States." *Northeast African Studies* 9/3, pp. 133–160.

Bähre, Erik (2007): *Money and Violence. Financial Self-Help Groups in a South African Township*, Leiden: Brill.

Bähre, Erik (2020): *Ironies of Solidarity. Insurance and Financialization of Kinship in South Africa*, London: Zed Books.

Balkan, Osman (2023): *Dying Abroad. The Political Afterlives of Migration in Europe*, Cambridge: Cambridge University Press.

Chacko, Elizabeth (2011): "Translocality in Washington, D.C. and Addis Ababa: Spaces and Linkages of the Ethiopian Diaspora in Two Capital Cities." In: A. Datta/K. Brickell (eds.), *Translocal Geographies: Space, Places, Connections*, Farnham: Ashgate Publishers, pp. 163–178.

Chacko, Elizabeth (2016): "Ethiopian Taxicab Drivers: Forming an Occupational Niche in the US Capital." *African and Black Diaspora: An International Journal* 9/2, pp. 200–213.

Chacko, Elizabeth/Cheung, Ivan (2011): "The Formation of Contemporary Ethnic Enclaves. Little Ethiopia in Los Angeles and Washington, D.C." In: John S. Frazier/Eugene Tettey-Fio (eds.), *Race, Ethnicity and Place in a Changing America*, New York: Global Academic Publishing, pp. 129–141.

Chacko, Elizabeth/Gebre, Peter H. (2017): "Engaging the Ethiopian Diaspora. Policies, Practices and Performance." In: Jack Magala (ed.), *Africa and its Global Diaspora. The Policy and Politics of Emigration*, Berlin: Palgrave/Springer, pp. 291–249.

Dejene Aredo (2010): "The Iddir: An Informal Insurance Arrangement in Ethiopia." *Savings and Development* 34, pp. 53–72.

Desalegn Amsalu/Bisaillon, Laura/Yordanos Tiruneh (2020): "'I Have Risen from the Place I Always Used to be': An Annotated Bibliography of the Ethiopian Iddir." Accessed March 18, 2022 (https://papers.ssrn.com/sol3/papers.cfm?abstract_id =3662537).

Eckert, Julia (2019): "The Solidarity of Concern." *Anthropological Theory Commons*. Accessed March 18, 2022 (https://www.at-commons.com/2019/12/17/the-solidarit y-of-concern/).

Featherstone, David (2012): *Solidarity. Hidden Histories and Geographies of Internationalism*, London: Zed Books.

Kaplan, Steven (2003): "Burial." In: *Encyclopaedia Aethiopica* 1, Wiesbaden: Harrasowitz, pp. 345–349.

Kaplan, Steven (2010): "Ethiopian Immigrants in the United States and Israel. A Preliminary Comparison." *International Journal of Ethiopian Studies* 5/1, pp. 71–92.

Lyons, Terence (2006): "Transnational Politics in Ethiopia. Diasporas and the 2005 Elections." *Diaspora: A Journal of Transnational Studies* 15/2, pp. 265–284.

Lyons, Terence (2007): "Conflict-Generated Diasporas and Transnational Politics in Ethiopia." *Conflict, Security & Development* 7/4, pp. 529–549.

Migration Policy Institute (2014): "The Ethiopian Diaspora in the United States." Accessed March 15, 2022 (https://www.migrationpolicy.org/sites/default/files/pu blications/RAD-Ethiopia.pdf).

Nida, Worku (2007): "African Religious Beliefs and Practices in Diaspora: An Ethnographic Observation of Activities at an Ethiopian Orthodox Church in Los Angeles." In: Jacob Olupona/Regina Gemignani (eds.), *African Immigrant Religions in America*, New York: New York University Press, pp. 207–228.

Pankhurst, Alula (2008): "The Emergence, Evolution and Transformations of Iddir Funeral Associations in Urban Ethiopia." *Journal of Ethiopian Studies* 41, pp. 143–185.

Solomon Addis Getahun (2007): *The History of Ethiopian Immigrants and Refugees in America, 1900–2000: Patterns of Migration, Survival, and Adjustment*, New York: LFB Scholarly Publishing.

Terrazas, Aaron Matteo (2007): "Beyond Regional Circularity: The Emergence of an Ethiopian Diaspora." *Migration Policy Institute*. Accessed August 8, 2023 (https://www.migrationpolicy.org/article/beyond-regional-circularity-emergence-ethiopian-diaspora).

Islands of hope
Informal savings associations among Ethiopian Israelis and the Ethiopian-Eritrean diaspora community in Israel

Kim Glück

Abstract *Informal savings associations (known as equb/qubye in the Ethiopian context) are a global phenomenon and a future-oriented practice that is ubiquitous in the diverse Ethiopian–Eritrean community in Israel. The heterogeneity of this community is reflected in the fact that it is divided into two groups, differentiated primarily by their legal status. On the one hand, there are Ethiopian Israelis, most of whom immigrated to Israel in the early 1990s and were naturalized under the Israeli Law of Return. Since their arrival in their long-awaited religious homeland, they have been an integral part of multicultural Israeli society. With security offered by the Israeli welfare state (e.g., pensions), state mortgages, and the possibility of house ownership, there is little need to save money urgently for an uncertain future (Kaplan 2010: 73). Yet, the equb practice is quite significant among Ethiopian Israelis. On the other hand, there are Ethiopian and Eritrean migrants who are in Israel as asylum seekers. They are temporarily tolerated, and Israel is mostly just a short-term stopover on the way to a future home elsewhere. For these migrants, belonging to an equb group is an important mechanism for maintaining and strengthening connections with the diaspora community and increasing financial security. This paper aims to offer a comprehensive understanding of hope in the context of the equb practice of Ethiopian Israelis as well as within the Ethiopian–Eritrean diaspora community in Israel, exploring its manifestations across various temporal, spatial, and social aspects.*

Introduction

"You know, we are still not safe; we do not have a comfortable life, for 17 years we have been living under these conditions. As long as you work, you're free, but my thoughts, [...] you're in prison, you can't go anywhere and you don't have papers to do what you want [...] especially for me, it's hard. I just want to be able to give my son a good life." (J., June 2, 2022: Interview)

I meet J.[1] on a Thursday morning before she goes to work. J. works as a housekeeper in a suburb of Tel Aviv, "where the rich people live", as she says. At the same time, she is training to be a graphic designer in an evening course run by an Israeli NGO, the African Refugee Development Center (ARCD). Since she has been in Israel, she has made her living mainly as a cleaner. She came to Israel 17 years ago by plane on a tourist visa. She cites political reasons as the main reason for her migration. Her legal situation has not changed since her arrival. She has to visit the United Nations High Commissioner for Refugees (UNHCR) centre in Tel Aviv every three to four months to apply for a new temporary residence permit.

J.'s story serves as an illustration of the lived experiences encountered by Ethiopian and Eritrean migrant workers in Israel. Amid the tension of temporary residence permits, precarious working conditions, the absence of social benefits, and an uncertain future, they try to build a more promising existence – an aspiration expressed in the notion of a 'good life', as J. herself says. This raises the fundamental question: What does this elusive concept of the 'good life' entail, and how is it achieved or realised? Edward F. Fischer (2014:2) defines the 'good life' as the ceaseless pursuit of an improved state that gives meaning to one's existence. This pursuit of meaning is deeply linked to individualized aspirations, significantly influenced by cultural values (Fischer 2014:7). The definition of a fulfilling life varies among individuals, raising questions about the criteria employed to delineate, comprehend, and grasp this inherently abstract and deeply personal notion. To capture the diverse and individual conceptions and aspirations of the 'good life', which depend on different life circumstances, it is crucial to consider non-material dimensions in addition to measurable, material parameters such as income, health, and security. These non-material dimensions include qualities such as aspiration, hope, dignity, fairness, imagination, and possibility (Fischer 2014:2).

An essential component to the notion of the 'good life' is its aspirational quality—an envisioning of life that is imagined and hoped for. This perspective draws upon Ernst Bloch's characterization of hope as a dream of a better life (Bloch 1977 [1959]:9). According to this view, hope perpetually reveals an insufficiency; it is aimed towards a state that is not yet present but has the potential to materialize in the future. Stef Jansen addresses this aspect and emphasizes that hope or hopeful actions inherently require an element of indeterminacy, without which hope would not exist (Jansen 2016:460). In his exploration of hope, Jansen stresses the linearity of the temporal argumentation of hope, adapting Bloch's teleological principle and its future-oriented aspect, which leads to an anticipated "not yet" (Jansen 2008:57f.; Jansen 2016:459f.). Further, Jansen differs between an intransitive and transitive use of the term hope. When hope is used in an intransitive manner, it relates to an emotional state (an *affect*), which can be described as hopefulness. In this context, the

---

1   To protect the personal rights of my interview partners, all names are anonymized.

emphasis is not on any specific hope directed towards a particular object. Hopefulness is rather vague, and it is employed with the expectation of acknowledgment, largely stemming from emotional resonance. When used in a transitive manner, the term hope is directed towards an object: individuals hope for something (in the case study: Israeli citizenship) or hope that something will occur (e.g., changes in migration laws in Israel). Both modalities may refer to the same condition but illuminate it from different perspectives (Jansen 2016:448f.). In this context, Jansen highlights that hope (for/that) does not necessarily have to have positive connotations. Hope can also be illusory in the sense that it will never be fulfilled or will be socially not accepted (Jansen 2016:454; Jansen 2009:46; 57f.).

Hope always directs its gaze towards future possibilities, which imbues it with an intrinsically future-oriented dynamic. Rebecca Bryant and Daniel M. Knight's analysis of hope contributes to the understanding of hope as an actively transformative force. They assume that hope is both an abstract and a general orientation towards the future, capable of bringing the not-yet into the present and inspiring present action (Bryant/Knight 2019:157). This perspective highlights the idea that hope comprises more than simply longing for a better life; it involves actively shaping one's future in the present, as the vision of the future ignites present actions and motivations (Bryant 2020:17). This means that when researching hope, not only aspirational visions of the 'good life' should be examined, but also present activities and actions with future-oriented goals that are specifically directed towards the realization one's own idea of a 'good life'.

My research aims to understand the strategies that individuals employ in the present to shape their futures and the available resources they use to fulfil their visions for a 'good life'. I adopt Jansen's approach and examine the spatial and temporal aspects of hope, as both places and time are charged with varying degrees of hope (Jansen 2016:456; Jansen 2008:58). Following Jansen's idea that the highly subjective state of hoping can be described through the lens of people's ordinary lives, I look at the practice of informal savings associations among Ethiopian Israelis (self-designated Beta Israel [house of Israel])[2] and Ethiopian and Eritrean[3] migrant workers[4] in Israel. Participation in informal savings associations such as *equb*[5] is the unifying characteristic of both groups, which it also distinguishes them from the rest of the Israeli population. However, the difference between both groups, which in turn affects future aspirations and notions of hope, lies in the socio-political realm.

To what extent does the hope for a better life and a secure future influence the current actions of these two groups, and how do these influences differ between them? What are their aspirations and goals? To answer these questions, an examination of their present circumstances, their dreams, desires, and hopes for the future is essential. Thus, a distinction can be made between those (e.g., Ethiopian Israelis) who wish to maintain or improve their current secure socio-political situation (e.g., holding Israeli citizenship) through financial investments and retirement planning and those (e.g., Ethiopian and Eritrean migrants) who aspire to improve their current situation and strive for a life of higher quality and fulfilment. The question of whether financial security can be considered equivalent to a 'good life' in that it facilitates the achievement of various goals is discussed, as well as the rationale for choosing *equb* as a means. The paper will provide insights into the different expressions of hope within the *equb* practice, encompassing temporal, spatial, and social dimensions. While the conception of a 'good life' remains highly personalized, akin to individual notions of hope, I also analyze certain parameters of *equb* among the Eritrean-Ethiopian diaspora community as well as among Ethiopian Israelis. In exploring these questions through the lens of the informal savings association practice *equb*, I will first give insights into the socio-political situation of the two groups and then present examples of *equb* groups and the way in which the *equb* practice is a hopeful activity that thrives on the realization of the ideas of a 'good life'.

---

2   This refers to Israelis with an Ethiopian-Jewish migrant background. In the following, I use their self-designation Beta Israel as well as the term Ethiopian Israelis. A decisive factor in the assignment of the term as well as the self-designation is the socio-historical background, i.e., whether the person belongs to the first immigrant generation that immigrated to Israel from Ethiopia as adults in the 1980s and 1990s, or to the second and third generation that was born and raised in Israel. The latter refer to themselves as Israelis, while the former tend to use the self-designation Beta Israel. Some researchers omit the attribution Ethiopian altogether and refer to Israelis of Ethiopian-Jewish migrant background as New Israelis – a term coined by Danny Admasu and brought up in a personal conversation in July 2023. A detailed discussion of external attributions is beyond the scope of this article (cf. Kaplan 2005; Kaplan/Rosen 1994; Hamilton/Benti 2007).

3   The Ethiopian diaspora community in Israel is rather small. The common cultural background of Eritreans and Ethiopians binds them together in Israel, thus *equb* groups in Israel often consist of Ethiopian and Eritrean asylum seekers.

4   In this article, the terms migrant worker and asylum seeker are used synonymously. For more information on the different classifications (cf. Willen 2019).

5   *Equb* is a so-called rotating credit association (ROSCAs).

Israel as the promised land

The Ethiopian Jewish community has been the subject of many studies since their religious recognition as Jews by Rabbi Ovadia Yosef in 1975[6] (Ashkenazi/Weingrod 1985; Hertzog 1999; Kaplan 1985; Salamon 1999). The recognition of their Jewishness marked a turning point in their immigration to Israel. As legal Jews, they now had the right to become Israeli citizens under the Law of Return, "[...] which sets the conditions for automatic citizenship for Jewish applicants" (Salamon 2003: 6; Levy/ Weingrod, 2006:698). The period from 1975 to the beginning of 1990 was marked by mass migration to Israel. This was in part due to external migration factors such as the repressive policies of the Derg regime (e.g., Ethiopian Jews were not allowed to own land; the regime selected Jews for forced conscription) and the drought and famine that affected northern Ethiopia, the home region of the Ethiopian Jewish community. Above all, the migration was driven by religious factors, particularly the community members' official recognition as Jews (Kaplan/Rosen 1994:62–66).

To manage this flow of immigrants, the Israeli government launched two major operations: Operation Moses in 1984 and Operation Solomon in 1991. During these operations, more than 20,000 Ethiopian Jews were airlifted from Ethiopia to Israel. By the end of 1993, the lives of the majority of Ethiopian Jews were centred in Israel (Kaplan/Rosen 1994:59). In the two waves of immigration, over 90 per cent (almost 45,000) of Ethiopian Jews immigrated to Israel.[7] After arriving in Israel, the Ethiopian Jews were obliged to live in an absorption centre for up to two years. This approach is still followed today (Association of Ethiopian Jews 2018; Keidar 2014). Israeli absorption centres are state institutions that focus on integrating immigrants (in Hebrew *olim* = those going up) who have made *aliyah* (Jewish immigration to Israel) and introducing them to the language, customs, and norms in Israel. The use of absorption centres is usually voluntary, but not in the case of Ethiopian Jews.[8] Absorption centres create a pattern of dependency (Hertzog 1999:194). The newcomers

---

6   The Sephardic Chief Rabbi of Israel at the time, Rabbi Ovadia Yosef, recognized them as descendants of the lost tribe of Dan. In 1975, the Israeli government accepted Rabbi Ovadia's ruling and recognized the Ethiopian Jews known as Beta Israel as Jews (Anteby-Yemini 2004:146).

7   In recent years, an increasing number of voices within the Ethiopian Jewish community have begun to tell their own immigration stories and emphasise that there had already been migrations of Jews from Ethiopia to Israel before these two state-organized campaigns. Before 1974, a relatively small group of Ethiopian Jews immigrated to Israel. They were mainly men who studied and came on a tourist visa and then stayed in the country illegally. As activists, they fought for their Judaism and pushed forward the religious recognition process (Yerday 2019).

8   It is known that *olims* from other countries who came to Israel at the same time as Ethiopian Jews (e.g., from Russia after the collapse of the former USSR in the early 1990s) were treated differently. They were not obliged to live in an absorption centre for the first 18–24 months

are completely dependent on the centre staff, who provide them with information, allocate money, etc. (Hertzog 1999; Kaplan 2010:79; Keidar 2014).

The Ethiopian Jews' reunification in Israel with other Jews was, and remains, challenging. Uneducated and from rural areas, they had to adapt to urban life in Israel's cities and acquire the professional qualifications needed to make a living. As Jewish citizens, however, they were directly integrated into the Israeli social system.

Among the Beta Israel, life in Ethiopia was considered a diaspora experience and Israel a home for which they had longed for centuries (Kaplan 2005:382). The immigration of Jews to Israel is closely linked to the Zionist idea and "[...] some would say the raison d'être of the State of Israel" (Kaplan 2010:72). Zionist ideology dictates that new immigrants (*olim*) must abandon the cultural customs adopted while living as part of the Jewish diaspora (i.e. while living in Jewish communities outside of Israel), and adopt an Israeli-Jewish identity (Anteby-Yemini 2019:23). Steven Kaplan points out that "in narratives and practices Ethiopian Israelis appear to dissociate themselves from such [an Ethiopian] diaspora consciousness in order to affirm their place as Jews returning from Diaspora" (Kaplan 2005:383). This paradox applies to almost all *olim* in Israel and is not peculiar to Ethiopian Jews (Anteby-Yemini 2019:27). The once Ethiopian-Jewish diaspora community, which relies on returning to the Jewish homeland for its very existence, has (now) arrived in the homeland and is caught up in the multicultural Israeli reality.[9]

The crux of the promised land

Today the Ethiopian community in Israel amounts to about 155,300 people, around 1.75 per cent of the Israeli population (CBS 2020). The Beta Israel are a small black minority within the ethnically mixed Israeli society (Kaplan 2013; Salamon 2003:3–4). While the promised land offered religious freedom and recognition, secure living and working conditions, the Beta Israel's lives there have been confronted with reality. Everyday examples show that the Jewish status of Ethiopian Israelis is still

---

but received monthly allowances directly from the Israeli state and could choose their own place of residence (Association of Ethiopian Jews 2018; Hertzog 1999:xxvi).

9   In this context, Lisa Anteby-Yemini refers to dynamics of de-diasporization, re-diasporization, and homing diaspora that are also found among other Jewish migrant groups to Israel, such as those from the former Soviet Union. These processes question the relationship between homeland and diaspora, especially considering their return as a Jewish migrant group to the promised land, where the Zionist idea excludes diasporic identity (Anteby-Yemini 2019:21f.). Ravit Talmi-Cohn, in her study on the immigration of Ethiopian Jews, highlights the fluidity of the shaping of place and time. She emphasizes that migrants move between a time continuum of being-time and meta-time: between the left homeland (Ethiopia) and the new homeland (Israel) maintained through certain practices, contact with family members in Ethiopia, and so on (Talmi-Cohn 2018; cf. Glück 2024).

highly contested. There are cases, for example, where Ethiopian Jews have been denied work in kosher restaurants or food production facilities because they were not considered "proper" Jews. Many Ethiopian Jews even had to undergo a strict conversion to be accepted as Jews. Only after going through the process of bloodletting[10] were they accepted as real Jews and naturalized under the Law of Return. Beta Israel fought against the procedure, which was abolished in the mid-1990s. Similarly, Rabbi Ovadia Yosef's 1975 decision was not officially recognised by the Chief Rabbinate of Israel until June 2020 (Yerday 2020).

Life in Israel is marked by racial tensions and stereotypes. Ethiopian Jews are confronted with structural racism,[11] which became clearly visible to the Israeli public in the blood scandal that became public in 1996, in which blood donations from Ethiopian IDF (Israeli defence force) soldiers were systematically sorted out and disposed of (Schmemann 1996; Seeman 2009; Levy/Weingrod 2006:699). Ethiopian Israelis reacted with a wave of outrage followed by protests (Anteby-Yemini 2019:27f.).[12] In 2015, protests increased as cases of racist police violence came to light, including the case of Ethiopian Israeli soldier Demas Fekadeh (Yerday 2017). Young people of Ethiopian descent are convicted of crimes more often than their non-Ethiopian peers, in percentage terms (Yerday 2019:3f.). Structural racism is evident, among other things, in the granting of mortgages on residential property. The state only offers Ethiopian Israelis mortgages for properties in certain areas. In this way, neighbourhoods are created where only Ethiopian Israelis live and which are usually located outside the city centres (e.g., in Israeli cities such as Rishon-LeZion, Kiryat Gat, Holon, and Netanya) (Kaplan/Salamon 2014:27f.). Efrat Yerday sees this as a clear paternalism on the part of the Israeli state, which determines where Ethiopian Israelis can live, giving them no choice in the matter.

---

10   Symbolic circumcision, in which a drop of blood is taken from the penis of a male Ethiopian immigrant during a ceremony by the Orthodox Jewish establishment to ensure his Jewishness. For women, the symbolic conversion means a ritual bath (*mikveh*, usually on the 7th "clean" day after menstruation). The bathing ritual was used by the rabbinate to recognize the Jewishness of Ethiopian women (Hertzog 1999:xiv).

11   Kaplan (2010) points out that in a small country like Israel, any mistreatment of Ethiopians is quickly labeled as racism in the national news. He notes that there is little evidence that Ethiopians are subjected to institutionalized racism. Further he notes that many Ethiopian Israelis have certainly experienced individual discrimination and racism (Kaplan 2010:84f.). Considering the events of 2015 and the existing discriminatory police violence against Ethiopian Israelis, this statement must be viewed critically. For more information on racial discrimination among Ethiopian Israelis in Israel cf. Kaplan 2013.

12   Kaplan cites other examples of racism against Ethiopian Jews besides the blood scandal mentioned above: "Discarding of blood donation because of fear of HIV, the dispensing of a particular form of birth control to Ethiopian women, or the refusal of a school to accept additional Ethiopian students quickly and vocals is condemned as racism" (Kaplan 2013:172).

In the southern city of Ashkelon, for example, there are neighbourhoods populated entirely by Ethiopian Israelis (Kaplan 2010:77; Yerday 2019).

Until the early 2000s, the stereotype of the naïve and vulnerable Ethiopian prevailed. The majority of Ethiopian Jews originally come from rural areas of Ethiopia. Many of them came to Israel illiterate and or only elementary education (Anteby-Yemini 2004; Kaplan/Salamon 2014:29). The Jewish Agency, which is responsible for the newcomers (*olim*), felt that the Ethiopian Jews needed special attention to be prepared for the Israel's industrialized, bureaucracy-ridden society (Kaplan/Salamon 2014:28; Keidar 2014:65). However, this supposedly well-intentioned attention quickly turned into paternalism and discrimination. This pattern was reinforced by academics, most of whom worked in the service of the Israeli authorities in the reception centres as social workers while collecting data for their own academic publications. Until the 2000s, most of the publications that emerged from this scenario portrayed Ethiopian Jews as dependent, out of touch with Israeli society, and naïve.[13] In recent years, the growing discontent within the Ethiopian Israeli community has come to light and is being publicly expressed by an emancipated second and third generation of Ethiopian Israelis born, raised, and socialized in Israel. They are fighting for social recognition and economic equality and are revising the image of "the naïve Ethiopian Jew" (cf. works by Efrat Yerday 2019/2020, Adane Zawdu Gebyanesh 2012/2020).

Saving for the future – Ethiopian and Eritrean migrant workers in Israel

Israel as workaround

According to the UNHCR, more than 80,000 people applied for asylum in Israel between 2006 and 2021. Of these, only 1 per cent were recognized as refugees (based on the definition of the 1951 Convention relating to the Status of Refugees)[14] or tolerated

---

13   Mistrust of researchers who do not belong to the Ethiopian Jewish community, especially white researchers, was expressed to me several times (Sharon Shalom, September 9, 2021: Interview). Although, as a non-Israeli, I was certainly quickly trusted, suspicious questions about my research interest and who would benefit from it, as well as statements like "a few years ago I would not have spoken to you, we are always misrepresented, and our voice is not taken seriously", were constant companions during my research.

14   Israel drafted and signed the Convention of Refugees in 1951 (Kritzman-Amir/Shumacher 2012:98).

under the terms relating to temporary group protection[15] (UNHCR 2021). The latter group includes Eritreans, among others (Kritzman-Amir/Shumacher 2012:102). Because it is difficult to gain the legal recognition as a refugee in Israel (Kritzman-Amir/Shumacher 2012:101–102), Israel has a relatively low number of asylum seekers compared to neighbouring countries. In most cases, asylum seekers are treated in a manner akin to undocumented migrant workers by the Israeli authorities (Hochman 2023:12). For most asylum seekers, Israel is therefore only a stopover on their journey to Europe or Canada. Most refugees come from African countries, especially Eritrea and Sudan. Their reasons for fleeing include escaping political and religious persecution in their home country and forced conscription into the army, which is the case for most young Eritrean men. Many of these young men are forced to flee their home country illegally and without valid travel documents. For their migration, they choose the dangerous land route via Sudan, Libya, and the Sinai Peninsula, risking imprisonment, torture, and sexual abuse (Anteby-Yemini 2015:347; Gidron 2020:133).[16] In doing so, they rely on human traffickers (mainly from Sinai) who charge horrendous prices. After the completion of the Egyptian–Israeli barrier in 2012, these prices rose from US$2000 in 2009 to US$50,000 in 2021. Human traffickers take advantage of the precarious situation, threatening torture or the sale of organs if families do not pay a ransom for their relatives (Kalir 2015:581; Kritzman-Amir/Shumacher 2012:105; S. October 4, 2021: Interview).

Precarious socio-political situation and contradictory legal status

The legal status of asylum seekers and refugees results in their precarious socio-political situation. In the following, I focus on Ethiopians[17] and Eritreans. The legal status of Ethiopian asylum seekers is complex. They do not fall under temporary group protection, do not receive refugee status, and always face deportation (Gidron 2020:138). According to my Ethiopian interviewees, most Ethiopians come to Israel on a tourist visa as part of a journey to visit the holy sights of Christianity

---

15 Temporary group protection is usually granted for two reasons: when an unexpectedly high number of asylum seekers come from one country; or when people must flee their home country, but the circumstances do not fall under the definition of refugee status in the Refugee Convention. If a group is under temporary group protection, UNHCR recommends that they be protected from deportation (Kritzman-Amir/Shumacher 2012:101–102).

16 Some of them try to reach Europe first via Libya and then across the Mediterranean. Most of them end up in detention and then decide to go via Sudan to Israel (S. October 4, 2021: Interview).

17 Ethiopian asylum seekers are either Orthodox Christians or Muslims. Ethiopian Jews are not included as they are entitled to Israeli citizenship under the Law of Return. See section on Ethiopian Jews/Ethiopian Israelis.

in Israel. Sarah Willen has named this approach the "tourist loophole".[18] For many asylum seekers, visiting Israel as part of a Christian pilgrimage with the intention of "overstaying" is the only way to circumvent the rigid Israeli migration regime (Willen 2007:14). Once in Israel, they seek asylum and receive a temporary visa, which they must renew every few months (statements vary). For this, they go to the UNHCR Centre in Tel Aviv, where there is explicit legal assistance to represent their case before the Israeli state. In most cases, their visa is extended for one year. After one year, they must repeat the procedure (L. October 3, 2021: Interview).

The legal status of temporary group protection for Eritreans seems to be somewhat more stable[19] than that of an asylum seeker without group protection, as is the case for Ethiopians. However, both Eritreans, and Ethiopians are not entitled to citizenship rights, work permits, social benefits, medical care, or access to benefits from the Israeli welfare state. Moreover, their status can be revoked at any time (Kalir 2015:586; Kritzman-Amir/Shumacher 2012:102).

Nevertheless, according to a ruling by the Israeli High Court, people under the legal status of temporary protection are allowed to work to meet their basic needs and expenses. Yet, this does not protect asylum seekers from exploitation by employers. A new Ministry of the Interior regulation (30 June 2022) has made the working conditions for asylum seekers in Israel even more difficult. The regulation came into force in October 2022 and caused a lot of concern and uncertainty among my interlocutors. According to it, asylum seekers who have received group protection from deportation (in this case Eritreans) are restricted to working in four settings: hotels, construction, agriculture and institutional nursing. The regulation affects 17 selected cities, mainly in the greater Tel Aviv area and all of which are home to the largest number of asylum seekers in Israel (Peleg 2022a).

Due to the lack of work permits and their uncertain legal situation, Ethiopians and Eritreans face discrimination by their employers and are often treated as undocumented migrant workers without rights. This leads to exploitative working conditions, including long working hours, low wages, and a lack of protection against dismissal (Kalir 2015:586). As a result, many asylum seekers work in several jobs at a time to support themselves and to save money for their own onward travel (e.g., to Canada) or that of their family members (L. October 3, 2021: Interview; S. October 4, 2021: Interview). For many, Israel is not the actual destination of their migration journey. My Eritrean interlocutors, for example, told me that they somehow got stranded in Israel on their journey to Europe. Most Ethiopian interlocutors, on the

---

18   In my case, the "tourist loophole" only applies to Ethiopians, as Eritreans in most cases do not have valid travel documents to officially cross country borders and enter as tourists.

19   Once asylum seekers cross the border with Israel, the Israeli Army takes them to the Saharonim detention centre in the Negev desert, where they go through a pre-reception procedure and receive a temporary three-month visa, which they can renew (Kalir 2015:586).

other hand, deliberately go to Israel to earn money for a while or to establish a long-term base there.

Equb in Israel – time and space in which money "is eaten"

> "*Equb* is temporary, with an amount of money agreed upon by members, they eat it up. If they want, they will continue, if it is finished it will be dropped. Those who want to continue proceed and those who can't drop in the middle … if there are nice people in the *equb*, it will be a platform for social life and they meet [regularly]." (D. May 14, 2022: Interview)

This excerpt from an interview with D., which I conducted in early summer 2022 in Tel Aviv, vividly exemplifies the temporal aspect and the social dimension of *equb* meetings. *Equb* is a common savings concept in Ethiopia. The Amharic term *equb*[20] refers to a rotating credit association (ROSCA), which is defined as "an association formed upon a core of participants who make regular contributions to a fund which is given in whole or in part to each contributor in turn" (Ardener 1995:1). In Ethiopia, it is common for a group of neighbours, colleagues, or friends to set up an *equb* together. They agree in advance on a monthly amount to be saved and commit to paying it on time. The main stabilizing and regulating factors are mutual trust and reputation. No one wants to be seen as unreliable, so everyone fulfils his or her obligation to pay in regularly. The *equb* practice among Ethiopian Israelis and those in the Eritrean-Ethiopian diaspora community in Israel is similar to that found in Ethiopia but has been adapted to the socio-political situation and everyday realities of life in Israel. In Israel, *equb*'s savings cycles are mostly medium-term and can extend over a period of four to 30 months, depending on the number of members in the group. The social dimension is evident in the meetings of friends and acquaintances emphasised by D., who highlights the friendly interactions that can take place. Furthermore, the social aspect is also marked in the language used, for example, in the use of the verb "to eat". Verbs such as "eat" and "drink" are quite commonly used in the context of *equb* savings. Salamon et al. highlight in their article on all-female *equb* groups in Israel that *equb* group members usually refer to *equb* meetings as "drink with money" (Salamon et al. 2009:399). The authors argue that the connection between *equb* savings and the concepts of eating and drinking implies that the recipient of the monthly instalment round becomes the provider ("feeder") for the group

---

20 Among Ethiopian Jews in Israel, the term *qubye* is very common. Most Ethiopian Jews originally come from the Ethiopian region of Amhara, especially from the area around Gondar. The term *qubye* is derived from the Amharic dialect spoken in Gondar (Anbessa Teffera October 3, 2021: Interview).

(ibid.:411). During my fieldwork, I noted that the one receiving the monthly kitty assumes the role of the provider by offering their own living space as a social gathering point but also by supplying drinks and food to *equb* members. The reference to food or drink can be traced back to initial forms of *equb* groups, in which *equb* savings were settled in kind items that were consumed, eaten, and drunk (see Nida as well as Pankhurst this volume). However, I would like to suggest another interpretation of the meaning of eating in relation to *equb*, namely, the consumption of the savings serves to metaphorically feed and nourish future plans and hopes. One nurtures and fosters one's hopes through the use (eating/drinking) of one's savings. Through the practice of *equb*, hopes are nurtured, and future visions flourish and taking on tangible forms. These hopes and visions of the future are very subjective but are influenced by external factors such as the socio-economic position or the legal status (e.g., asylum seeker; Israeli citizen) of the individual.

In this context, *equb* has established itself as a common savings concept and future-oriented practice in the Ethiopian–Eritrean diaspora community. The daily life of many Eritreans and Ethiopians migrants in Israel is characterized by working several jobs and saving money (Si. October 15, 2021: Interview). In the diaspora community, *equb* parameters are complex and ambivalent. On one hand, it is challenging to find trustworthy individuals, particularly for asylum seekers who find themselves navigating Israeli society independently. On the other hand, cultural practices such as *equb*, along with shared experiences of seeking refuge, a common heritage originating from Eritrea or Ethiopia, shared language, and religious affiliations, can provide a sense of unity.

Engagement in *equb* groups also encompasses practical considerations. For instance, upon arrival in Israel, not all migrants possess immediate access to a bank account. Many also encounter limitations imposed by financial institutions, which restrict their eligibility to access certain services, such as loan facilities. Willen emphasizes that it is often also due to the incompetence of bank employees that migrants are prevented from opening bank accounts or securing loans, even though they have the right, in principle, to such things (Willen 2019:260). As a result, people often keep the money they save on them, hidden about their person, and refuse to deposit it anywhere (ibid.:56).[21] Thus, migrants circumvent these situations by, among other things, paying into *equb* groups.

Ethiopian and Eritrean migrants often actively participate in multiple *equb* groups, which enables them to save significant sums of money. For instance, D., a 36-year-old man, is a member of three *equb* groups. His immigration trajectory involved arriving in Israel as a tourist in 2008, seeking asylum, and marrying an

---

21   Willen made this observation among her interlocutors during her research on undocumented West African (Nigerian and Ghanaian) and Filipino migrants in the south of Tel Aviv (Willen 2019:56, 260).

Ethiopian Jewish woman in 2011, despite being an Orthodox Christian himself. The marriage granted him a permanent residence permit and an official work permit in Israel. D. has established himself as a successful entrepreneur. He owns a thriving clothing shop for traditional Ethiopian dresses and suits situated in Tel Aviv's central bus station, which serves as a gathering place for the Ethiopian–Eritrean diaspora community. Within these *equb* groups, D. can accumulate 9000 shekels per month, approximately equivalent to 2500€, as part of his savings strategy. D.'s *equb* practice is driven by a sense of obligation to consistently allocate funds and fulfil payment responsibilities, thereby upholding his reputation as a reliable participant and member of the diaspora community. It also serves as a deterrent against frivolous expenditures on non-essential items like clothing and alcohol. Moreover, D. finds banking institutions' exorbitant interest rates on loans to be unfavourable, and this feeds his preference for *equb* groups. Another advantage of participating in *equb* groups lies in the expedited access to funds. During financial emergencies, the established order of disbursements can be altered, allowing members in urgent need to receive their share of the monthly pay-out ahead of schedule (D. November 2, 2021: Interview).

Within the diaspora community, the motivations behind saving money through *equb* exhibit significant diversity. For instance, D. is engaged in saving funds with the aim of acquiring property, specifically a house, in Israel (D. November 2, 2021: Interview). For S., along with numerous Eritrean asylum seekers, *equb* serves as a viable means to accumulate finances for his onward journey. Many asylum seekers in Israel aspire to relocate to Canada in pursuit of better opportunities and a 'good life'. The naturalization process in Canada is relatively straightforward, but it requires a considerable sum of money. S. intends to save up to US$ 30,000 through *equb*, which is the amount required as a deposit for a refugee sponsorship program. By collaborating with Canadian human rights organizations, the possibility of immigrating to Canada emerges. After one year of residence and having demonstrated proficient English language skills and secured a permanent job, he will attain Canadian citizenship (S. October 4, 2021: Interview).[22] Additionally, some individuals employ *equb* as a financial mechanism to support their relatives' migration to Israel or Europe across overland routes or even to pay ransoms to human traffickers.

Within the Ethiopian–Eritrean diaspora community, the act of saving through *equb* has additional significance beyond mere monetary accumulation. It serves as a symbolic representation of a migrant's agency and determination to shape their

---

22 In September 2022, S. was able to fulfil his long-awaited dream and immigrated to Canada with the support of a Canadian friend. His friend, who worked with S. at an Israeli NGO in Tel Aviv, found a group of volunteers to act as guarantors for S. In addition to the guarantee, S. saved over US$30,000, which served as a deposit for his first year in Canada, allowing him to settle in and find a permanent job.

own destiny. The commitment to saving reflects their conscious effort to take control of their future and pursue a path that aligns with their aspirations for a free and fulfilling existence, for a 'good life' (Fischer 2014:202). *Equb* serves as a crucial tool for Ethiopian and Eritrean asylum seekers in Israel, allowing them to save money in preparation for a more secure future. This financial strategy is driven by the pursuit of a 'good life', encompassing equal rights, citizenship, and a clear understanding of their ultimate objectives. Through their engagement in *equb*, Ethiopian and Eritrean asylum seekers actively exercise agency and assert their desire for a life that is not only economically stable but also reflective of their values and aspirations for political freedom and wellbeing (i.e., to be able to move freely, to be in possession of valid papers/citizenship) (Fischer 2014:207–211).

The socio-political context of Ethiopian Israelis, who are Israeli citizens and many of whom were born in Israel, differs significantly from that of Ethiopian and Eritrean asylum seekers. The practice of *equb* among Ethiopian Israelis is quite prevalent, and its fundamental aspects, such as the rotating principle, common trust, and oral agreements, remain the same as the *equb* practice in Ethiopia. However, the sociological aspects of forming an *equb* differ. For Ethiopian Israeli participants, *equb* gatherings resemble meetings with friends from Ethiopia who also migrated to Israel during the same period, neighbours, or even family members. The formation of an *equb* group consisting exclusively of family members represents a distinctive characteristic of Ethiopian Israeli *equb* groups in Israel.[23] This phenomenon highlights the significance of family cohesion and the transmission of Ethiopian cultural values within the context of *equb* activities in the Ethiopian Israeli community. In this context, the spatial aspect of hope refers quite explicitly to coming together and sharing experiences. Here, the focus is on the preservation of Ethiopian values and tradition, and on the associated desire that future generations will appreciate and preserve these morals (Glück 2024).

The use of savings acquired through *equb* varies greatly, yet distinct patterns can be observed. What they have in common is that the savings tend to relate to the immediate future and embrace short- to medium-term life plans. Often, individuals employ the funds for substantial purchases, such as a new sofa or a new car, or for meeting considerable medical expenses (e.g., obtaining new dentures). Others choose to allocate their savings to facilitate a journey back to Ethiopia, where they can reunite with former friends and family members for an extended period, often spanning one to two months—a possibility typically available only after retirement. Furthermore, some *equb* participants indicate that they utilize their accumulated savings for joint ventures. By pooling their monthly contributions at the end of

---

23 See Sebhatleab Tewolde Kelati in this volume, who made similar observations among Eritrean *equb* groups in Germany.

the savings round, a group might go on a weekend getaway together or plan a brief holiday.

In addition to its economic implications, participation in *equb* groups encompasses a social dimension. Being part of an *equb* is crucial to many because it fosters a sense of community, providing a safety net that prevents people from feeling lonely (Sharon Shalom September 30, 2021: Interview). The establishment of trust-based relationships among members fostered through repeated interactions, yields social benefits and accumulates social capital (Ardener 2014:4). The shared financial arrangement necessitates the cultivation of stable relationships among group members, fostering bonds of trust and mutual support during times of both financial and social need. Financially, the agreed-upon sequence of *equb* rotations can be altered to accommodate individual circumstances, allowing members in need to receive their share of funds in advance, thereby offering quick financial assistance without resort to borrowing. This approach eliminates the need for loans while ensuring access to future savings ahead of time. Socially, group members typically maintain close and amicable relationships, helping one another in various ways, such as organizing funeral services (Salamon et al. 2009:402).

In the following sections, I discuss the spatial and temporal dimensions of hope, through an analysis of the *equb* practice among Ethiopian Israelis and Eritrean and Ethiopian migrant workers in Israel. The spatial aspect refers to the creation of a social network through gatherings where individuals find themselves in a familiar environment that creates an atmosphere where hopes can be nurtured, and which helps build trust. The temporal dimension takes on particular importance in the context of Ethiopian and Eritrean migrants. It relates to the temporary nature of their stay in Israel, which imposes a temporality on hope. The latter is evident in the pursuit of future aspirations through the financial security and opportunities provided by informal savings systems. In addition, however, an intersection of the social and temporal dimensions of hope is also evident here. *Equb* meetings can sometimes serve as a pathway to attaining citizenship, as they present opportunities to encounter future partners who might ensure a secure and legal stay in Israel through marriage. They thereby foster a foundation for building hopes and visions of a fulfilling life.

Temporality of hope – *"Equb* takes care of you 365 days a year"

The temporal and social components of hope come into light in the fact that *equb* plays a role in fostering connections between members of the Ethiopian Jewish community and Ethiopian (mostly Christian-Orthodox) asylum seekers. Regular *equb* meetings offer opportunities for social interaction and mixing between these two groups, often leading to relationships and eventually marriage, as seen in the case of D. (see above). Notably, Ethiopian Israeli men, particularly those who have migrated within the last 15 years, may not be seen as prospective partners by Ethiopian Israeli women, who value independence and emancipation, and live non-traditional lifestyles. Conversely, these men may find potential partners among Ethiopian migrant women, who still adhere to traditional values and patriarchal societal structures and have recently arrived in Israel. For these young women,[24] maintaining a relationship with an Ethiopian-Israeli man offers the prospect of obtaining permanent residency and even Israeli citizenship.[25]

Nonetheless, this process does not guarantee the realization of their aspirations for a better life. In fact, it may even result in shattered dreams and torn future visions. During my field research, I met L., who shared her initial plans for using the savings from *equb* with me. L., who has resided in Israel for five years, allocates her savings towards an imminent return to Addis Ababa, Ethiopia. Her plan involves establishing a personal business venture, a hairdressing salon specializing in human hair wigs[26] (L. October 3, 2021: Interview). In 2022, I met her again, she told me that she had started dating an Ethiopian-Israeli man whom she had met through her friend and *equb* group leader, F. They got to know each other and eventually fell in love during the regular *equb* meetings. A few months later, L. became pregnant, and her plans to return to Ethiopia with her savings vanished. The change in her circumstances brought up the possibility of acquiring Israeli citizenship (through marrying an Israeli citizen), but also concerns about her future, as she desired to raise her child in Ethiopia. She will not be able to fulfil this wish, as her fiancé will not allow her to travel alone with the child to Ethiopia. L. refers to instances where children visit their family in Ethiopia, Europe, or the USA with their mothers and do not return (L. June 17, 2022: Interview).

Fischer emphasizes that the efficiency of aspirations and agency is often constrained by the opportunity structures in place, which include social norms, legal regulations, and market access mechanisms that either limit or facilitate certain

---

24 This phenomenon is not limited solely to Ethiopian migrant women; indeed, many Ethiopian migrant men also marry Ethiopian Israeli women (see the case of D.).

25 The process of obtaining Israeli citizenship is defined by the concept of an "ethnonational migration regime" as outlined by Willen (2019:24), which relies on the legal basis of the Law of Return. The Law of Return restricts immigration to individuals who are of Jewish origin or possess a bureaucratically recognized connection to the Jewish people (Willen 2019:24). There are three possibilities through which Israeli citizenship can be acquired: being Jewish or of Jewish descent (subject to approval by the Rabbanut); being married to a Jewish individual; or converting to Judaism (a process also overseen by the Rabbanut) (Willen 2019:24f.). Obtaining Israeli citizenship beyond these frameworks is exceedingly challenging. This limited pathway to citizenship creates difficulties for integration into Israeli society, the labour market, and other facets of life (Willen 2019:25).

26 She learned this craft mainly in Israel, where the market for human hair wigs is booming. For Jewish Orthodox women, covering the main hair is a religious custom. Instead of a scarf or beret, many prefer to wear real hair wigs (called *Scheitel* in Yiddish).

behaviours and aspirations. While willpower is important, there must also be a viable pathway (Fischer 2014:6). In the case of Ethiopian and Eritrean asylum seekers, this means that legal status affects opportunity structures, but that by participating in *equb*, it is possible to create new opportunity structures or, sometimes, circumvent restrictions. Further, *equb* groups play a pivotal role in fostering marriages and serving as a pathway to Israeli citizenship. However, this intertwining of personal aspirations and legal status can also lead to complex and life-altering decisions for individuals, as exemplified in L.'s case.

The temporality of hope is evident in multiple aspects related to *equb* savings. On one hand, it is reflected in the objectives pursued through these savings, particularly when they are utilized for ongoing migration journeys, such as those aimed at relocating to Canada. In this sense, hope is transitive, as it involves aspiring to obtain either Israeli citizenship through marriage or the opportunity to travel to alternative destinations like Canada with the assistance of *equb* savings. However, the temporality of hope can also be disrupted from external factors, such as changes in migration laws implemented by the Israeli state. This disruption may lead to temporary setbacks for migrants, including deportation, or challenges in securing employment in Israel, altering their future prospects. In addition to these considerations, the migrants also face the constraint of a limited timeframe to remain in Israel, adding another layer to the temporality of hope.

The spatial component of hope is equally significant, as the aspiration for a better life is intricately linked to specific locations and countries, be that Israel, other potential migration destinations, or Ethiopia. Moreover, hope is distinctly intertwined with the social and temporal sphere of *equb* meetings, as these gatherings serve as a crucial setting where hopes and aspirations are nurtured and shaped.

Trust in hope – Hope in trust

The following examples emphasize the issue of trust among *equb* group members and intend to underscore the social aspect of hope. Being hopeful or having hope for something, believing that something will occur, change, or endure, is closely intertwined with the concept of trust within the *equb* groups discussed here.

"Why should I trust the state?"

Trust is one of the key elements of *equb* groups. Thus, trust is cultivated through repeated interactions among members, leading to the accumulation of social capital and reinforcing solidarity (Ardener 2014:4). This sense of trust becomes especially crucial in the selection of new members and the establishment of stable relationships within the group.

The overall trust network within *equb* groups among the Ethiopian–Eritrean diaspora community is noticeably fragile and depends heavily on the legal status of individual members. An uncertain legal position, such as group protection or asylum seeker status, does not play a role in an individual's initial acceptance into an *equb* group. However, in certain cases, this uncertain legal status can be used against members. For example, individuals with group protection status or even Israeli citizenship (since some *equb* groups are composed of individuals with different legal statuses) can exploit their stronger position. After receiving their savings instalment, such members may decide not to contribute further to the group and, when questioned by other members, falsely claim that they never received any money. In the absence of written agreements (they rely solely on verbal agreements), they may then threaten to involve the Israeli authorities and accuse others of defamation. Such actions can, in the worst case, lead to the deportation of certain individuals. During my research, I encountered such incidents at least three times, with one case already before the courts at the time of the investigation (A. May 17, 2022: Interview). The different emphasis on trust and relationships within *equb* groups in Ethiopia and in the diaspora is reflected, among other things, in the fact that in Ethiopia, everyone knows each other, and non-payment is avoided due to the involvement of one's family and the risk of damaging one's reputation. In the diaspora, however, *equb* sometimes lacks precisely this social factor, this strong sense of familiarity and mutual accountability, according to my interlocutors. This is because participants have limited knowledge of each other, and this leads to a deficiency of trust and the possibility of a fraudulent member absconding after receiving his/her share (B. April 27, 2022: Interview). Attempts are made to mitigate such risks by ensuring that new members are the last in the round to receive their *equb* savings. In this way, the trust of the members is put to the test.

Despite these risks, active participation in *equb* groups remains for many Ethiopian and Eritrean migrants the only means of effectively planning for a future in Israel that is unpredictable because so much depends on the Israeli state's approach to their legal status. In addition, the Israeli state signals that Israel is intended to be only a temporary stopover for asylum seekers through its restrictions on their labour (see examples above) and the fact that it withholds 16 per cent of each asylum seeker's monthly salary and does not return the withheld amount until the individual leaves the country (Peleg 2022b). This practice can be seen as an indication that, from the Israeli state's perspective, there is no long-term future for asylum seekers in Israel. As one interviewee pointed out, this practice undermines trust in the Israeli state, as asylum seekers feel that the state is withholding their hard-earned money: "Why should I trust the state? They are keeping our hard-earned money" (T. & L. October 6, 2021: Interview).

The *equb* practice among Ethiopian and Eritrean asylum seekers in Israel shows how trust and mistrust are intertwined and mutually dependent. Both feed on the dynamics of uncertainty – in this case an uncertain financial, socio-political, and individual future – and lead to an active approach to this situation (Mühlfried 2018:1). This active approach leads to hopeful action, like setting up *equb* groups, since, to refer to Jansen (2016:460) again, for hope or hopeful thoughts to exist, a kind of indeterminacy is required. Further, trust nourishes hopeful dreams, acts as a stabilizing factor within *equb* groups, and exerts a significant influence on the social dynamics and relationships between *equb* members. Nonetheless, the dynamics of uncertainty also contribute to shaping *equb* activities. In particular, the legal status of Ethiopian and Eritrean asylum seekers, which depends on the decisions of the Israeli state, is characterized by uncertainty. In this context of uncertainty, the practice of *equb* provides a reliable network for individuals, one which nurtures their hopes (Bryant/Knight 2019).

"I don't trust anything institutional"

The practice of saving with *equb* is widespread among Ethiopian Israelis. What is interesting about *equb* practices among Ethiopian Israelis is the basis on which these groups are formed. What parameters are considered unique to *equb* and lead people to engage in informal savings associations, despite the existence of formal insurance and financial institutions in Israel? Furthermore, the question arises as to what factors sustain *equb* activities, what dynamics are induced by group cohesion and mutual trust, and to what extent do these, in turn, influence notions of hope or, conversely, emerge from them. By examining this question and considering the sociological nature of *equb* groups, I trace the social component of the notion of hope and highlight how this, in turn, influences actual activity in *equb*.

I have consistently attended meetings of a women's *equb* group comprising 19 members, which was established 18 years ago. All members reside within the same neighbourhood and contribute 600NIS (equivalent to 160€) per month towards their savings. The primary focus of this group centres around social exchange. Through my regular attendance at these meetings, I became aware of a woman from the neighbourhood who sought membership primarily to stay informed about the local news and gossip, such as recent marriages, deaths, or individuals purchasing new cars. A lively discussion ensued, as the woman desired to join during an ongoing active savings round, which meant she would have to pay a substantial joining fee to compensate the existing members who had already received their allocated funds. Eventually, she was admitted into the group, after having agreed to compensate each member accordingly.

The woman's admittance to the group raised the issue of trust. In many instances, positions within the group were inherited: when a member died, her daughter would assume the vacated spot. Trust has been cultivated and reinforced over the course of years and even across generations. So, questions were raised about who would vouch for the credibility of the new member, and whether her reliability could be assured.

In discussions with my interlocutors concerning trust and mistrust, particular attention was directed toward the distinct characteristics of *equb* groups. It was highlighted that these groups are regarded as reliable networks. Individuals experiencing financial difficulties or requiring immediate access to funds prefer to establish an *equb* group with friends or neighbours rather than seek a loan from a bank. The members of these groups exhibit a lack of trust in banking institutions, deeming them exploitative entities. The imposition of interest charges or account maintenance fees by banks is condemned as usury or a fraudulent practice. In contrast, savings accumulated within *equb* groups are associated with positive connotations. Group members possess comprehensive knowledge regarding their savings amounts and the expected disbursements, thus avoiding any unpleasant surprises.

The disposition of Ethiopian Israelis to exhibit mistrust towards Israeli authorities and institutions can be attributed to their experiences when they first arrived in Israel. Their early encounters have a lasting impact on their positioning within the multicultural fabric of Israeli society, as well as their perceptions of Israeli authorities and institutions. Factors such as the struggle for religious recognition, the intricate socio-cultural dynamics within Israeli society, instances of racism, and the sense of not being recognized as independent and self-determined citizens (manifested, for instance, through their dependence on authorities and the existence of absorption centres) have contributed to the cultivation of a deep-rooted mistrust of state authorities and official organizations, including financial and insurance institutions (Association of Ethiopian Jews 2018). This sentiment of mistrust is particularly prevalent among the older generation of Ethiopian Israelis who arrived in Israel prior to the 1990s, as evidenced by their substantial scepticism towards state authorities (Salamon et al. 2009:412). Consequently, their mistrust is reflected in behaviours such as refraining from depositing savings in banks and swiftly withdrawing funds from accounts once their monthly pensions are received. Instead, they tend to direct their money or savings towards informal saving associations like the *equb*. They rarely engage in savings schemes offered by financial institutions or participate in stock market investments (Salamon et al. 2009:402). Interview statements from my younger interlocutors attest to this prevailing sentiment of mistrust. They recount, for instance, stories of parents refusing to trust institutional entities, as evidenced by their lack of credit card usage and their reluctance to deposit money in bank accounts. I often heard statements like "But they [the older generation] don't trust. My mum doesn't have a credit card, she doesn't trust anything institutional" (E. September 30, 2021: Interview) or "They [parents] have a bank account, but they don't deposit money there" (Z. October 14, 2021: Interview).

According to Salamon et al.'s investigation into exclusively female *equb* groups in Israel, the practice of *equb* does not serve as a substitute for formal banking systems but, rather, operates in a symbiotic relationship with them. The women involved in these groups express their perception of Israeli banking institutions as exploitative and deceitful. Simultaneously, they rely on the monthly pensions, such as the National Insurance funds, which are deposited into their bank accounts as the primary source of financing for their monthly contributions to the *equb* (Salamon et al. 2009:402–404). Similar observations were made during my own field research among the aforementioned female *equb* group.

Furthermore, my example of a women's *equb* group highlights the significance of trust within the *equb* framework. This sense of trust becomes especially crucial in the selection of new members and the establishment of stable relationships within the group. Choosing informal savings associations over formal banking systems reveals the pervasive sense of mistrust towards formal financial institutions and state authorities among Ethiopian Israelis. Their experiences during the migration process (*aliyah*) have contributed to this scepticism, leading them to seek alternative means of savings, such as *equb*, rather than entrusting their funds to banks. However, it is not only mistrust towards institutions but also a lack of knowledge about bureaucratic processes that leads to this reliance on familiar and informal networks (especially among the older generation).

The mutual trust cultivated in *equb* groups, where members have faith in regularly coming together as a group to contribute their savings and become integral parts of the social community, paves the way for hopeful thinking, planning, and ultimately achieving one's version of a 'good life'.

Conclusion

Equb serves as a catalyst for hope and future aspirations, creating a platform for individuals to envision a better life and work towards its realization. By participating in *equb*, participants are encouraged to imagine and work towards their desired future. *Equb* provides a platform for various hopes and aspirations that are strongly influenced by the prevailing socio-political context. Here, I have explored the temporal and spatial dimensions of hope, revealing the essential role of social dynamics in *equb* alongside the tangible benefits that the practice offers. As a trusted network, *equb* fosters a sense of support and community among its members and serves as a reliable source of hope and encouragement in difficult times.

The uncertainty in which Ethiopian and Eritrean asylum seekers find themselves motivates them to actively participate in *equb*. This engagement is driven by the hope of improving their lives, whether by seeking a change of legal status in Israel, exploring options for further migration, or considering a return to Ethiopia with financial security. Their experiences and challenges cause them to dream, hope, and strive for a better life that may seem out of reach in their current circumstances in Israel. For

Ethiopian Israelis, *equb* meetings create Ethiopian-Israeli cultural spaces in which Ethiopian values are upheld and passed on to the next generation and trustworthy networks are created that are important for the social cohesion of the group. The social facet of *equb* is also reflected in the amicable and even marital connections that arise from the encounter of Ethiopian Israelis and Ethiopian asylum seekers during *equb* meetings.

Equb functions as a transformative practice that creates islands of hope in participants' lives. It offers a popular alternative to state and financial institutions, as my examples show. *Equb* groups provide a predictable time frame and social space that enables the creation of concrete goals for a 'good life'. However, their presence and appearance, akin to an island, are contingent on external influences, whether they stem from realpolitik (e.g., decisions by the Israeli state concerning migration laws) or occur at an individual level (e.g., insufficient income to save money for the future within *equb* savings groups). *Equb* is a future-oriented practice, it creates space and time in which hopeful actions aimed at fulfilling the 'good life' flourish.

Bibliography

Anteby-Yemini, Lisa (2004): "Promised Land, Imagined Homelands. Ethiopian Jews' Immigration to Israel." In: Fran Markowitz/Anders H. Stefansson (eds.), *Homecomings. Unsettling Paths of Return*, Lanham: Lexington Books, pp. 146–163.

Anteby-Yemini, Lisa (2015): "Criminalisation, Israélisation et Couleur de Peau. Les Demandeurs D'asile Africains en Israël." *Ethnologie Française* 45/2, pp. 343–352.

Anteby-Yemini, Lisa (2019): "From a Returning Jewish Diaspora to Returns to Diaspora Spaces. Israeli Ethiopians Today. Israel: A Diaspora of Memories." *Quest. Issues in Contemporary Jewish History* 16, pp. 19–44.

Ardener, Shirley (1995): "Women Making Money Go Round. ROSCAs Revisited." In: Shirley Ardener/Sandra Burman (eds.), *Money-Go-Rounds. The Importance of Rotating Savings and Credit Associations for Women*, Oxford: Berg (Cross-Cultural Perspectives on Women, 14), pp. 1–19.

Ardener, Shirley (2014): "Credit Unions and Money Clubs (ROSCAs)." *Anthropology Today* 30/4, pp. 3–6.

Ashkenazi, Michael/Weingrod, Alex (eds.) (1985): *Ethiopian Jews and Israel*, New Brunswick: Transaction Publishers.

Association of Ethiopian Jews (2018): "Absorption". Accessed March 8, 2024, (https://iaej.co.il/language/en/absorption/).

Bloch, Ernst (1977 [1959]): *Das Prinzip der Hoffnung* (vol. 5, ch. 1–32), Frankfurt am Main: Suhrkamp.

Bryant, Rebecca (2020): "The Anthropology of the Future." *Ethnofoor* 32/1, pp. 11–22.

Bryant, Rebecca/Knight, Daniel M. (2019): "Hope". In: Rebecca Bryant/Daniel M. Knight (eds.), *The Anthropology of the Future*, Cambridge: Cambridge University Press, pp. 132–157.

Central Bureau of Statistics (CBS) (November 11, 2020): "The Population of Ethiopian Origin in Israel Selected Data Published on the Occasion of the Sigd Festival". Accessed March 8, 2024, (https://www.cbs.gov.il/he/mediarelease/DocLib/202 0/358/11_20_358e.docx).

Fischer, Edward F. (2014): *The Good Life. Aspiration, Dignity, and the Anthropology of Wellbeing*, Stanford, California: Stanford University Press.

Gidron, Yotam (2020): *Israel in Africa. Security, Migration, Interstate Politics*, London: ZED.

Glück, Kim (2024): "When I'm with Them, I'm at Home". Informal Savings Associations and the Process of Home-making Among Ethiopian Israelis and Ethiopian Migrants in Israel." In: Sophia Thubauville/Kim Glück (eds.), *Home and Future Making in the Ethiopian Diaspora*, Addis Ababa: Centre français des étdues éthiopiennes.

Hage, Ghassan (1997): "At Home in the Entrails of the West. Multiculturalism, Ethnic Food, and Migrant Home-Building." In: Helen Grace/Ghassan Hage/Lesley Johnson/Julie Langsworth/Michael Symonds (eds.), *Home/World: Space, Community, and Marginality in Sydney's West*, Annandale: Pluto Press, pp. 99–153.

Hamilton, Ruth Simms/Getahun Benti (2007): "Redefining a Collective Identity in the Struggle for State and National Identity in Ethiopia and Israel. The Case of Ethiopian Jews (Beta Israel)". In: Ruth Simms Hamilton (ed.), *Routes of Passage. Rethinking the African Diaspora* Vol. 1, Part 2, East Lansing, Michigan: Michigan State University Press, pp. 135–167.

Hertzog, Esther (1999): *Immigrants and Bureaucrats. Ethiopians in an Israeli Absorption Center*, New York; Oxford: Berghahn books.

Hochman, Oshrat (2023): "Introduction." In: Oshrat Hochman (ed.), *Immigration and Integration in Israel and Beyond*, Bielefeld: transcript, pp. 9–20.

Jansen, Stef (2008): "Hope and the State in the Anthropology of Home. Preliminary Notes." *Ethnologia Europaea* 39/1: pp. 54–60.

Jansen, Stef (2016): "For a Relational, Historical Ethnography of Hope. Indeterminacy and Determination in the Bosnian and Herzegovinian Meantime." *History and Anthropology* 27/4, pp. 447–464.

Kalir, Barak 2015: "The Jewish State of Anxiety: Between Moral Obligation and Fearism in the Treatment of African Asylum Seekers in Israel." *Journal of Ethnic and Migration Studies* 41/4, pp. 580–598.

Kaplan, Steven (1985): "The Beta Israel (Falasha) in the Ethiopian Context." In: Michael Ashkenazi/Alex Weingrod (eds.), *Ethiopian Jews and Israel*, New Brunswick: Transaction Publishers, pp. 9–18.

Kaplan, Steven/ Rosen, Chaim (1994): "The Ethiopian Jews in Israel." *The American Jewish Year Book* 94, pp. 59–109.

Kaplan, Steven (2005): "Tama Galut Etiopiya. The Ethiopian Exile is Over." *Diaspora: A Journal of Transnational Studies* 14/2–3, pp. 381–396.

Kaplan, Steven (2010): "Ethiopian Immigrants in the United States and Israel. A Preliminary Comparison." *International Journal of Ethiopian Studies* 5/1, pp. 71–92.

Kaplan, Steven (2013): "Ethiopian Immigrants in Israel. The Discourses of Intrinsic and Extrinsic Racism." In: Efrayim Sicher (ed.), *Race, Color, Identity. Rethinking Discourses About "Jews" in the Twenty-First Century*, New York, Oxford: Berghahn books, pp. 167–181.

Kaplan, Steven/Salamon, Hagar (2014): "Ethiopian Immigrants in their Israeli Context. Some Introductory Framings." In: Eliezer Witztum/Nimrod Grisaru (eds.), *Social, Cultural and Clinical Aspects of the Ethiopian Immigrants in Israel*, Beer-Sheva: Maor Wallach Press, pp. 21–36.

Keidar, Mira (2014): "Insights Regarding the Absorption of Ethiopian Immigrants, July 2011." In: Eliezer Witztum/Nimrod Grisaru (eds.), *Social, Cultural and Clinical Aspects of the Ethiopian Immigrants in Israel*, Beer-Sheva: Maor Wallach Press, pp. 65–84.

Kritzman-Amir, Tally/Shumacher, Yvette (2012): "Refugees and Asylum Seekers in the State of Israel." *Israel Journal of Foreign Affairs* 6/3, pp. 97–111.

Levy, Andre/Weingrod, Alex (2006): "Paradoxes of Homecoming. Jews and Their Diasporas." *Anthropological Quarterly* 79/4, pp. 691–716.

Mühlfried, Florian (eds.) (2018): *Mistrust. Ethnographic Approximations*, Bielefeld: transcript.

Peleg, Bar (June 30, 2022a): "Israel Bars Asylum Seekers from Most Jobs in Major Cities". Accessed March 8, 2024, (https://www.haaretz.com/israel-news/2022–06–30/ty-article/.premium/israel-bars-asylum-seekers-from-most-jobs-in-major-cities/00000181-b5e3-da42-abdd-b7e71a540000).

Peleg, Bar (December 12, 2022b): "Gov't Audit Reveals Gap of Millions of Shekels in Deposits for non-Israeli Workers". Accessed March 8, 2024, (https://www.haaretz.com/israel-news/2022-12-04/ty-article/.premium/govt-audit-reveals-gap-of-millions-of-shekels-in-deposits-for-foreign-workers-in-israel/00000184-dbea-dc05-adae-fffb08040000).

Salamon, Hagar (1999): *The Hyena People. Ethiopian Jews in Christian Ethiopia*, Berkeley: Univ. of California Press.

Salamon, Hagar (2003): "Blackness in Transition. Decoding Racial Constructs Through Stories of Ethiopian Jews." *Journal of Folklore Research* 40/1, pp. 3–32.

Salamon, Hagar/Kaplan, Steven/Goldberg, Harvey (2009): "What Goes Around, Comes Around. Rotating Credit Associations Among Ethiopian Women in Israel." *African Identities* 7/3, pp. 399–415.

Schmemann, Serge (January 29, 1996): "Ethiopian in Israeli Riot Over Dumping of Donated Blood". Accessed March 8, 2024, (https://www.nytimes.com/1996/01/2 9/world/ethiopian-in-israeli-riot-over-dumping-of-donated-blood.html).

Seeman, Don (2009): *One People, One Blood. Ethiopian-Israelis and the Return to Judaism*, New Brunswick; New Jersey; London: Rutgers University Press.

Talmi-Cohn, Ravit (2018): "Time Making and Place Making. A Journey of Immigration from Ethiopia to Israel." *Ethnos* 38/2, pp. 335–352.

UNHCR (2021): "Israel Factsheet". Accessed March 8, 2024, (https://www.unhcr.org /il/wp-content/uploads/sites/6/2022/01/9b.-Israel-EXCOM-Factsheet-September-2021.pdf).

Willen, Sarah S. (2007): "Toward a Critical Phenomenology of 'Illegality', State Power, Criminalization, and Abjectivity among Undocumented Migrant Workers in Tel Aviv, Israel." *International Migration* 45/3, pp. 8–38.

Willen, Sarah S. (2019): *Fighting for Dignity. Migrant Lives at Israel's Margins*, Philadelphia: University of Pennsylvania Press.

Yerday, Efrat (2017), "Recognising the discrimination Ethiopian Jews face in Israel is a step in the right direction." Accessed March 8, 2024, (https://www.middlee asteye.net/opinion/recognising-discrimination-ethiopian-jews-face-israel-ste p-right-direction).

Yerday, Efrat (2019): "Weiße und 'andere' jüdische Menschen." Accessed March 8, 2024, (https://www.rosalux.org.il/aschkenasim/).

Yerday, Efrat (2020): "Ethiopian Jewish community in Israel." Accessed March 8, 2024, (https://www.youtube.com/watch?v=hvPr_dL4EvA).

Zawdu Gebyanesh, Adane Eitan (2019): *When Rituals Migrate: A Study of the Relationships Between Collaborative Cultural Practices and Social Ties Among Ethiopian Immigrants in Israel*, Doctoral Dissertation, University of Connecticut (https://openco mmons.uconn.edu/dissertations/2334).

Zawdu Gebyanesh, Adane Eitan/Nissim Mizrachi (2012): "Between Global Racial and Bounded Identity. Choice of Destigmatization Strategies Among Ethiopian Jews in Israel." *Ethnic and Racial Studies* 35/3, pp. 436–452.

"Trust a man after you bury him"
Trust and the status of informal saving associations among Ethiopians in the United Arab Emirates

Kelemework Tafere Reda

Abstract *This contribution focuses on trust dynamics in informal saving institutions (equbs) among Ethiopians residing in the United Arab Emirates (UAE). The main objectives of the study were to examine the distinctive features of equbs and identify the salient factors in trust and trust responsiveness within these informal associations. Trust is an important asset for solidarity, cooperation, and collective action, but trust becomes difficult to achieve in an environment of chaos, disorder, and uncertainty as well as a lack of familiarity and safety. Goffman's theory of interaction order (Misztal 2002) notes that trust materializes well with normality. The trust–commitment theory also argues that trust and commitment are fundamental ingredients in the process of building effective relationships (Morgan/Hunt 1994). In the context of an insecure and highly mobile diaspora population in the UAE, trust becomes difficult to envisage, and informal saving institutions are compelled to develop their own idiosyncratic qualities in response to this reality.*

Introduction

Informal financial institutions in Ethiopia have been the subject of anthropological and sociological inquiries for many years (Aredo 1993; Bekerie 2003; Yitbarek 2008; Abegaz 2014; Bazezew/Chanie 2015). Institutions such as *equbs*[1] are often considered viable options for micro-level economic transactions in Ethiopia because they are easily accessible, people-oriented, and participatory (Bekerie 2003). These dynamic institutions have significantly contributed to the establishment of strong social and economic support networks, enhancing community cohesiveness and social solidarity (ibid. 2003).

---

[1] An *equb/iqqub* is an Ethiopian Rotating Savings and Credit Association (ROSCA) organized voluntarily to mobilize financial resources. They are popular among almost all sections of society (Aredo 2004).

Contemporary modern society is facing a 'crisis of trust'. Western society is particular implicated in this crisis, but in the era of globalization, a lack of trust has become pervasive. Trust is the most cherished value in society (Corsín-Jiménez 2011; Mühlfried 2021), but at the same time it is "one of the most endangered social resources at the present time" (Mühlfried 2021:201). The melting down of such an important social virtue is evident in the formal sectors of government and politics (ibid. 2021). This empirical study addresses the question of trust in the context of the informal sector, about which little is hitherto known in previous studies.

A good deal of literature is already available on informal financial institutions in urban and rural Ethiopia. However, data on the essence of trust in those institutions especially among diaspora communities has hitherto remained scant. Although old ethnographies have adequately discussed issues related to difference and solidarity, particularly in small-scale societies, the role of anthropology in recent debates on trust has been marginal (Coates 2018). It is, therefore, timely to address the issue of trust as a research agenda because it is a crucial asset in social, economic, and political life. In view of this, this study sets out to examine how *equb* saving associations function in diaspora settings, while identifying the factors in building trust and the contemporary challenges associated with it.

The research was conducted in the United Arab Emirates (UAE) between May and September 2022. Data collection took place in Dubai and Sharjah states.[2] The study followed a qualitative approach in which ethnography was used as a principal method of scientific inquiry. Semi-structured interviews, informal chitchats, and small group discussions were conducted with purposively sampled key informants to harness first-hand information about migrants' personal experiences. Besides, a review of secondary data (both published and grey literature) obtained from different sources was made.

Some theoretical considerations

Trust and mistrust

Theorizing trust is not new. It has, for example, been central to the social contract theory since it was first advocated by classical writers of the nineteenth century (Mühlfried 2018). Sociologists such as Simmel would argue that trust is what binds people together in society and that it has a lot to do with putting confidence in others; it reflects a hypothesis about future behaviours eliciting certain practical actions (Frederiksen 2012). Both trust and mistrust are attitudes that help us deal with uncertainty. The difference is that the former presupposes a condition in

---

2   The two locations were selected given the high concentration of Ethiopian migrants there.

which risk is accepted while deferring feelings of doubt; in the case of the latter, risk avoidance tendencies are pursued (Luhman 1973, cited in Mühlfried 2018).

The establishment of trust between parties presupposes the formation of binding links, that is, the personal and social relationships that ultimately create a friendly environment between the two parties. This relates to the notion of social honour and the moral obligation to remain mutually trustworthy in the context of existential risk, especially in the informal sector (Mühlfried 2018). Similarly, the Trust–Commitment Model argues that relationships within the framework of institutions work best when there is trust and commitment. In a business and marketing environment, this theory argues that, paradoxically, even in the world of competition, cooperation is a key Instrument—or success in the context of functional networks (Morgan/Hunt 1994).

In socio-cognitive models, trust is often seen as a reflection of attitudes shaped by such cultural and demographic factors as personality, income, age, and class. According to Dasgupta (1988), the decision to trust a person or not depends on the reputation of that person. For contracts to hold, there should be a credible threat of punishment by a trustworthy agency against those who break agreements between parties. The trust towards a person depends on the trust one puts in the enforcing agency.

According to Good (1988) it is important to consider the economic and political fabric of society and its impact and consequences on relationships to understand the individual as a trusting agent. Individuals can pursue either competitive or cooperative strategies, but trusting others and being trustworthy are closely related to the wellbeing of the individuals involved in such relationships. Good (1988) explains that cooperation is a manifestation of trust, which is a protective mechanism that prevents anomaly from occurring by ensuring feelings of familiarity, and an assurance of the feeling of being safe in the context of social order (Goffman 1983).

Dasgupta (1988) argues that trust depends on some form of agency that is mandated with regulation and enforcements of contracts. Trust is considered a rational strategy as long as subsequent actions are revised based on experience and an assessment of the past performance of the trusted (ibid. 1988).

Ethiopian Middle East migration trends

The migration of Ethiopians to the Middle Eastern countries like Bahrain, Lebanon, Qatar, Jordan, Saudi Arabia, and the United Arab Emirates has a long history. However, there has been an increasing mobility trend since the early 1990s, most of which tends to be irregular (Adugna 2021). The Emirates is one of the key migration destinations for young, uneducated migrants from Ethiopia. There are over 160,000 Ethiopians currently living in the UAE, with over 65 per cent living in Dubai and the Northern Emirates (MFA 2023). However, it is difficult to get official statistics and exact numbers given that quite a number of Ethiopian migrants reside in the country illegally. Many work as housekeepers, labourers, civil servants, and in small businesses.

In 2013 the Ethiopian government put a temporary ban on travel to the Middle East in a bid to encourage legal migration and deal with the deportation of large numbers of migrants from those countries. The ban was lifted after five years, after new labour recruitment regulations were imposed on hiring agencies (Adugna 2021).

The majority of my informants said they had come to the UAE with economic aspirations and resorted to migration as a way to escape poverty in their home country. However, their expectations of a better life are largely not being fulfilled: finding secure jobs is not easy; remuneration is lower than expected and often comes erratically; and the cost of living in the host country is high. Illicit migrants also face the risk of being deported at any time. Feelings of economic and social insecurity, which result in low levels of trust, prevent people from establishing long-term commitments in informal savings associations such as *equbs*.

Some features of *equb* associations in the Emirates

The series of interviews[3] with Ethiopians in the study area shows that the basic characteristics of *equbs* in the UAE are the same as in Ethiopia. They are voluntary associations in which people organize themselves for savings purposes; members pay in a fixed amount of money at a certain interval (daily, weekly, or monthly) and the collected money is dispensed back to the members on a turn basis. As in Ethiopia, *equbs* in the UAE have their own bylaws, which relate to the amount of contributions, timing, defaulting etc. When membership is based on kinship and close social relations, the rules and procedures are simple and straightforward, without elaborate structures and hierarchies. *Equb* associations are often led by those who initiate them, although an election process can also take place to determine the chairperson and other members of the management. In some cases, the chairperson may be salaried/commissioned; in some, they offer their services free; in others, the chairperson is given priority in the lots (for example, by being offered the first payout). Headship is a temporary position, with individuals taking turns at different times. Whether a secretary and treasurer are needed partly depends on the size of the *equb*.

---

3   I stayed in an Ethiopian-run hostel throughout the research period and travelled across Dubai and Sharjah to meet people and discuss their experiences through formal interviews and informal chitchats. I also observed people's activities in the workplace, social gatherings, restaurants, and shops and formed intimacies with some of the informants.

Otherwise, only a chair is sufficient to ensure that institutional rules are observed and financial resources are properly mobilized and distributed to the winners. Winners are determined based on a lottery system, but sometimes those with an urgent need of money may be given priority.

However, there are also significant differences: the size of the associations is usually much smaller than in Ethiopia. While the large groups in Ethiopia may be made up by people who do not know each other, in the UAE, *equb* associations often involve highly cohesive social groups linked by blood ties, friendship, or business relations. The number of members is kept as small and manageable as possible to minimize risk. In a similar recent study conducted in Berlin, Germany, Tadesse (2023) also notes that *equb* associations are common among diaspora Ethiopians who know each other very well and are close friends. The number of members in UAE *equbs* is often limited to minimize risk. One of the *equb* associations, for example, consists of only three members (all women working in the same company). One of the members told me:

> "The bigger the equb association, the richer we would have become [...] we could have covered so many of our expenses with equb money [...] but we could not expand our equb to include other members because things are so unpredictable in this country. The amount we pay in monthly is equal to our salary, which is 2,000 dirhams."[4] (A., female, age 35, 2022: Interview)

Risk is also avoided by lowering the contributions and raising the frequency of rotation. *Equb* associations in the UAE are short-lived and encounter frequent interruptions. In fact, it is not easy to find associations that continued for even a couple of years. Unlike those in Ethiopia, some of which function for several years uninterrupted due to the established residence status of members. In addition, unlike in Ethiopia, face-to-face meetings are minimized because of access to digital technologies for communication. The *equbs* use digital platforms not only for communication but also for transferring money. For example, WhatsApp is commonly used for internal communications among members, while a few people use the Workxon app[5] to transfer *equb* money to winners.

---

4   In addition to their status as employed workers, members often had diverse sources of income. For example, renting out hostel rooms, commissions paid for helping newcomers get jobs, brokerage, etc.

5   This is an app that is not well known, but the company describes itself as a digital platform with a wide range of uses including forex trading, digital media, and real estate development since 2021 (Workxon LinkedIn page).

Equb in the UAE is also not ritualistic,[6] in the sense that it is often not accompanied with the sharing of food and drinks in a ceremonial way as is the case in Ethiopia. *Equb* members meet to exchange *equb* money and occasionally discuss issues (not necessarily related to their association) over coffee or tea. However, this is entirely voluntary.

The significance of ROSCAs[7] for Ethiopians in the Emirates

Ethiopians form their own communities in the host countries and maintain their economic and social networks. Through the *equb*, they mobilize their financial resources for specific purposes. According to informants, the *equb* is a good alternative to modern banking because the latter tends to be more top–down and bureaucratic. When opening a bank account, a number of requirements have to be met. For example, in addition to residency, a certain minimum monthly income is often mentioned as a key criterion for opening a savings account with some banks in the UAE. *Equb* associations, on the other hand, tend to be more flexible, transparent, and participatory.

In a more general sense, the most obvious significance of the *equb* as an informal institution lies in its tendency to discourage extravagant behaviour. Once someone is a member of the *equb*, they know that a fixed amount of money is expected from them in a certain period. Therefore, consumption is cautious and unreasonable spending is kept in check.

The benefits of *equb* money are complex. Many migrants had to borrow the money to pay for the visas and transport costs[8] of their movement the UAE. Their top priority is often to repay these debts before they start saving to invest money for future use. Others use the money to help family members back home. The conflict in northern Ethiopia (2020–2022), for example, put additional pressure on migrants, especially those from the Tigray region, as they had to pay money to transmitters to send money home informally following the closure of all government services in the region. Azam et al. (2016) also note that diaspora communities make foreign remittances of various forms to alleviate poverty and ensure a safe future in their home countries.

---

6   Involvement in social rituals such as prolonged feasts and related events are kept to a minimum because people are very busy with matters pertaining to their livelihoods. The rush of life in Dubai does not allow people to spend much time on ceremonial occasions.

7   Rotating Savings and Credit Associations.

8   The cost of a three-month tourist visa to Dubai can cost up to US$300–400 via the different agents.

Studies show that informal saving and credit associations have the potential to finance small and micro enterprises (Herr/Nettekoven 2017). However, in the UAE, a negligible proportion of diasporic Ethiopians (especially the economically better off) use *equb* money to open businesses or expand existing ones both in the country of origin and the host. There is often a wide gap between what people aspire to and what they can achieve in reality. Many still struggle for bare survival.

In addition to economic functions, informal institutions such as *equbs* serve to build support networks that are crucial for building a sense of security in the new environment. *Equbs* therefore facilitate social cooperation among members of the Ethiopian diaspora. The social interaction in *equbs* also expedites communication and information-sharing, which enable integration into the culture and norms of the host country. Knowledge and skills are passed on from those who have lived in the UAE for a long time to newcomers. Through *equb* networking, people also share crucial information that can be used for personal growth.

However, no matter how much money goes into it, participation in an *equb* is a luxury for those whose bare survival is in question because of unemployment or marginal income. Many of the women who work as nannies in the UAE's so-called 'madame houses' do not have secure jobs. Some have been dismissed due to disagreements with their employers, and the exploitation and extortion of house cleaners are commonplace experiences, as Senait's story illustrates:

Senait[9] came from a remote rural area in northern Ethiopia. She was employed as a maid in Abu Dhabi for a few months before her employer decided to dismiss her due to disagreements about the quality of her work (the owner complained that the household utensils were never clean enough). It was a difficult time for her because at first it was difficult for her to find people from her hometown to stay with until she found another job. Fortunately, she met an Ethiopian woman from her region who ran a hostel in the Dera district (a busy neighbourhood in Dubai). She took her home and stayed with her until she finally found another job. At the hostel, she cleaned the living quarters, kitchen, and bathroom and in return received free food and accommodation from the owner. (S., female, age 27, 2022: Excerpt from an interview)

Some informants also reported that Ethiopian and other African migrants are discriminated against when it comes to access to jobs and remuneration in the domestic sector. For example, one informant reported that her Filipina colleague enjoyed better pay and treatment. The precariousness of Ethiopian lives in the UAE can affect the decision to join an *equb*.

---

9   Not her real name. The identities of informants have been concealed for the sake of privacy.

Elements of trust in saving institutions

Trust is an important factor in the establishment of *equb* associations among Ethiopians in the UAE. Informants generally indicate that they trust an institution more than individuals particularly on matters involving economic transactions. They believe that the presence of several people in an institution such as an *equb* increases the trustworthiness of its members because the relationships are more or less structured and there are checks and balances. People will avoid cheating while under the watch of others because they risk negative consequences in the form of name-calling and social exclusion. One of the informants said:

> "Any transaction with isolated individuals draws less public attention. If your partner cheats on you, you complain, but it goes unnoticed and the untrustworthy person takes advantage of it; it may not be easy for other people to determine who is telling the truth. In institutions like equb, this is a remote possibility." (B., male, age 36, 2022: Interview)

The following elements are important to understanding trust in the context of *equb* associations among the Ethiopians in the UAE:

Mobility and residency status: There are no asylum programs for immigrants in the UAE. Therefore, it is not possible for many Ethiopians to lead a stable life in the country. During informal conversations, some informants often used expressions such as *ke bahar yawata asa* ("fish out of the pond"), *maheja yat'a* ("not knowing where to go") etc. to describe their situation in the Emirates. Frustration with the lack of inclusive, migrant-friendly policies in the Emirates is forcing Ethiopian migrants to consider returning to their country of origin or emigrating to countries in Europe and North America. Faced with these challenges, migrants often do not make long-term commitments in the host country. Joining *equb* associations is much easier for those who have a residence permit and are less mobile because they are likely to stay in one place, build assets, and establish some networks, all of which are important for trust.

Relationships and intimacy: According to informants, intimacy leads to cooperation and solidarity and vice versa, and is a key factor in trust. The exchange of ideas among friends in close circles often leads to the establishment of a voluntary self-help association or other joint business ventures for mutual economic benefit. Often *equbs* are initiated by a few intimate friends and expand gradually by co-opting others on a case-by-case basis.

Equb members regularly meet and chat to advance their relationship further. However, regular contact is also pursued as a strategy of surveillance and monitoring to make sure that everyone is around and remains committed to the saving institution. This reflects Sahin and Taspinar's (2015) argument that the emotional attachment established between the trusting and the trusted is fundamental for the former as they ponder whether the relationship is worth the risk. In explaining the need for intimacy in trusting others, one of the informants said:

> "When you meet and talk to people, you know who is who because you have the opportunity to learn more about their behaviour and personal qualities, so much so that you can tell if someone is honest or not. Therefore, you form friendships with many but you become intimate with a few of them." (G., male, age 29, 2022: Interview)

Therefore, it is imperative that potential members demonstrate good behaviour. As a requirement for membership, he/she must be well known to at least one of the other members who then make a recommendation that they join the *equb*. Background checks often become mandatory in the process of determining membership into these informal institutions. A good reputation for honesty and trustworthiness is an added asset, while greedy behaviour is highly discouraged. Trust-building in the context of the *equb* involves rationally choosing the right partners in a way that minimizes risk. Some informants would argue it is not worth taking risks even with intimate friends because the future behaviour of members cannot be predicted from their present behaviour. According to M. (male, 32), "somebody may look honest and trustworthy now but some challenges in the future may force him to become a different person."

Asked if they would like to continue with their membership in the *equb* associations, some informants said they wanted to withdraw as soon as the first cycle was over. The main reasons for frustration were defaulting, late contributions, and having to worry about possible dropouts and the mischievous behaviour of members. Some who want to avoid risk at all costs use the Amharic proverb as a guiding principle in their relations with others: *sawn wdadaw enji atmanaw* ("you can like but never trust a person").

Livelihood: *Equb* associations are not necessarily meant for the poor only. The relatively richer sections are also interested in forming their own associations in order to expand businesses, open up new ones, or initiate other projects in the country of origin and host country. There are separate *equb* associations for taxi drivers, restaurant owners, coffee and shisha houses, and company employees. Those with the economic capacity to make multiple financial contributions may also engage in several *equb* associations at the same time. A notable example is T., who lives in Sharjah, and his colleague A., a restaurant owner, who currently run two *equb* associations: one comprising members from within the UAE; and the other, a digital one, involving people from areas as far as the USA. Of late, there have been efforts to digitize *equbs*. For example, an app called eQub[10] has been introduced to modernize the system while retaining its fundamental traditional features (Getachew 2020).

According to informants, being Ethiopian (or Eritrean)[11] does not automatically guarantee a person membership of an *equb*. Access to a regular income is mentioned as one of the key factors for participation. Those who can provide guarantors and have a stable income (e.g., a monthly salary) would be considered for enrolment. The financial competence of members also helps ensure the sustainability of the saving institution. Unfortunately, fluctuations in income, which are typical of many Ethiopian migrants in the UAE, puts sustainability at stake. The result is that it is not easy to find *equb* associations that last long.

Often members come from the same economic sector, e.g. those working in the same organization or running similar businesses. For example, one of the saving associations covered in this study consists of taxi drivers who work in the same company. One of my interviewees stated:

> "We all work in a taxi company in Dubai. We all know each other at work. We also know where each of us lives in the city. We see each other almost every day. I am not willing to take the risk of going beyond my circle and joining other groups." (Excerpt from an interview with B., female, age unknown, 2022: Interview)

According to informants, difficult circumstances at the place of origin and destination (i.e., political and economic hardship in Ethiopia and the skyrocketing cost of living in the host country, particularly Dubai) negatively affect trust responsiveness. One informant said: "People know untrustworthy behaviour is unacceptable. But what can they do when their survival is threatened?" Many of the informants stated that poverty at home, along with unfulfilled expectations, create frustration among many of the Ethiopian migrants residing in the UAE, and this has negative implications for trust. The current political crisis in Ethiopia has also divided people along ethnic lines, contributing to a general lack of trust towards one another, with possible trickledown effects on other aspects of social life.

The overall slowdown in economic activities in the post-COVID-19 period also made informal institutions of saving weak and fragile. Business has gone down, many small ventures collapsed, and many have been unable to get back on track. In fact, some coffee and shisha houses have been closed permanently.

---

10 This is not commonly used among the Ethiopians in the Emirates.

11 Often Ethiopian and Eritreans associate themselves as *habesha* and maintain good social relations. But political upheavals in the countries of origin often limit the extent to which mutual trust is established although personal relations, and intimacy rather than ethnicity remains a much strong factor.

The overall breakdown of cultural norms

Another issue consistently raised by informants is the increased vulnerability of members to the exploitative behaviour of others. Untrustworthy people may take advantage of the vulnerability of people to satisfy their greed, informants explained, weakening trust and contributing to the overall breakdown of social values and norms that characterizes Ethiopian society today. This is worse in a context of migration because of the absence of societal sanctions in a foreign land. One of the informants stated:

> "When we were in our home country, if someone became unreliable, we would often go to a person who could mediate and solve the problem for us. Here, in a foreign country, whom would you turn to in times of betrayal and dishonest behaviour? In our country, no one will speak to you if you do. Here, no one will hold you accountable for your bad behaviour." (H., male, age 32, 2022: Interview)

On one hand, there are those who generally do not want to risk trusting others. On the other hand, there are those who have had a real experience of untrustworthy behaviour and whose attitudes have changed over time. For example, F., a restaurant owner in Sharja state, shared her own experience:

> "Two years ago, I was the chairperson of an equb. The members came to Sharjah from different parts of Ethiopia, but we did not know each other before [...] the fact that we were all Habesha (from Ethiopia) was reason enough to trust each other [...]. As Ethiopians we simply trusted each other. A certain man got the first lot and we gave him 20,000 Dirhams [...] but he disappeared with the money [...] nobody heard from him afterwards [...]. So I had to pay that amount out of my own pocket. Things have taken a turn for the worse [...]. Now, I have organized a small equb for my employees in the cafeteria [...] the contributions come from their monthly salaries." (F., female, age 42, 2022: Interview)

Diminishing trust also deters non-members from establishing their own informal saving associations. In an informal conversation, I asked an informant about his overall thoughts regarding *equb* in Dubai and whether he would consider becoming a member in the future. He replied:

> "I have no intention whatsoever of becoming a member of an equb [...] I no longer have confidence in anyone [...] some time ago we elected a person to raise money for humanitarian causes, the guy disappeared with the money ... and his whereabouts are unknown to date, [...] except that he is still active on Facebook [...] And pretending to be religious [...] saw maman kabro naw ("trust a man after you bury him")." (T., male, age 28, 2022: Interview)

Informants stress that trust has become a very scarce resource even within kinship groups. For example, one group of migrants (mainly women) who had transferred the money they had saved for years to relatives in Ethiopia for future projects were badly let down when the recipients behaved dishonestly.

Conclusion

The findings show that Rotating Savings and Credit Associations (ROSCAs) and *equbs* in particular continue to play a significant role in financial mobilizations among diasporic Ethiopians in the UAE. This informal platform provides a good alternative to modern banking in a foreign country because many of the migrants have non-resident status and earn marginal income. In the UAE, *equb* associations often involve highly cohesive social groups tied by blood, friendship, or business relations that help build a sense of trust. The relationships, income, and occupational status of members are, therefore, key factors in trust formation. Where *equb* associations are formed based on kinship and social relationships, the rules and procedures become simple and straightforward often not involving meticulous hierarchies. In recent times, such self-help associations have been threatened significantly by eroding trust, arising, in part from, the highly mobile nature of the Ethiopian diaspora population in the Middle East. The overall slowdown in economic activities in the host country following the COVID-19 pandemic generally made informal savings institutions weak and fragile.

Equb in the UAE does not function well as the environment is characterized by suspicion and a lack of trust caused by mobility and insecurity. Member numbers are often limited to minimize risk. *Equb* associations tend to be more ad hoc and less permanent. Other features of *equb* in the Emirates include strict inclusion/exclusion criteria, smaller size, higher frequency of rotation, and lower financial contributions. Diminishing trust also means that the very survival of such institutions hangs in the balance. *Equb* associations are less rampant today compared to in the past as the importance of a sense of morality has declined and there have been more frequent violations of cultural norms. The weakening of such institutions has a far-reaching impact on the extent of social interaction and communication among migrants, which are key to establishing social and economic wellbeing in the host country.

Bibliography

Abegaz, Kassech (2014): *The Role of Iddir in Development for City Slum and Frontier Subcities of Addis Ababa: The Case of ACORD Intervention Areas*. MA Thesis, Addis Ababa University.

Adugna, Girmachew (2021): "Once Primarily an Origin for Refugees, Ethiopia Experiences Evolving Migration Patterns." Migration Policy Institute, Accessed March 8, 2024, (https://www.migrationpolicy.org/article/ethiopia-origin-refugees-evolving-migration).

Aredo, Dejene (1993): *The Informal and Semi-Formal Financial Sectors in Ethiopia: A Study of the Iqqub, Iddir, and Savings and Credit Co-Operatives*. African Economic Research Consortium, Nairobi: Zakuna printers Ltd.

Aredo, Dejene (2004): "Rotating Savings and Credit Associations: Characterization with Particular Reference to the Ethiopian Iqqub." *Savings and Development* 28/2, pp. 179–200.

Azam, Muhammad/Haseeb, Muhammad/Samsudin, Shamzaefa (2016): "The Impact of Foreign Remittances on Poverty Alleviation: Global Evidence." *Economics and Sociology* 9/1, pp. 264–281.

Bazezew, Arega/Chanie, Wubliker (2015): "Iddirs as Community-Based Social Capital in the Amhara Region of Ethiopia: Case Study in Gende Woin Town of East Gojjam." *The Ethiopian Journal of Social Sciences* 1, pp. 3–13.

Bekerie, Ayele (2003): "Iquib and Idir: Socio-Economic Traditions of the Ethiopians." *Tadias Magazine*. Accessed March 8, 2024, (http://www.tadias.com/v1n6/OP_2_2003-1.html).

Coates, Jamie (2108): "Trust and the Other: Recent Directions in Anthropology." *Social Anthropology* 27/1, pp. 1–6.

Corsín-Jiménez, Alberto (2011). "Trust in Anthropology." *Anthropological Theory* 11/2, pp. 177–196.

Dasgupta, Partha (1988): "Trust as Commodity." In: Diego Gambetta (ed.), *Trust: Making and Breaking Cooperative Relations*, Oxford: Blackwell, pp. 49–72.

Frederiksen, Morten (2012): "Dimensions of Trust: An Empirical Revisit to Simmel's Formal Sociology of Intersubjective Trust." Current Sociology 60/6, pp. 733–750.

Getachew, Samuel (2020). "Digital Equb". *The Reporter*. Accessed March 8, 2024, (https://www.thereporterethiopia.com/10645/).

Good, David (1988): "Individuals, Interpersonal Relations, and Trust." In: Diego Gambetta (ed.), *Trust: Making and Breaking Cooperative Relations*, Oxford: Blackwell, pp. 31–48.

Goffman, Erving (1983): "The Interaction Order: American Sociological Association." *American Sociological Review* 48/1, pp. 1–17.

Herr, Hansjorg/Nettekoven, Zeynep M. (2017): "The Role of Small and Medium-sized Enterprises in Development What Can be Learned from the German Experience?". Friedrich Ebert Stiftung, Accessed March 8, 2024, (https://library.fes.de/pdf-files/iez/14056.pdf).

Ministry of Foreign Affairs (MFA) (2023): "Consulate General of the Federal Democratic Republic of Ethiopia." Accessed March 8, 2024, (https://dubai.mfa.gov.et/the-embassy/).

Misztal, Barbara (2002): "Normality in Trust in Goffman's Theory of Interaction Order." *Sociological Theory* 19/3, pp. 312–324.

Morgan, Robert M./Hunt, Shelby (1994): "The Commitment-Trust Theory of Relationship Marketing." *Journal of Marketing* 58/ 3, pp. 20–38.

Mühlfried, Florian (2018). "Introduction, Approximating Mistrust." In: Florian Mühlfried (ed.), *Mistrust: Ethnographic Approximations*, UK: Dover Publications, pp. 8–22.

Mühlfried, Florian (2021): "The Spectrum of Mistrust." *Journal of Social and Cultural Anthropology* 146/1, pp. 201–218.

Şahin, Ali/Taşpınar, Yasin (2015). "Citizens' Trust in Public Institutions: A Field Study." *Conference paper, International Congress of The International Institute of Administrative Sciences*, June 22–26, 2015, Rio de Janerio, Brazil.

Tadesse, Michael Emru (2023): "Rotating Savings and Credit Associations as a Financial Commons: A Case Study of an Ethiopian Equub in Berlin." In: U. Nothdurfter/F. Zadra/A. Nagy/C. Lintner, (eds.), *Promoting Social Innovation and Solidarity Through Transformative Processes of Thought and Action*, Bozen: Bozen-Bolzano Press, pp. 73–96.

Yitbarek, Elias (2008): "The Role of Iddir in Neighborhood Upgrading in Addis Ababa, Ethiopia." *Journal of Ethiopian Studies* 4/1–2, pp. 187–197.

Savings (*equb*) and insurance (*iddir*) associations of Eritreans in Germany

Sebhatleab Tewolde Kelati

Abstract *With more than 70,000 members, Germany hosts the third-largest Eritrean population in the world. The objective of this contribution is to explore and describe the establishment, activities, and administration of savings (equb) and insurance (iddir) associations in this community. The investigation contextualizes their utilization within the framework of the migration experience. The associations are organized based on trust to help members solve their economic and social challenges. Trust is established through family, religious, or ethnic affiliations, and this helps the associations have a less formal administrative structure. Though most are not registered as non-profit organizations, they have binding internal regulations.*

Introduction

A wealth of literature exists on savings (*equb*) and insurance (*iddir*) associations within Ethiopia and Eritrea (Dejene Aredo 2010; Pankhurst/Damen 2000; Elliesie 2017; Gebremichael/Ruys 2006; Gebreyesus Abegaz Yimer et al. 2018) and in the Ethiopian diaspora (e.g. Michael Emru Tadesse 2023). However, to my knowledge, there is no literature on Eritrean savings and insurance associations in the Eritrean diaspora.

By the end of 2022, 73,805 Eritrean diaspora community members resided in Germany.[1] Most of them live in Hesse, especially in the metropolitan area of Frankfurt. The Eritrean population in Germany is the third largest in the world, after Eritrea itself and its diaspora in Sudan and Ethiopia. Accordingly, it has been of interest to several studies (Conrad 2010; Santos 2019; Treiber 2017).

In this contribution, I want to look at how Eritreans in Germany have established social interaction and cooperation in the form of savings (*equb*) and insurance (*mahiber* or *iddir*) associations and how they instrumentalize these associations to work towards a 'good life' and 'good future' (cf. Fischer 2014; see introduction to this

---

1   According to Statistisches Bundesamt (https://www-genesis.destatis.de/).

volume). While *equbs* revolve around building up future investment, *iddirs* provide insurance for important, future life-course rituals such as burials and wedding ceremonies.

In both *equb* and *iddir* associations, members meet regularly and contribute a fixed amount of money. The difference between them lies in the objective for which the contributed money is used. *Equb* associations are a type of rotating savings and credit association (ROSCA), which are informal institutions that provide saving and lending facilities (Geertz 1962). The money is repaid to members in turn. *Iddir* associations, also called *mahiber* by the Eritrean and Tigrinya speaking communities, are broadly community associations that employ forms of risk-sharing and risk-pooling: members pool their resources as a protection from the high costs associated with important life-cycle events like weddings and burials. Each member contributes money each month, and this accumulates until a member or one of their close family gets married or needs burial, at which point an agreed amount of money is paid out.

Research objective and methodology

Most of the data for the current study was collected during the first quarter of 2022. I distributed questionnaires to members of 21 *equb* and *iddir* associations (see Table 1). I additionally collected evidence from sources such as the associations' by-laws, direct observation, and interviews.

In designing the questionnaires, I prepared a list of questions for each variable in the main outcome measures listed below. Care was taken so that all the relevant questions were asked, but that there was enough flexibility to allow the natural flow of ideas and events. Before distributing the questionnaires, a pilot test was conducted with five members of *equb* or *iddir* associations to check the clarity and relevance of the questions. Finally, I took a sample of 21 associations from five cities in Germany (see Table 1 below for more information). The main outcome measures I used to study were the following:

- The background of the associations: I asked how long their association had been established, the objective of its establishment, its membership numbers, and criteria for membership.
- The activities of the associations: Here I asked for the types of activities that the associations routinely perform, such as periodic meetings, money contributions, and helping members and relatives back in Eritrea.
- The administrative setup of the associations: which includes the administrators' status, election criteria, duties/tasks, and how they manage conflicts.

- Internal regulation and official registration: I inquired if the associations have written or oral internal regulations and if they are registered with the relevant government offices.
- The effects of the Covid-19 pandemic: I studied the effects of the Covid-19 pandemic on the activities of the associations and on the approaches they used to solve or minimize the effects.

Eritrean communities in the diaspora at a glance

The state of Eritrea (independent from Ethiopia since 1993) is geographically located in the Horn of Africa. According to the United Nations World Population Prospects, Population Division and Worldometer (2022), the estimated population of Eritrea is 3,748,901. Particularly following the 1998–2000 Ethio–Eritrea war, a large percentage (10%–20%) of its population migrated to many countries across the world (United Nations 2022). Figure 1 shows the top five destinations for Eritrean migrants, in which about 70 per cent of the migrant community live.

Figure 1: Top 5 destinations for Eritrean migrants (2020)

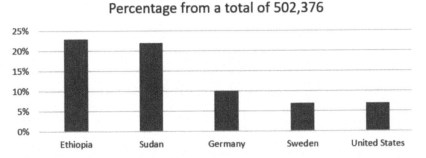

Source: World Population Prospects – Population Division – United Nations 2022

Emigration out of Eritrea has increased dramatically in the last 10 to 15 years. Germany, particularly since 2015, has attracted a very large number of migrants and refugees (Rietig/Müller 2016), a sizable number of which are Eritreans. With regard to the diaspora communities in Germany, reference to the Statistisches Bundesamt (2020) shows that the East African community in general and particularly the Eritrean population in Germany continuously increased from 2013 to 2020. By 2020 about 10 per cent of the migrant Eritreans worldwide, that is 75,735 people, were residing in Germany (Statistisches Bundesamt 2020) (see Figure 2 for more information).

Figure 2: The East African community in Germany 2013 to 2020

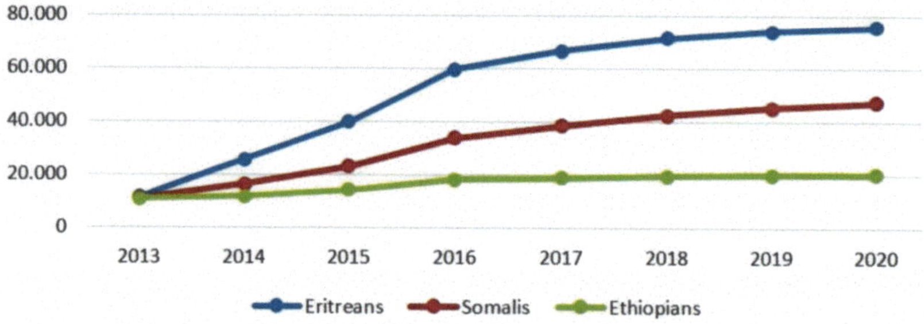

Source: Statistisches Bundesamt (2020)

Figure 2 indicates that the Eritrean community increased from 11,655 in 2013 to 75,735 in 2020. Only 1,415 Eritrean migrants live in Berlin, the capital of the Federal Republic of Germany. The largest Eritrean communities are found in four federal states in Germany: Hesse (with an Eritrean population of 17,020), North Rhine Westphalia (14,045), Bavaria (11,640), and Baden-Wurttemberg (8,270) (Statistisches Bundesamt, 2020). Thus, I took samples from the following metropolitan cities (cf. table 1):

Table 1: Eritrean diaspora communities in Germany

State and sampled city	Eritrean diaspora Population		Number of Eritrean associations		
	Size	Percentage of total population	*equbs*	*iddirs*	total
Hesse – Frankfurt	17,020	22	3	10	13
North Rhine Westphalia – Cologne	14,045	19	-	1	1
Bavaria – Nuremberg	11,640	15	2	2	4
Baden-Wurttemberg – Stuttgart	8,270	11	1	1	2
Berlin – Berlin	1,415	2	-	1	1
Total population sampled	52,390		6	15	21
Total Eritrean population in Germany	75,735				

Source: Statistisches Bundesamt (2020)

Research findings on *equb* and *iddir* associations in Germany

As shown above (Figure 2), most Eritreans arrived in Germany recently (since 2013). It is therefore not surprising that most of the associations under study are quite young. About 67 per cent of *equbs* and 53 per cent of the *iddirs* from my sample are ten years old or less (cf. table 2).

Table 2: Age of sampled equb and iddir associations

	1–5 years	6–10 years	11–15 years	16–20 years	More than 21 years
equb associations	3 (50%)	1 (17%)	1 (17%)	-	1 (17%)
iddir associations	5 (33%)	3 (20%)	4 (27%)	1 (7%)	2 (13%)

To give a better insight into why these associations are thriving in the growing Eritrean population in Germany, I will start my findings with three case studies.

Case 1: Mahiber Qudus Michael (Saint Michael) of Segheneiti

According to my interview with its chairman Mr. T., the Mahiber Qudus Michael association was founded in 2004 with many members. However, the chairman said the association currently has only ten actively participating families, who live mostly in the cities of Frankfurt and Stuttgart. The criteria for membership are willingness, trust, commitment to making the monthly contribution, and being a Catholic from the village of Segheneiti, which is located in the southern part of Eritrea, where the population is Tigrayan. The main objective of Mahiber Qudus Michael is to provide financial and material support for mourning and funeral ceremonies, and to provide opportunities to meet and socialize. Members also coordinate fundraising activities to help people in the village of Segheneiti and maintain its parish church, St. Michael Church.

The Mahiber Qudus Michael is very formal in its administration. It has the three executive positions often seen in formal organizational structures: chairperson, secretary, and treasurer. Money is deposited in the bank as soon as it is collected. The *mahiber* has written regulations and is registered as a non-profit organization with the Frankfurt city administration. Members meet once a year, during June, at the meeting hall of St. Maria-Hilf (a Roman Catholic church) in the city of Frankfurt. After taking mass, the members share Eritrean food and drinks. The members all come with their children, and friends and other relatives are also invited. The meeting lasts for three days: Friday, Saturday, and Sunday. Apart from the annual meeting, the members' main activity is to collect funds to pay for burials or mourning. Mr. T. said that each member is liable for a fixed amount of Euro 5 per month, which they pay annually. The members make a higher contribution to cover the costs of the annual meeting and in the event of deficits at funerals and memorial services. In the case of a death of a member's family, the association pays that member Euro 500.

Case 2: The Mahiber Mehazut (Association of Friends)

The Mahiber Mehazut is a hybrid of an *equb* and *iddir*. Members contribute Euro 110 per month. The Euro 100 is an *equb* contribution, and Euro 10 an *iddir* contribution. The association has seven members and was founded in 2010. According to an interview with one of its members, Mrs. H., all seven members go to the Eritrean Catholic church in Frankfurt. Furthermore, they belong to the Tigrinya language-speaking or Tigrayan ethnic group that hails from the southern part of Eritrea bordering the Tigray region of Ethiopia. The *mahiber* is therefore not only based on friendship, but also on a common religion and regional origin in Eritrea.

The main objectives of the Mahiber Mehazut's members are to help each other with funeral and marriage arrangements and to meet and socialize. Members take turns to host the monthly meeting, where the members make their monthly payments, celebrate the three rounds of the Eritrean cultural coffee ceremony (which takes about three hours), and discuss their situation in Frankfurt and families back home in Eritrea.

The Mahiber Mehazut has no formality in its administration. Its members consider no need for internal controls because any money is deposited in a bank as soon as possible. Their long-term objective is to start a business together, although no business plan so far exists and socializing seems to be the main reason for the association. From each member's monthly contribution, Euro 100 per member is saved as seed money for that business; the remaining Euro 10 contributions are saved as insurance for unexpected expenditure during mourning and funeral events. With the collected contributions of Euro 10, some of their members received financial support of Euro 500 to travel to Eritrea and attend the funerals of their close relatives there.

Case 3: The *equb* family Tesfa Giorgis

Like the *mahiber* in case 2, the Equb Tesfa Giorgis is a hybrid of a *mahiber* and *equb*. The *mahiber* and *equb* started by seven middle-aged, male cousins and their wives living in Frankfurt and its vicinity. They organized a *mahiber*, whose main purpose is to meet four times per year with their wives and children. Apart from the meetings, the *mahiber* regularly collects a small amount of money, and the members assist each other in organizing life-cycle events like weddings graduation ceremonies and a joint trip outside Frankfurt once a year.

The male cousins felt that meeting four times per year was not enough for them to update each other about family news and looked for a reason to meet more regularly. Therefore, they started an *equb* together, meeting monthly on the last Sunday of every month. Although all the members are related, they usually meet in a church where one of the members is a member of the congregation and a close friend of the church administrator. They do not meet at their homes, so as not to burden their wives with hosting the meeting with three rounds of cultural coffee ceremony. Their *equb* has a cycle of seven months and a monthly contribution of Euro 100. According to the members, the main purpose of the *equb* is to socialize, the small amount of money that is saved is secondary and is not enough for larger purchases or investments.

Considering the above-mentioned case studies, it is interesting to note that there are notable differences between *equb* and *iddir* groups back in Eritrea or Ethiopia and those among the Eritrean diaspora in Germany. First, the German groups are often made up of close family members of friends, whereas *equbs* in Ethiopia are often made up of colleagues and very rarely made up of family members, while *iddir* groups are mostly made up of neighbours (Dejene Aredo 2010; Pankhurst/Damen 2000; see Glück this volume). Second, the main purpose of *equb* groups in the Eritrean diaspora in Germany is to socialize, while back in Eritrea or Ethiopia, the purpose is to save or invest (Dejene Aredo 2010; Pankhurst/Damen 2000). Third, in the Eritrean diaspora in Germany many hybrids of *equb* and *iddir* groups exist, something that is not usual in Eritrea or Ethiopia. These hybrids are a product of the limited number of possible members in the diaspora, where neighbourhoods and colleagues are made up of other nationalities. As can be seen from the above examples, apart from providing ways to save (*equb*) and finance life-cycle events (*iddir*), the associations are also important in helping members to socialize and to send money to Eritrea to help relatives there.

In my 21 samples, I observed that *equb* associations are generally smaller than *iddirs*. The memberships of *equb* associations range from 4 to 13 individuals, while those of *iddir* associations are between 20 and 200 (see Table 3). Each time members of an *equb* meet, they have a draw to determine who will take the month's contribution. Therefore, all the money is paid to the lucky member of the month; this continues until they have all had a turn. Therefore, *equbs* demand a higher level of trust, as more money is contributed and remains with individual members, who have already received the total contribution. Conversely, in *iddir* associations, the risk of losing money is smaller, as the contribution of money is less and the shared funds are kept in a bank account.

174 Saving and being safe in the Ethiopian diaspora

Table 3: Size of membership of sampled equb and iddir associations

number of members	*equb* associations	*iddir* associations
200	-	1 (10%)
100	-	3 (30%)
60	-	1 (10%)
40	-	1 (10%)
30	1 (17%)	2 (20%)
20	-	2 (20%)
15	-	-
13	1 (17%)	-
12	1 (17%)	-
8	1 (17%)	-
7	1 (17%)	-
4	1 (17%)	-

The findings, especially from the case studies, lead us to the conclusion that the focus in *equb* associations in Germany is, in the main, short term, and that these associations seldom help members make financial investments for future development in Germany. Many members send their *equb* money back home to Eritrea to help relatives or to buy (or build) a house there (provided they pay the 2 per cent tax).[2] The findings show that *iddir* associations in Eritrea share a common purpose with their German counterparts in helping their members during funeral and marriage events, as well as providing opportunities to meet and socialize. However, those in Germany have the additional purpose of sending money to Eritrea, for the same reasons as the *equb* associations, that is, to help relatives back home. When money is sent to Eritrea for a common purpose, such as to help a village, the money is sent in the name of the association. However, when it is sent to financially help relatives, individual members send it to their respective relatives.

In both *equb* and *iddir* associations, members are admitted based on trust that is established due to affiliations, such as extended family, friendship, co-working, region (in Eritrea), or religion. Additional membership criteria in *equb* associations include the ability to pay the monthly money contribution.

---

2   Eritrea charges two per cent tax on the income of all Eritreans who live outside Eritrea. If an individual does not pay the tax, they cannot receive consular services from an Eritrean embassy or consulate.

The administration of *equb* and *iddir* associations

In this section, I consider the associations' administration, including their main operations, administrative structures, and criteria for election to administrative duties, along with how they resolve conflict.

Equb associations in Germany have less formality in their administration compared to *iddir* associations. About 33 per cent of those sampled in Germany have the three primary executive positions in a formal structure, that is, chairperson, secretary, and treasurer; 17 per cent have only one executive position (treasurer); and 50 per cent have none. However, about 93 per cent of the *iddir* associations have all three executive positions (chairperson, secretary, and treasurer) and only 7 per cent have none. This shows that *equb* associations consider there to be less need for internal controls. Since *iddir* associations have a longer life span compared to *equb* associations, they have long-term objectives, so they see the need for a more formal structure (see Table 4).

Table 4: The administrative structure of the sampled equb and iddir associations

	chairperson, secretary and cashier	only cashier	no chairperson, secretary and cashier
equb associations	2 (33%)	1 (17%)	3 (50%)
iddir associations	14 (93%)	-	1 (7%)

Here again, both *equb* and *iddir* associations use multiple criteria to choose their administrators. In *equb* associations, the main criteria[3] for election to an administrative position is trust (33 per cent), willingness (33 per cent), good relations with members who actively participate (33 per cent), and leadership ability (17 per cent). *Iddir* associations emphasise willingness (40 per cent), leadership ability (40 per cent), good relations with members who actively participate (40 per cent), trust (33 per cent), and majority vote (27 per cent). Other criteria include the ability to read and write Tigrinya and German (13 per cent), and seniority in the association or years of service as a member in the association (17 per cent) (see Table 5).

---

3 The criteria were specified by the author in his questionnaire.

Table 5: Criteria for electing administrators in equb and iddir associations

	trust	willingness	leadership ability	good relationship with others	seniority	majority vote	ability – German language
equb associations using this criterion	2	2	1	2	-	-	-
percentage using this criterion from 6 *equbs*	33	33	17	33	-	-	-
iddir associations using this criterion	5	6	6	6	1	4	2
percentage using this criterion from 15 *iddirs*	33	40	40	40	17	27	13

Members of about 66 per cent of the sampled *iddir* associations could not clearly identify the main duties/tasks of their administrators. However, some of them mentioned that follow-up and coordinating activities (17 per cent) and establishing internal regulations (17 per cent) were among their duties. With *iddirs*, following-up and coordinating activities (50 per cent), sending money to Eritrea (25 per cent), control and making annual report of payments (21 per cent) were cited as the administrators' main duties.

I also asked respondents if their associations encountered conflicts and, if so, how they resolved them. All *equb* associations reported that they had not had any conflict so far. Similarly, 79 per cent of the *iddir* associations had experienced no conflict so far. The three *iddir* associations (21 per cent) that had experienced conflict (for example if the deceased family member is close enough to the member to be paid money from the association) solved it amicably (67 per cent) or by calling a general meeting (33 per cent).

Internal regulations and official registration

The following explores the question of whether the associations have internal regulations and, if so, whether they exist in written or oral form. Furthermore, I enquire if the associations are registered officially at the relevant government office as a non-profit organization.

I found that among *equb* associations 50 per cent have only oral, 17 per cent only written, and 33 per cent both oral and written internal regulations. From the *iddir* associations, 54 per cent have only written, 31 per cent only oral, and eight per cent have both written and oral internal regulation. I observed that both types of association have internal regulations. In addition, oral regulations are considered as binding as written regulations.

My findings show that 83 per cent of the *equbs* are not registered at the relevant government office as non-profit organizations (or Eingetragener Verein or e.V., German for NGO). From the *iddir* associations, 67 per cent are not registered. I observed that many of them are not registered because, as some reported, registration will subject them to strict government control such as annual reporting of activities for tax and other control purposes.

Members' contributions and payments to members

As defined at the beginning, both *equb* and *iddir* associations are community organizations where members meet regularly and contribute a fixed amount of money. But how much money and how often does each member contribute to the association, and how much money and how often does the association pay their members?

Of the *equb* associations, 67 per cent reported that each member contributes Euro 100 per month. I also found that members in one association contribute Euro 300 each month. In another *equb* association, members do not need to contribute the same amount of money: if someone wants to contribute more, he or she can pay multiples of one share, or they can share a share with other members to pay less. The payment to members at *equb* associations depends on their monthly contribution and the number of members: the higher the amount contributed by each member and the more members in each association, the more the monthly payment to a member. In *equb* associations, members can choose how to use the money they receive. However, most of members send it to Eritrea to help their relatives because they have an obligation to repay the financial support given by family members to help pay for their migration. In addition, most family members in Eritrea depend on the remittances sent by relatives in the diaspora.

About 53 per cent of *iddir* associations reported that members contribute Euro 5 monthly, or Euro 60 annually, to the association. Among the other four (27 per cent) *iddir* associations, payments differed. One *iddir* association reported that members pay Euro 100 each month. Accordingly, the pay-outs of *iddir* associations to members differ greatly, ranging from Euro 500 to Euro 4,000 for a funeral or marriage ceremony. In *iddir* associations, the monthly contributions are always the same, and the amount paid out is set by the associations' regulations. The events that trigger a payment do not occur regularly, so contributions can accumulate. However, it is also possible for the association to run short of money and ask members to make special, irregular contributions.

The Covid-19 pandemic and its effect on associations' activities

During my research, I enquired into whether Covid-19 pandemic affected the activities of the associations, and how they managed these effects. In response, about 83 per cent of the *equb* associations reported that Covid-19 had greatly affected their activities, and only 17 per cent said it did not affect them at all. All those whose activities were affected stopped their periodic meetings and their overall activities. Similarly, all of the *iddir* associations reported that Covid-19 had affected their activities. Therefore, they had no periodic meetings (100 per cent) and their activities were stopped (93 per cent) or greatly decreased (93 per cent) (see table 6 for more information).

In *iddir* associations, the activities, particularly the marriage ceremonies, were either interrupted or kept to a minimum. Obviously, however, burial events were out of the associations' control, and members had to make special contributions, while participation at these events was kept to a minimum.

Table 6: Covid-19's effect on the activities of equb and iddir associations

	affected	
were activities affected?	yes	no
from 6 *equb* associations	5 (83%)	1 (17%)
from 15 *iddir* associations	15 (100%)	-
	effect		
effect on the activities	no periodic meetings	decreased activities	decreased contribution
from 6 *equb* associations	5 (33%)	5 (33%)	5 (33%)
from 15 *iddir* associations	15 (100%)	14 (93%)	14 (93%)

To mitigate the effects of the pandemic, all the associations used different methods. Half of the affected *equb* associations said they would wait for the Covid-19 pandemic to end in order to resume their normal activities. Some also used social media, such as Zoom (33 per cent) and WhatsApp (17 per cent), telephones (17 per cent), and the banking system (12 per cent) to solve the effects. Similar, about 67 per cent of the *iddir* associations waited for Covid-19 pandemic to end. Similarly, some of the *iddirs* used social media, such as Zoom (7 per cent) and WhatsApp (13 per cent) (see Table 7 for more information).

Table 7: Solutions to the Covid-19 pandemic used by equb and iddir associations
Others*– Created opportunities for online meetings/asked for government help/no idea

equb and iddir associations	waiting	use media					others*
social media used		WhatsApp	telephone	Zoom	banking system		
equb	3	1	1	2	1		-
per cent from 6 equb associations	50	17	17	33	17		-
iddir	10	2	-	1	-		4
per cent from 15 iddir associations	67	13	-	7			27

Conclusion

I started my study with the objective of answering the questions: How do the Eritrean diaspora communities' *equbs* and *mahibers* or *iddirs* (1) establish their social interaction and (2) manage their activities once the interaction is established?

Based on experiences in Eritrea, I expected that the purpose of *equb* associations would be to collect money for future investment. However, my research data shows that the main objective of *equb* groups within the Eritrean diaspora in Germany is to socialize. In addition, they raise funds to send home to support their relatives in realizing their individual visions of a 'good life'. This is, for example, because migrants have obligations to repay family members who helped them in their migration journey. I also observed that, mostly, the amount of money contributed in *equbs* is not enough to make meaningful investments, mainly because the financial power of members is weak.

On the other hand, the example of Mahiber Mehazut (Association of Friends) demonstrates that *equb* savings can be used to set up a joint business. The future-oriented practice of *equb* is evident both in its social and financial aspects. The social quality shows in how *equb* associations foster gatherings, share ideas, and support relatives. The financial factor is evident in the financial support that can improve the

180 Saving and being safe in the Ethiopian diaspora

quality of life of relatives back in Eritrea or contribute to entrepreneurial endeavours in Germany. The example of the Mahiber Mehazut further shows that hybrids of *equb* and *iddir* associations exist in the diaspora, especially among homogenous circles of friends. This is a clear difference to Eritrea, where *iddirs* exist with large numbers of members and are neighbourhood associations.

The findings show further that *iddir* associations in Eritrea and their counterparts in Germany share a common purpose of helping each other during funeral and marriage ceremonies, and to meet and socialize. However, the associations in Germany also have the additional responsibility of sending money to Eritrea.

Compared to associations back in Eritrea, both kinds of associations in Germany give less emphasis to formality: they generally have no formal administrative structure and are often not registered with government offices. Associations and their members place more emphasis on trust, friendship, or family relations. Conflicts rarely happen and are solved amicably.

When looking at the effects of the Covid-19 pandemic, we see that the activities of the associations decreased, but at the same time digital ways of communicating, which remain useful today, were taken up.

Figures

Figure 1: Top 5 destinations for Eritrean migrants (2020)
Figure 2: The East African community in Germany 2013 to 2020

Tables

Table 1: Eritrean diaspora communities in Germany
Table 2: Age of sampled *equb* and *iddir* associations
Table 3: Size of membership of sampled *equb* and *iddir* associations
Table 4: The administrative structure of the sampled *equb* and *iddir* associations
Table 5: Criteria for electing administrators in *equb* and *iddir* associations
Table 6: Covid-19's effect on the activities of *equb* and *iddir* associations
Table 7: Solutions to the Covid-19 pandemic used by *equb* and *iddir* associations

Bibliography

Conrad, Bettina (2010): *"We Are the Prisoners of our Dreams": Long-Distance Nationalism and the Eritrean Diaspora in Germany*. PhD Thesis, University of Hamburg.

Dejene Aredo (2010): "The IDDIR: An Informal Insurance Arrangement in Ethiopia." *Savings and Development* 34/1, pp. 53–72.

Elliesie, Hatem (2017): "Traditional Forms of Social Protection in Africa: Selected Examples from Ethiopian and Eritrean Societies." *Recht in Afrika* 20, pp. 28–73.

Fischer, Edward F. (2014): *The Good Life. Aspiration, Dignity, and the Anthropology of Wellbeing*, Stanford, California: Stanford University Press.

Gebremichael Kibreab Habtom/Ruys, Pieter (2006): "Traditional Risk-Sharing Arrangements and Informal Social Insurance in Eritrea." *Health Policy* 80/1, pp. 218–235.

Gebreyesus Abegaz Yimer/Decock, Wim/Mehreteab Ghebremeskel Ghebregergs/ Gebrehiwot Hadush Abera/Gidey Seyoum Halibo (2018): "The Interplay Between Official and Unofficial Laws in Rotating Savings and Credit Associations (*Eqqub*) in Tigray, Ethiopia." *The Journal of Legal Pluralism and Unofficial Law* 50/1, pp. 94–113.

Geertz, Clifford (1962): "The Rotating Credit Association: A Middle Rung in Development." *Economic Development and Cultural Change* 10/3, pp. 241–263.

Michael Emru Tadesse (2023): "Rotating Savings and Credit Associations as a Financial Commons: A Case Study of an Ethiopian Equub in Berlin." In: Urban Nothdurfter/Franca Zadra/Andrea Nagy/Claudia Lintner (eds.), *Promoting Social Innovation and Solidarity Through Transformative Processes of Thought and Action*, Bozen: bu press, pp. 73–96.

Nolting, Nina von (2010): *Nation im Exil? Eritreer in Deutschland*, Köln: Köppe.

Pankhurst, Alula/Damen Haile Mariam (2000): "The Iddir in Ethiopia: Historical Development, Social Function, and Potential Role in HIV/AIDS Prevention and Control." Northeast African Studies 7/2, pp. 35–57.

Rietig, Victoria/Müller, Andreas (2016): "The New Reality: Germany Adapts to its New Role as a Major Migrant Magnet." *Migration Information Source*, August 31, 2016.

Santos, Beatris de Oliveira (2019): *Eritrean Diaspora in Germany: The Case of the Eritrean Refugees in Baden-Württemberg*, PhD Thesis, University of Lisbon.

Statistisches Bundesamt (2020): *Fachserie 1, Reihe 2*.

Treiber, Magnus (2017): *Migration aus Eritrea. Wege, Stationen, informelles Handeln; Mensch werden, Mensch bleiben*, Berlin: Reimer

United Nations (2022): *World Population Prospects*, Population Division.

Saving and being safe beyond Ethiopia

Spatial manifestation of self-governance groups
Addis Ababa x Nairobi

Yasmin Abdu Bushra

Abstract *According to official figures from the Ethiopian Central Statistics Agency, the urban population of Ethiopia is projected to nearly triple from 15.2 million in 2012 to 42.3 million in 2037, growing at 3.8 per cent a year (World Bank 2018). Urban Kenya is experiencing similarly dramatic growth, with its population soaring and boundaries expanding. However, urban local government institutional systems and infrastructure have not kept pace with rapid urbanization (UN Habitat 2017, 2022). Despite progress over the last decade in building institutions and providing infrastructure and services across all sectors, urban service delivery remains weak to this day, as urban reform remains one of Ethiopia's greatest challenges. In both Addis Ababa and Nairobi, parallel varieties of self-initiated community organizations exist, among which iddirs and resident associations are the most widespread. Primarily established to provide mutual aid in difficult times or for important events, increasingly they have been observed to address other community concerns (Pankhurst 2008; and this volume). This research applies the constructivist grounded theory method to birth a theory that explains the terms of engagement of these community organizations with local state actors through open coding, focused coding, and theoretical coding procedures. A co-production framework has been crafted from the data embedded in the experiences and perceptions of realities within participants. The co-creation, co-operation, and co-optation modes of iddir engagements pave the way for the prospect and understanding of a restructuring of power relationships among iddirs, resident associations, and local governments for an empowering exercise of the right to the city.*

Introduction

"Spatial Manifestation of Self-Governance Groups" is a research in progress that explores the disconnect across three unique African urban realities: the rapid growth of urban spaces; the inability of states to meet the basic needs of existing and emerging demographics; and the spatial effects of community organization activities. It explores how those different realities can come together and form socio-spatial resilient practices.

The intention of this research is therefore to present an indication of the economic, social, and political potential of self-initiated community organizations in Addis Ababa and Nairobi while understanding their capacity to strengthen urban service delivery and management equitably and sustainably. It also attempts to investigate the interactions of self-initiated community organizations, social movements, local governments, and state agencies around urban service delivery and their role of collective participation in citizen empowerment and engagement. The research also maps the involvements of selected community organizations in the provision of urban services and uses these engagements to understand the conditions needed for co-production.

The research investigates the connections between high urbanization rates, poor urban service delivery, and strong community-led organizations. It explores the possibility of longer-lasting ties between state actors and society, and documents *iddirs* in Addis Ababa and resident associations in Nairobi and their engagement in urban service delivery in these two rapidly densifying African cities.

Methodology and case studies

In the absence of documentation on the participation of *iddirs* in the process of urban service delivery, this investigation applies Constructivist Grounded Theory, an inductive qualitative research method in which a set of structured but flexible rules for conducting inquiry are applied with the overarching intention of developing a theory. It also utilizes other methodologies, such as Discursive Grounded Theory, which focuses on the language used in data collected (McCreaddie/Payne 2010). This methodology recognizes that language produces reality rather than merely representing it, whereby social realities and relationships are constituted in language.

Theoretical sampling is used to allow the researcher to follow leads in the data by sampling new participants that provide relevant information. This process allows the final developed theory to remain grounded in the data. Consequently, the theoretical sampling method is intended for the development of a theoretical category, as opposed to sampling for population representation.

Section I: Addis Ababa

According to the most recent figures, the urban population of Ethiopia is projected to nearly triple from 15.2 million in 2012 to 42.3 million in 2037, growing at 3.8 per cent a year (World Bank 2018), with 30 per cent of the population living in urban areas by the year 2028, and 37.5 per cent by the year 2050 (Ethiopia 2050/BRP 2020).

Urban local government institutions have not kept pace with this rapid urbanization (UN Habitat 2017). Despite progress over the last decade in building institutions and providing infrastructure and services across all sectors, urban service delivery remains weak. In urban Ethiopia, 80 per cent of the overall housing stock needs either upgrading or replacing (Marrengane/Croese 2020). Currently, only half of the urban structures have private or shared water connections. The government estimates that 35 per cent of urban solid waste is never collected, while only 10 per cent of the population report using a municipal waste collection system (Tsega G. Mezgebo 2021). The public sector is unable to provide sustainable services to the current urban residents and is expected to struggle even further with the new urban influx.

Several self-initiated community organizations have stepped into the gap with a focus on solving various urban challenges in the city of Addis Ababa (Solomon Dejene 2009). A variety of community organizations exist, of which *iddirs* are the most widespread institutions in both urban and rural areas. *Iddirs* are community entities that are formed for social resilience. They operate within self-crafted guidelines that outline membership rights and responsibilities, terms of membership, the rights and responsibilities of the *iddir*'s leadership, election terms and requirements, areas of operations, and suchlike. The guidelines for each *iddir* are written and ratified by its members through a democratic process, therefore the intricacies of each *iddir* varies depending on the activeness of its leadership and members through the years.

Iddirs are primarily established to provide aid in burial matters (Pankhurst 2008). However, in recent years *iddirs* have evolved to cover functions related to urban service delivery and maintenance. Membership in community organizations such as *iddirs* (funeral associations), *equbs* (saving/credit groups), and *mahibers* (other groupings based on monthly religious celebrations, relatives, colleagues, and others) is indispensable for low-income households as it provides an essential web of economic and social security needed to compensate for the weak social-security networks provided by the government.

Geographic and substantive focus

The Addis Ababa Bureau of Labor and Social Affairs has documented 7856 active and operating *iddirs*. The geographic focus of this research covers the *iddirs* inside the city of Addis Ababa and their role and engagement in urban service delivery processes.

From the data collected, certain patterns of how *iddirs* behave with their local administration have emerged. Their behaviour can be divided into three main categories based on their mode of engagement with their local authorities: co-operation, co-creation, and co-opting. Co-creating *iddirs* often work and have a negotiating relationship with local authorities: they ask and negotiate for their needs. Co-operating *iddirs* often act as assistants to local authorities: they help with the activities and plans already set by the local authorities. Co-opting *iddirs* often perform their social services completely independent of local authorities. The following explores these three categories and the differences between them, and touches on case studies of *iddirs*' activities in the city.

Co-creating *iddirs*

Co-creating *iddirs* engage actively in the provision of social services within their communities. Some of their services include the designation of access roads as one-way streets to manage community disturbances and requesting regular policing rounds to manage security issues. The *iddirs* in this category exhibit strong relationships with their respective local governments; they have surpassed the level of consultation and are in a position to negotiate with their local authorities. This relationship stems from the recognition of *iddirs* as highly influential pillar institutions within the community.

One case study for the co-creating *iddirs* is located adjacent to the new Adey Abeba Stadium. The residents of the 25tu Mahiberat *iddir* first came to the area as a result of the Derg's 1981 campaign to house public servants whose income was considered moderate, that is between 300 and 500 birr per month (US$1032 to US$1720 today, taking inflation into account). The area was named 25tu Mahiberat for the 25 smaller cooperatives that were formed to construct the houses. 25tu Mahiberat is today an *iddir* with close to 478 member families, each contributing 40 birr every month.

In the past decade, the *iddir* has become the primary body responsible for the neighbourhood's upkeep. It actively regulates, maintains, and provides the necessary equipment for the upkeep of the neighbourhood's designated open spaces. Over the course of twelve years, the *iddir* has managed to build a fully standardized tennis court and a basketball court. It has also bought and operates a children's playground and general open space amenities such as open-air seating and waste disposal equipment within the open space compound. The rest of the area is planted with fruit trees such as mango, avocado, false banana and papaya, the fruits of which are later sold back to the community at lower than market prices at community gatherings.

The *iddir* has recently expanded its efforts to farm an idle space that used to be open-air garbage. The *iddir* representatives that served from 2018 to 2020 managed to negotiate and convince the local administrative representatives to temporarily allow them to make use of an area estimated to be about 8688 square metres of linear space (24m x 356m) for urban farming, with produce being offered to the area's residents at lower prices.

Figure 1: Ethnographic mapping of a weekend meeting at the 25tu Mahiberat iddir

Source: illustration and observation Yasmin Abdu Bushra

Figure 2: Geographic mapping of the 25tu Mahiberat iddir

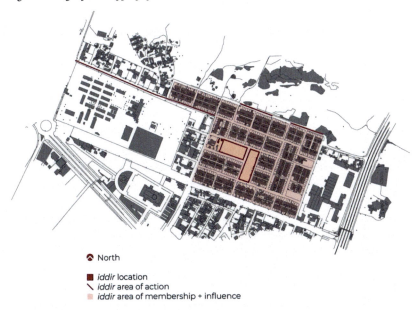

Source: base map GIS Edits by Yasmin Abdu Bushra

190 Saving and being safe beyond Ethiopia

Figure 3: Ethnographic mapping of one of the edible gardens at 25tu Mahiberat iddir

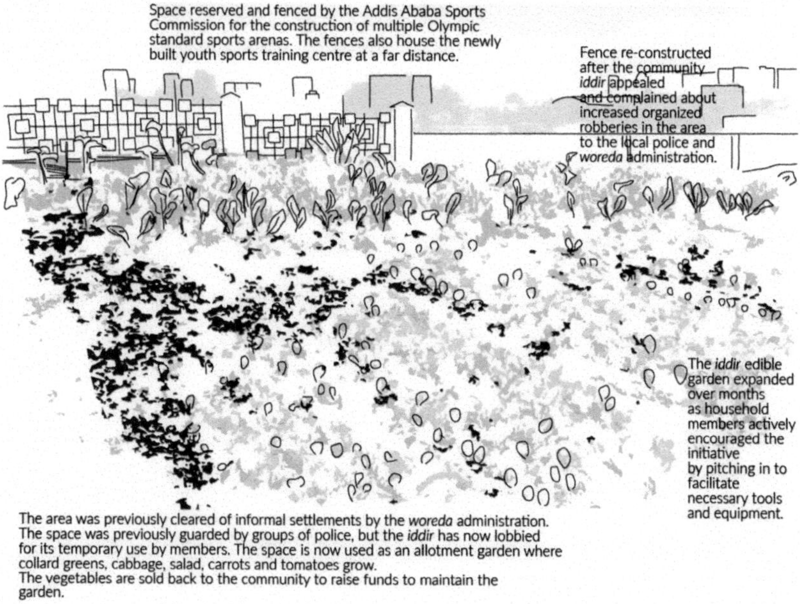

Space reserved and fenced by the Addis Ababa Sports Commission for the construction of multiple Olympic standard sports arenas. The fences also house the newly built youth sports training centre at a far distance.

Fence re-constructed after the community iddir appealed and complained about increased organized robberies in the area to the local police and woreda administration.

The iddir edible garden expanded over months as household members actively encouraged the initiative by pitching in to facilitate necessary tools and equipment.

The area was previously cleared of informal settlements by the *woreda* administration. The space was previously guarded by groups of police, but the *iddir* has now lobbied for its temporary use by members. The space is now used as an allotment garden where collard greens, cabbage, salad, carrots and tomatoes grow. The vegetables are sold back to the community to raise funds to maintain the garden.

Source: illustration and observation Yasmin Abdu Bushra

Co-operating *iddirs*

This category is set apart by the presence of a clear hierarchy within the relationship that defines its engagement with local administrative bodies, as they engage with their local administrations as assistants. Co-operating *iddirs* often mobilize communities and disseminate local authorities' information, as they have a great reach within the community. Examples of their services include the stocking and management of local libraries built by local administrations. While co-creating *iddirs* play a role in making the activities they choose to engage in, the co-operating *iddirs* only contribute to actions proposed by the local administrators.

The selected case for the co-operation type of engagement, Andinet *iddir*, is located in one of the founding *sefers* of the city of Addis Ababa. Serategna *sefer* is adjacent to a building registered as a heritage site by the Arada sub-city administration and Addis Ababa's Culture and Tourism Bureau. Its members estimate Andinet *iddir* to have been there for around two decades, with an average of 275 permanent members. Andinet is based adjacent to the Mussie Minas residence in the burnt and damaged section (date unknown).

Figure 4: Ethnographic mapping of Andinet iddir location

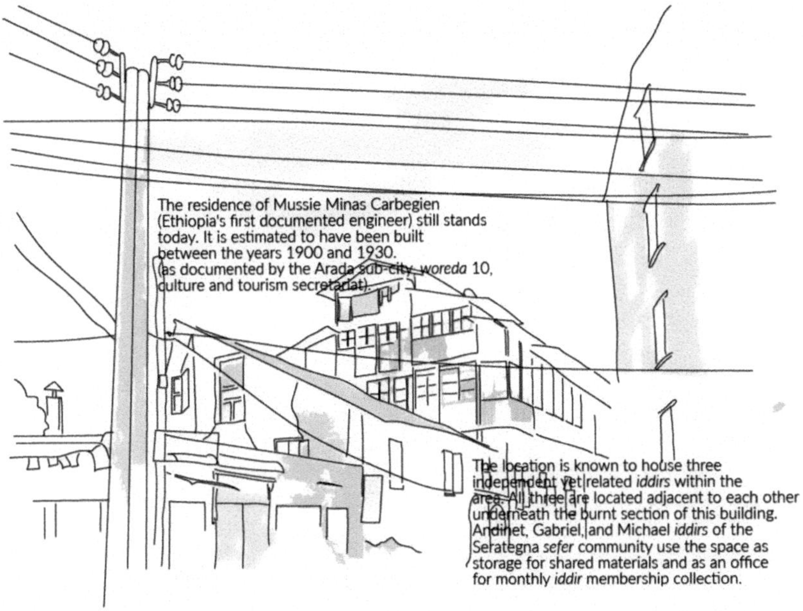

Source: illustration and observation Yasmin Abdu Bushra

This *iddir*, like others, was primarily established to provide mutual aid for vital events and emergencies among member families. Prominent members within Andinet emphasized that while the *iddir*'s main function is to come to the rescue of families at times of emergencies, the contribution of one *iddir* might not be enough to address all the different family needs. Thus, many families join multiple *iddirs* to get different benefits, prompting leading *iddirs* to specialize and address specific community needs.

The Andinet *iddir* is the most prominent one in Serategna *sefer*. The *iddir* makes a substantial contribution to the public library found just in front of its shared storage unit. The library is said to have opened about 30 years ago and has since served to nurture students in the area. While the *woreda*[1] 10 education bureau of Arada sub-city allocates an annual stipend to the library, the *iddir* closely follows the day-to-day operations of the public facility, helping maintain damaged books and sagging shelves, and repair leaky roofs, broken desks and chairs, etc. It also maintains close contact with the librarians to ensure that the library offeres a generally pleasant

---

1   A *woreda* is the lowest entity in the governance structure of the city of Addis Ababa. The city is governed by the Addis Ababa City Administration under which 11 sub-cities exist. Then come the *woredas*, which are assigned jurisdictions under the sub-city.

environment for students. Generally, while the *iddir* does not single-handedly contribute to the management of the public library by physically maintaining the library space, it continues to directly contribute to the preservation of a neglected modern urban heritage where a public facility directly benefiting the community is housed.

Figure 5: Geographic mapping of Andinet iddir

Source: base map: GIS Edits Yasmin Abdu Bushra

Figure 6: Ethnographic mapping of the interior of woreda 10 education bureau library

Source: illustration and observation Yasmin Abdu Bushra

Co-opting *iddirs*

Co-opting *iddirs*, similar to co-creating and co-operating *iddirs*, have a significant role in performing activities to service the community. However, they are set apart by their engagement with local governments. Co-opting *iddirs* recognize and actively engage in the provision of social services but mostly work as independent entities without much co-operation or co-creation with the local government. The decision opt out of working with the government can be exclusively attributed to members' fear of the *iddir* being used as an instrument to perform agenda that are politically charged. Eyob Balcha Gebremariam (2020) notes that *iddirs* are spaces where political entities attempt to mobilise voters especially during election seasons.

Ye Hiwot Meseret *iddir* is based in the central-eastern part of the city. It was founded 35 years ago and now has around 100 family membership. This *iddir* is seen as the 'deciding body' for mobilization of monetary and human capital when it comes to the neighbourhood. It actively participates in the upkeep of the neighbourhood's cobblestone roads, footpaths, speed bumps, etc. However, its communication with the *woreda* administration is very limited, and its representatives show no interest in forging relationships with the administration.

Figure 7: Geographic mapping of Yehiwot Meseret iddir

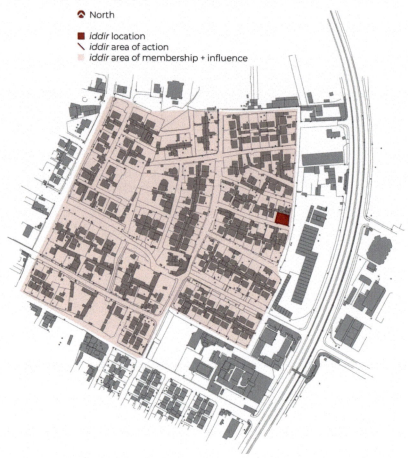

Source: base map: GIS Edits Yasmin Abdu Bushra

Figure 8: Ethnographic mapping of the compound location of Yehiwot Meseret iddir

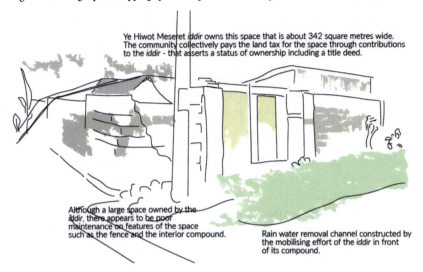

Source: illustration and observation Yasmin Abdu Bushra

Figure 9: Ethnographic mapping of one of the monthly meetings of Yehiwot Meseret iddir

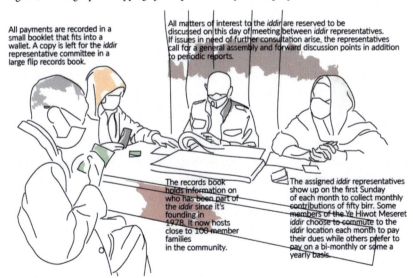

Source: illustration and observation Yasmin Abdu Bushra

Section II: Nairobi

The emergence of residents' associations is a recent development that has shaped urban centers throughout Kenya and Nairobi in particular (Chitere/Ombati 2004). An urban residents' association is a group of neighbours who get together and share their ideas, thoughts, and feelings for the purpose of cooperation for the betterment of their immediate neighbourhood (Mitrofanova 2004).

The weakened capacity of local government, excessive pricing from private service providers, and the indifference of community groups are all contributing to bad urban service delivery in the city. In response to the challenges this raises, neighbohrhood-level associations in low, middle, and high-income areas have emerged. With their increasing numbers and visibility, they have the potential to shape the landscape of urban service provision in Nairobi.

The research examines the functions of residents' associations in urban service delivery. It investigates the relationship between residents' associations and local administrative groups in urban service delivery, and examines the challenges encountered by residents' associations. It goes on to categorize the associations based on their mode of engagement with local state elements.

Logic of organization

According to Jonas (2005), participation in neighbourhood associations in Nairobi is important because it offers increased access to information between residents and local governments and allows the co-identification of development options. It also enables residents, who represent an array of community interests, to give priority to their individual and collective needs, identify resources for these needs, and develop their collective capacity.

Urban residents' associations have a brief history in Kenya, which dates back to 1994 and the formation of the Buru Buru and Komarock residents' associations (Echessa 2010). The recent increase in the number of residents' associations can be traced to the reduced capacity of urban authorities to provide basic services to residents (Chitere/Ombati 2004). Urban residents' associations stimulate people's involvement in the design and delivery of common basic services. As observed with the *iddirs* in Addis Ababa, these associations represent the efforts of urban residents to meet the challenges of declining basic service provision through collective action.

Residents become members of associations upon payment of registration fees and monthly contributions. George Echessa (2010) found that registration fees differed across income groups and according to whether members were homeowners, tenants, residents, or organizations. Apart from registration fees, members also pay to get services like garbage collection, plumbing services, trimming of hedges, and security monitoring. In terms of membership size, Echessa (ibid.) reports that associations in middle-income areas had the highest registered average: 5155 members. The average membership size in high-income communities was 141 members, while it was 112 in low-income communities. There was an enormous disparity in membership size among associations in middle-income neighbourhoods that ranged from 210 to 15,000 members (ibid.).

The reason why associations in middle-income areas have a high number of members could be the high population density in the area. However, in the city of Nairobi, low-income areas have the highest population density (Ngigi 2003). The membership numbers are, in fact, often influenced by reasons other than the neighbourhood density, including the issues addressed, modes of mobilization, membership composition, relations with the local authority, and modes of mobilization (Coelho 2006). Small membership also enhances the quality of the internal administration of rewards and penalties.

Membership sites are also controlled by the ability of an association to forge an interesting and community-engaging agenda for the neighbourhood. The low-income associations are largely unable to forge a broad agenda as they have a lower capacity to raise resources or engage with other stakeholders (Baiocchi 2003). Likewise, low-membership associations have to bear the consequences of having a limited sphere of influence due to significantly reduced social capital.

Members often benefit enormously from their membership in these associations, but benefits often differ from one association to another because of each association's agenda, funds, and resources. For instance, an association in a high-income area can easily raise funds for hiring guards to help with security issues, while associations in low incomes areas cannot, making the benefits reaped from the association in a high-income area much higher (Mwaura 2000).

Echessa (2010) indicates that different associations have initiated various projects to improve residents' living conditions. High-income and middle-income associations are addressing basic needs, such as security, the environment, and social amenities. Associations in low-income areas fulfil the welfare needs of members and act as a social safety net. They are also known to respond to the efforts of state entities to address insecurity and environmental challenges in the area, and provide important information to the local administration on security and crime.

The Co-production framework

Making use of the framework crafted as a result of data collected in Addis Ababa, the cases observed in Nairobi appear to fall into similar patterns of co-production of urban services between local state actors and self-initiated community organizations.

Co-operating community organizations

The Muthaiga Neighbourhood Association is a residents' association located in an upper-middle-class neighbourhood in the district of Muthaiga. It was founded in 1997 by early residents of the district with a mere 22 members and now has 280 household members. The organization's administration is independent and is community-funded through membership fees. It mainly engages in security provision to the district as well as ecological upkeep of the area. It also delivers and manages protected green spaces, playgrounds, and golf courses. While some are protected spaces to be used by members only, others remain public and part of the Nairobi city landscape. The association has gained prominence within the community and serves residents by delivering a strong voice to the Nairobi County administrative bodies. It also makes sure all newly planned renovations and developments within the district comply with the zoning laws of the area and it maintains a close relationship with the Nairobi County planning bureau.

Figure 10: Ethnographic mapping of one of the streets maintained by the Muthaiga residents' association

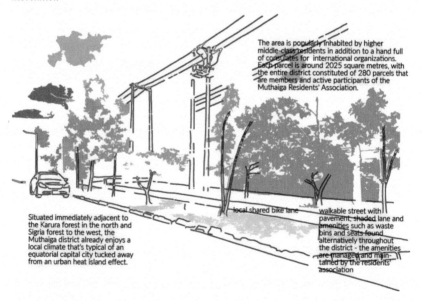

Source: illustration and observation Yasmin Abdu Bushra

Co-opting community organizations

Futbol Mas Kenya is a prime example of a community organizing to fill urban service delivery gaps. In one of the two largest slums in Nairobi, named Mathare, the youth of the neighbourhood have come together and founded Austin's Grounds. Initiated by an ex-footballer, Austin's Grounds used to be a nameless, abandoned waste dumpsite for the slum of Mathare in general and the immediate informal residential concoctions in particular. Over the past six years, the area has been converted into an open, multi-purpose space that can fulfil some of the needs of the community. On weekends, Austin's Grounds serves as a sports venue for children and youth. The space is maintained by an administrative group that comes from the community and assigns tasks to teams of individuals from Mathare to take care of the makeshift football pitch, wash motorcycles and cars to generate income, rent out carts for the movement of goods, etc. The group further generates income from voluntary monthly contributions that have neither minimums nor caps. Futbol Mas has an average of 280 contributing members who regularly use Austin's Grounds. Even though this community organization is disadvantaged by being located in one of the most deteriorating urban spaces in the city of Nairobi, it is able to address community needs, such as the need for public open space and a reliable supply of clean water.

Figure 11: Ethnographic mapping of Austin's Grounds on a Sunday

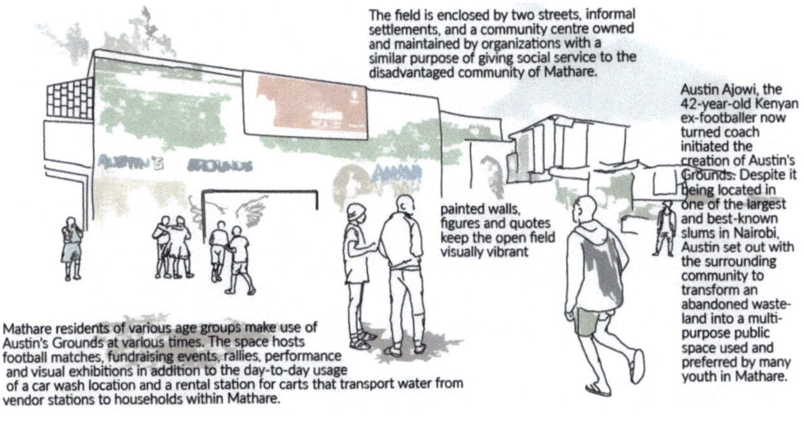

The field is enclosed by two streets, informal settlements, and a community centre owned and maintained by organizations with a similar purpose of giving social service to the disadvantaged community of Mathare.

Austin Ajowi, the 42-year-old Kenyan ex-footballer now turned coach initiated the creation of Austin's Grounds. Despite it being located in one of the largest and best-known slums in Nairobi, Austin set out with the surrounding community to transform an abandoned waste-land into a multi-purpose public space used and preferred by many youth in Mathare.

painted walls, figures and quotes keep the open field visually vibrant

Mathare residents of various age groups make use of Austin's Grounds at various times. The space hosts football matches, fundraising events, rallies, performance and visual exhibitions in addition to the day-to-day usage of a car wash location and a rental station for carts that transport water from vendor stations to households within Mathare.

Source: illustration and observation Yasmin Abdu Bushra

Figure 12: Photograph of Austin's Grounds on a Sunday

Source: image: © Sebastian Gil Miranda

Figure 13: Photograph of the interior wall of the Mathare Social Justice Center's dance hall

Source: image © Yasmin Abdu Bushra

Near Futbol Mas Kenya is another community organization, the Mathare Social Justice Center, which has made a big name for itself by making use of mass media in the radio and digital means such as social media to attract members. The centre was founded to promote social justice in the Mathare community. It works as an advocacy centre, providing various services such as creative development, communication skills, performance arts, and others that appear and disappear depending on need. The centre provides an open and accessible space that caters to the youth residing in Mathare and its surroundings.

The Mathare Social Justice Center is an interesting case study for this investigation due to its ecological justice program, which is led by the founders of the community group. The ecological justice program is engaged in cleaning up the neighbourhood (collecting and disposing of improperly disposed waste), planting trees that are indigenous to the Nairobi environment, undertaking yearly river audits that are made public, and planting bamboo trees along the banks of the Mathare river to help clean the river.

Figure 14: Ethnographic mapping of the riverbank in Mathare

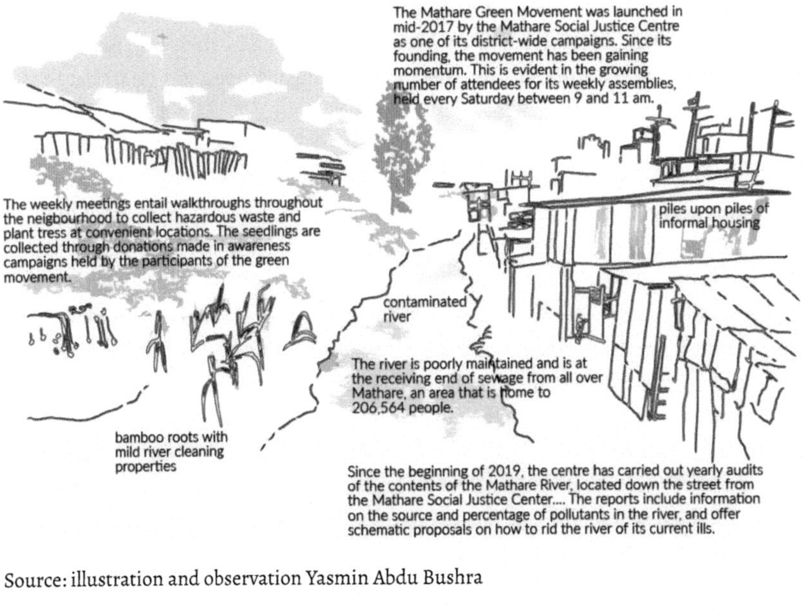

Source: illustration and observation Yasmin Abdu Bushra

Conclusion

The "Spatial Manifestation of Self-Governance Groups" investigated the potential of local self-initiated community organizations to be major actors in the practice of service delivery in the urban space. By taking particular cases in the cities of Addis Ababa and Nairobi, the research attempted to formulate a theory to reconcile three unique realities. The first is a high rate of urbanization in both Nairobi and Addis Ababa. The second is exceptionally weak urban service delivery that cannot cope with the demands of the present and upcoming population. The third is the presence of self-initiated community organizations that play a strong role in urban service delivery. The research set out to investigate those self-initiated community groups, their varying degrees of engagement with their local authorities, their spatial influence in their neighbourhoods, and their role in urban service delivery in the cities of Addis Ababa and Nairobi.

The research highlighted three main aspects of these community organizations: the various degrees of engagement with local authorities; the effect of the neighborhood's income level and social status on the organization's influence and interventions; and their spatial interventions in urban spaces. The Addis Ababa case studies showed how co-operating *iddirs* choose to work within their local authorities' overall agendas and operate more or less as assistants to their local authorities, while co-creating *iddirs* have more of a negotiating relationship with their local authorities and often communicate their needs. On the other hand, co-opting *iddirs* choose to operate independently from the authorities and formulate their own projects and spatial interventions. Through the three modes of engagement, it is clear that the *iddirs'* interventions in service delivery are positive.

In the case of Nairobi, while the case studies operate more or less under the same modes of engagement with local authorities, the effect of each neighbourhood's level of income is the main factor shaping the influence that each organization has on urban service delivery. While higher-income organizations are able to provide all the security needs of their community, smaller organizations are not able to raise funds nor effect action from other stakeholders to move their agendas forward.

In both cities, self-governed community organizations seem to be influencing the community positively. Their spatial effects can be seen clearly in the neighbourhoods, in libraries, football fields, allotment gardens that feed communities, and dry-waste collection systems. Citizens are stepping up and coming together to fill gaps left by the local authorities. How their relationships with local authorities will evolve and how much influence these groups will have in shaping urban realities is something that is worth studying in the future.

Figures

Figure 1: Ethnographic mapping of a weekend meeting at the 25tu Mahiberat *iddir*

Figure 2: Geographic mapping of the 25tu Mahiberat *iddir*

Figure 3: Ethnographic mapping of one of the edible gardens at 25tu Mahiberat *iddir*

Figure 4: Ethnographic mapping of Andinet iddir location

Figure 5: Geographic mapping of Andinet *iddir*

Figure 6: Ethnographic mapping of the interior of *woreda* 10 education bureau library

Figure 7: Geographic mapping of Yehiwot Meseret *iddir*

Figure 8: Ethnographic mapping of the compound location of Yehiwot Meseret *iddir*

Figure 9: Ethnographic mapping of one of the monthly meetings of Yehiwot Meseret *iddir*

Figure 10: Ethnographic mapping of one of the streets maintained by the Muthaiga residents' association

Figure 11: Ethnographic mapping of Austin's Grounds on a Sunday

Figure 12: Photograph of Austin's Grounds on a Sunday

Figure 13: Photograph of the interior wall of the Mathare Social Justice Center's dance hall

Figure 14: Ethnographic mapping of the riverbank in Mathare

Bibliography

Baiocchi, Gianpaolo (2003): "Emergent Public Spheres. Talking Politics in Participatory Governance." *American Sociological Review* 68/1, pp. 52–74.

Chitere, Preston O./E. Ombati (2004): *Urban Governance and Neighborhood Associations in Nairobi: Performance and Future Prospects*, Nairobi: IPAR.

Coelho, Karen (2006): *Neighbourhood Associations as Urban Collective Actors*, Unpublished. India.

Echessa, George (2010): *The Role of Residents' Associations in Urban Service Delivery: The Case of Nairobi City*, Kenya: Jomo Kenyatta University.

Ethiopia 2050/BRP (2020): "Ethiopia 2050 Grand Challenges and Opportunities." Accessed March 8, 2024, (https://ethiopia2050.com/).

Eyob Balcha Gebremariam (2020): "The Politics of Dominating Addis Ababa (2005–2018)." *Effective States and Inclusive Development Working Paper* No. 148.

Jonas, R. (2005): *From Urban Management to Urban Governance. Towards a Strategy for the New Millennium*. Unpublished: Geneva.

Marrengane, Ntombini/Croese, Sylvia (2020): *Reframing the Urban Challenge in Africa: Knowledge Co-Production from the South*, London and New York: Routledge.

McCreaddie, May/Payne, Shiela (2010): "Evolving Grounded Theory Methodology: Towards a Discursive Approach." *International Journal of Nursing Studies* 47/6, pp. 781–793.

Mitrofanova, Helen (2004): "Neighborhood and Community, How to Organize a Neighborhood Association." Nebline Newsletter, Nebraska.

Mwaura S. R. (2000): Emergence of Neighbourhood Associations in Nairobi City: Case of Juja & Huruma Estates, Faculty of ADD, University of Nairobi.

Ngigi, C. M. (2003): *Neighbourhood Associations: their Role in the Management of the Urban Commercial Built Environment. Case of Nairobi Central Business District (NCBDA) within the Nairobi Central Business District (CBD)*, Faculty of ADD, University of Nairobi.

Pankhurst, Alula (2008): "The Emergence, Evolution and Transformations of Iddir Funeral Associations in Urban Ethiopia." *Journal of Ethiopian Studies* 41/1–2, pp. 143–185.

Solomon Dejene (2009): "Exploring Iddir: Toward Developing a Contextual Theology of Ethiopia." *International Conference of Ethiopian Studies*, pp. 535–548.

Tsega G. Mezgebo (2021): "Urbanization and Development: Policy Issues, Trends and Prospects". In: Mengistu K./ Getachew D. (ed.), *State of the Ethiopian Economy 2020/2021: Economic Development, Population Dynamics and Welfare*, Addis Ababa: Ethiopian Economic Association.

UN Habitat (2017): "The State of Addis Ababa 2017: The Addis Ababa We Want." Accessed March 8, 2024, (https://unhabitat.org/the-state-of-addis-ababa-2017-the-addis-ababa-we-want).

UN Habitat (2022): "Envisaging the Future of Cities." Accessed March 8, 2024, (https://unhabitat.org/sites/default/files/2022/06/wcr_2022.pdf).

World Bank (2018): "Ethiopia Urbanization Review." Accessed March 8, 2024, (https://documents.worldbank.org/en/publication/documents-reports/documentdetail/543201468000586809/ethiopia-urbanization-review-urban-institutions-for-a-middle-income-ethiopia)

Caring for the future
Social insurances, and the notion of time and trust

Sabine Klocke-Daffa

Abstract *For the social insurance industry, Africa is considered to be a market of the future where "the scramble for African customers" has just begun. With a share of more than 80 per cent of all insurance sales, the southern African countries of South Africa, Namibia and Botswana dominate the life insurance market. Namibia, though only a small country in respect to its population size, represents the "new targets" of insurers, where more life premiums than non-life premiums are sold and accounted for more than US$1 billion of sales in 2021. Life insurance, including funeral coverage that provides for the entire family, has turned out to be a bestseller. Customers appear to have considerable confidence in their insurers and have found a way to merge company requirements, culture-specific preferences, and national inheritance laws. This contribution looks at the backdrop of increased sales and redirected monetary flows and argues that caring for the afterlife by way of formal life insurance impacts not only informal support networks but also on notions of time and the relations between the living and the dead.*

The new scramble for African customers and the quest for social security

This contribution focuses on a particular aspect of social insurance and savings, namely funeral insurance and life cover. Alongside the established informal support systems and savings associations documented in this book, formal insurance is increasingly in demand on the African continent. From the perspective of the insurance companies, the African continent is a market of the future, where "the new scramble for customers" (PwC 2018:44–45) is underway and investment prospects are good (KPMG 2022; Swiss Re 2020). Despite the fact that less than 20% of the population in Sub-Sahara Africa is said to be covered by social protection benefits (ILO 2021:19), and regardless of the marked drop in the year-on-year average growth rate of 2.9 per cent between 2018 and 2019 (World Bank 2022), the insurance industry appears confident. It will stay one of the most important drivers of economic development in Africa. With a share of more than 80 per cent of all insurance sales, the southern African countries of South Africa, Namibia, and Botswana dominate the life insurance market (Signé/Johnson 2020:9).

Namibia, although being a country with a small population of just slightly over 2.5 million inhabitants (World Data 2023), represents one of the "new targets" of insurers. The number of life premiums exceeds the one of non-life premiums, and sales per year amounted to more than US$1 billion in 2019 (Signé/Johnson 2020:9) and were equally high in 2021 (Global Data 2023). Financial products such as funeral insurances and life covers are sold separately or in a package, with funeral insurance being in much higher demand nationwide. For customers who sign up for the more comprehensive life cover, funeral insurance is usually included; the insurance companies call it "the final expense", and it is paid before the remaining sum is due for payout.

Given the overall economic importance of social insurance, the growing number of African customers and the financial volume involved, anthropological research on this interesting topic is, as yet, relatively scarce, as Dekker (2008) so rightly stresses. A large part of the anthropological literature on care and security tends to be focused on the traditional forms of *informal security*. There is a comprehensive literature that testifies to their historical nature. Even where the state does not provide much welfare help – as is the case in many West African states, where a substantial part of the non-sedentary population is barely covered by any kind of welfare regime – there are powerful systems in place to minimize risks such as those faced by nomadic populations living with the threat of environmental hazards (van Dijk 1994). In war-torn East African countries with failing states and hundreds of thousands of refugees crammed into refugee camps, the informal value transfer system of Xawilaad (which operates worldwide and is also called Hawala) is remarkably efficient at handling remittances sent for social support by members of diaspora communities. It is a kind of underground banking system based on the concept of honour, shame, and trust that reaches the most remote places (Horst 2006; Lindley 2010:53–80). Similarly, traditional forms of mutual aid (Zacher 1988) as well as locally based financial mutuals, also known as "money-go-round" self-help associations (ROSCAs), are well-established ways to accumulate financial resources where bank credits are unavailable, formal insurance is out of question, and government welfare schemes are fragmentary (cf. the contributions in this volume; Ardener 1964; Bähre 2007; Kedir/Ibrahim 2011; Kimuyu 1999; Thomas 1991). For women in urban and rural contexts, rotating credit associations – also called village savings and loan associations (VSLAs) – may constitute a particularly valuable form of extra-familial social support beyond the financial backing they provide (cf. the edited volume of Ardener/Burman 1996; Ashong-Katai 2011; and Buijs 1998 for South-Africa; Deubel/Boyer 2020 for Mali; Gugerty 2007 for Kenya; Kedir/Ibrahim 2011 for Ethiopia). Michael Aliber claims that the efficacy of ROSCAs as a form of group lending is mainly to be attributed to social pressure "to reduce the probability that people will fall short on their commitment to themselves" (Aliber 2010:136). We will see later that insurance companies operate with similar strategies in order to keep their customers from lapsing.

Religious communities deploy their own forms of charity and gifting (cf. De Bruijn 1994; Weiss 2020 on Zakat and faith-based organizations in Muslim societies in Africa). However, the kind of security provided by the "gift" in religious contexts is questionable (De Bruijn/Van Dijk 2009 on Pentecostalism and West African Sufi groups), since the causes of inequality and poverty usually remain unchallenged and might even be intended to basically remain untouched. Nevertheless, international financial funding of church congregations and "church shopping" of church members between congregations, forming *vertical alliances* of formal institutions, which provide unilateral support, and *horizontal alliances* of interpersonal relations within the congregations (Rohregger 2009) allow for the establishment of a support structure. It exists in parallel to government-financed welfare systems and formal security institutions and can be used as an additional source of care.

Where governments do provide for the fundamental needs of the poor, a quite substantial percentage of the population may indeed be covered. For example, in South Africa and Namibia, more than a quarter of the population – mainly from special risk groups like the disabled, orphans, and vulnerable children, war veterans, and pensioners – is reckoned to receive some kind of social grant (Bähre 2011 on social grants; Devereux 2001 and Pelham 2007 on state pensions). The southern African countries are surely in a privileged position compared to many other African nations with regard to state provision of social assistance schemes, but they are in no way outstanding. All countries of Sub-Saharan Africa have introduced formal security schemes, most notably pensions for the elderly paid for either by mandatory contributory schemes, non-contributory elderly assistance schemes, occupational schemes, or civil service schemes (for an overview cf. Abels 2016; Bailey/Turner 2008; Dorfman 2015; Gillion et al. 2000). One of the oldest such schemes on the continent, after that of South Africa, is Ghana's, which dates to the 1946 Pension Ordinance (Gockel 1996:35).

What needs to be emphasized is that informal, semi-formal, and formal social protection systems in many countries exist side by side, as Stephen Devereux, Melesse Getu, and the contributors to their edited volume (2013) demonstrated. We also find forms of integrated state and non-state systems operating simultaneously, for example, where informal familial support systems are strengthened by government benefits paid to kin or non-kin caregivers who take responsibility for the needy, such as orphaned children (Midgley 2000:224–227 on several social security programs), or provide ample opportunities for a complementary system of non-formal social protection (Mupedziswa/Ntseane 2013 on Botswana). With formal social insurance gaining ground, we find more and more hybrid forms of individual provisioning with regard to securing a good life and peaceful afterlife. This has led to an increase

208 Saving and being safe beyond Ethiopia

in anthropological inquiries focusing on the intersection of the formal and the informal sides of care and security, and their relation to concepts of life and death. Given the dominance of multinational insurers in the southern part of the continent, it is no surprise that recent publications on social insurance have focused on this area. They vividly illustrate the cultural factors that need to be considered when we talk about social insurance. Among them we find work on the impact social insurance may have on social network cohesion or disruption (Bähre 2012; 2020 for South Africa), specific forms of individual coping strategies when navigating between personal risk provisioning and social values of solidarity (Klocke-Daffa 2016 on funeral insurance; 2022 on life cover and last wills in Namibia), and the remaking of kinship ties (Golomski 2015 on life insurance in former Swaziland).

Research outline

I argue that cultural values always impact the demand for and use of formal insurance even if invisible at first glance. Furthermore, funeral insurance as well as life cover have some features in common that should be given particular attention in anthropological research: the notion of time, since both are generally paid out only after the death of the policyholder, and the importance of *trust* on both the customer and insurer sides because the economic and social success ultimately relies on the customers' willingness to pay into contracts on a fairly regular base. This paper will particularly focus on the importance of trust within the context of life insurance in Namibia.

I will use a relational approach to analyse the everyday interactions of insurance brokers and customers in view of the question of caring for one's afterlife. The overarching research question is: What are the intersections of social insurance, cultural values, and trust in relation to life cover as a means of safeguarding the present and the future? A number of additional questions for investigation emerged with regard to the Namibian case study. How do Namibian customers manage to merge their individual interests regarding safeguarding their own incomes with the social obligations of care? For whom is social security to be provided? What are the key factors for imparting trust and confidence that one will be fairly treated in formal social insurance?

To analyse my data, it appears promising to link two strands of theoretical approach. The first is that developed by Morton Pedersen and Martin Holbraad on time and security (2013). The authors claim that concepts of (un)security are folded into concepts of time and visions of the future. Applying this approach to the study of life insurance policies seems even more promising because life cover explicitly addresses the aspect of time since it is usually paid out after the death of the policyholder. So, when is the time of security, and for whom? The second approach concerns the notion of trust. With regard to financial institutions such as insurance, Stephné Herselman (2008) suggests that we should include research results from the anthropology of marketing and examine the extent to which marketing strategies and trust are interrelated in the demand for life insurance. In his own research on purchasing power in the so-called "emerging markets" in South Africa, which include the insurance market, he investigated the impact of trust and face-to-face relations on the buying behaviour of customers. Herselman claims that the success of the life insurance industry heavily depends on the acknowledgement of cultural phenomena.

The research presented here was part of a broader project on social security in Namibia that started in 2010. Originally, I focused on informal, government, and church safety services (Klocke-Daffa 2012; 2016; 2017). However, it soon became apparent that formal insurance was increasingly in demand. This necessitated separate research with insurance companies, which was carried out between 2017 and 2019 (prior to the Covid-19 pandemic), during three consecutive fieldwork periods over a span of six months. Qualitative interviews were held with a number of customers who make use of financial products such as funeral and life cover. Special attention was given to insurance brokers and independent sales agents, as well as legal advertisers. These are the people who not only sell financial products but also operate at the interface between customers and companies; they have hitherto been quite neglected in the anthropological literature. In total, 30 semi-structured interviews were undertaken in six different institutions where life insurance is sold (Old Mutual, Sanlam, Metropolitan Life, Bank Windhoek, Standard Bank, First National Bank). To get an impression of regional differences, about half of the interviews were done at the companies' local branches in Oshakati, Otjivarongo, Rehoboth, and Keetmanshoop; the other half at the main offices in the capital, Windhoek.

Namibia and the market for social insurance – What makes it so attractive to Namibian customers?

Historical background

To understand the overall situation of insurers and their customers, it seems indispensable to consider the recent history of the country. In 1990, after more than 100 years of colonial domination by German and South African authorities, the former Southwest Africa became independent as the Republic of Namibia (for a historical overview up to independence cf. Wallace/Kinahan 2011). Until then, the political system was deeply entrenched in the discriminatory concepts of Apartheid, which entailed the political, economic, and social segregation of the population into 'whites', 'coloureds', and 'blacks' (the terms are widely used in Namibia until this

210 Saving and being safe beyond Ethiopia

day). Apartheid was as much the political program of successive governments as it was the base of national law. According to its regulations, civil rights were granted or deprived according to racial categorization. Most of the 'non-white' population lived in reservations characterized by economic and social neglect. In urban settlements, separate locations were assigned to each group, each with their own nurseries, schools, hospitals, and working places. The majority of the population had no right to vote and was kept away from better-paid positions in government, public institutions, private companies, banks, and insurance. They were literally excluded from large parts of the economy. While 'whites' enjoyed the advantages of privileged elites, all others were held 'apart' from them. When Apartheid ended, most Namibians did not possess a bank account or real estate; they had no access to bank loans and were not permitted access to social insurance. Aside from the state pensions granted to all persons above the age of 60, only informal support systems provided for social security (cf. Klocke-Daffa 2001 for the Nama). The state pensions were also graded according to the racial category of the beneficiaries, with monthly payments as low as 92 NAD/month in 1992 (c. 24 EUR), which were raised to 120 NAD (c. 29 EUR) in 1994. Racial disparities were only abandoned in 1994, and the standard rate of 135 NAD (c. 40 EUR) was imposed for all social pensioners in 1994[1]; it was raised to 160 NAM (c. 27 EUR) in 1996 (Devereux 2001:10–11).[2]

With the onset of independence, the newly elected government was eager to overcome the legal, social, educational, and economic relics of past decades. One of the priorities was to open the financial market to those who were formerly excluded. However, up to and even after independence, the Namibian banking and insurance sector was heavily regulated by the South African Reserve Bank. The "legacy of institutional dependence", as Odén (1991) called it, continued for some time. In 1991, four out of five commercial banks and all insurance companies were still controlled by South African entities (1991:6). For years, the banks maintained "credit apartheid" (James/Rajak 2014) by refusing to grant loans to customers unless they had salaried employment or collateral to offer – requirements that most of their prospective customers were unable to fulfil. Since insurers demand direct-debit orders, enabling them to take the monthly premiums from customers' salaries, they considered those with very low incomes and no bank account, such as domestic staff and farm workers, as 'uninsurable'. However, following political appeals for the democratization of

---

1 For pensioners of the white minority, who had been used to receiving pensions up to seven times as much as the 'black' population, this meant a reduction of almost 70 per cent at a stroke (Devereux 2001:11).

2 Due to the importance of social security, not only to the elderly, pensions have been continuously raised ever since. Currently, they stand at 1.100 NAD (c. 56 EUR) per person per month for all Namibian residents over 60 years of age. Despite the increase, pensions may have lost in relative value, for example, between 1994 and 1996 because of the weakness of the Namibian currency (historical currency convertor, https://fxtop.com).

credit and the "banking of the unbanked" (James/Rajak 2014:457), and not least to overcome their own legacy of racial and social discrimination, banks and insurance companies finally drafted new programs to include the 'mass market'. Among the products they offered was cheap funeral cover, which in the beginning was bound to membership of a particular group, such as, the employees of government institutions, schools, hospitals, or companies (i.e. group schemes). Many years passed before the insurance companies opened their portfolio to all customers, and again it was quite long before the formerly 'unbanked' were able to afford the expensive life insurance.

The attractiveness of formal social insurance

Against the backdrop of the discriminatory experiences and racist treatment of the past, one would expect to find considerable scepticism and distrust towards banks and insurers on the part of the population. However, this is not generally the case. On the contrary, Namibians today appear to be more concerned with the trustworthiness of their government than that of the financial institutions of the country. There are, of course, those who are suspicious of any kind of long-term contract urging them into a new kind of dependency, such as those required by life cover. A few of my interlocutors from banks and insurance companies reported that some of their customers were reluctant to buy financial products for lack of trust. In Oshakati, the new economic hub in Namibia, which has a flourishing financial scene, a legal advisor working at a bank mentioned that in some cases it was difficult to sell life cover in particular. Elderly customers would suspect banks of following the (white) "money makers' schemes" and blame insurers for not being trustworthy when contracts lapsed, saying: "You are stealing from us" (A., Oshakati, September 9, 2018: Interview). In Rehoboth, a small town with a predominantly 'coloured' population, the local insurance agent found customers to be particularly sceptical of long-term financial obligations such as life insurance due to a general mistrust of banks and insurance. They would neither believe that life cover provided much security nor that the insurance company would be reliable enough to pay out the money in due time. Selling insurance policies turned out to be hard work there, she claimed: "You have to struggle to advise them. You face many challenges and you have to overcome them every day" (P. Rehoboth, September 7, 2018: Interview). These voices, however, may not reflect the overall situation at the time of recording, and the general opinion has certainly changed in the meantime, as shown by the rising number of life cover policies being taken out.

Despite all the scepticism, as much as this may have been justified at that time as it is today, there is one insurance that outperforms all others: funeral cover has been in high demand since the post-independence insurance market opened to the general public. Young people leaving home after school in search of a job with a regular income, which provided access to the insurance market, quickly made use of the new product because it offered the opportunity to share in the costs associated with death and burial within the extended families. As early as the beginning of 1990s, several of my elderly interlocutors, who were far from considering funeral cover for themselves at that time, confirmed: "Yes, our children are modern now, they have death benefits." With relatively low deposits and reliable disbursements, funeral cover allows people to bear a portion of the unpredictable financial burden and ever-increasing debt that can accompany a death within the family. Insurers allude to precisely this situation in their advertising posters (fig. 1).

Figure 1: "Funerals do not always come on payday." Advertising funeral insurance on the main street in Windhoek 2017

Source: Klocke-Daffa

With increasingly diversified offers, funeral insurance became a bestseller. This was in part because insurers not only lowered the price down to as little as 9.99 NAD per person per month but also allowed customers to contract a policy for the entire family (*family cover*) of up to 12 or more members[3] (fig. 2).

Figure 2: "Honour your loved ones." Advertising family funeral cover, 2018

Source: Klocke-Daffa

Today, most Namibians possess one or more funeral cover policies,[4] and many may additionally opt for the more comprehensive life insurance, which entails a 'death benefit' and relatively high financial disbursement. Most life cover policies are requested either as *term life insurance*, paid for a specific term of life, or *whole life insurance*,[5] which covers not only one's own funeral costs with a quick pay-out but also provides a larger sum to cover outstanding debts and provide financial resources for those left behind. Whole life insurance means that the kind of security obtained generally affects only the heirs or beneficiaries since it pays out only after the policyholder passed.

---

3   Bonlife Namibia offers a family plan for up to 14 people in an extended family. To make it more attractive, the insurance grants an additional "tombstone benefit" (https://www.bonlifenam.com/benefits/).
4   Unfortunately, no statistics on the number of life insurance policies sold in Namibia are available.
5   Whole life insurance is usually only paid until the retirement age of 65.

Insurers have flexibly responded to the dynamics of the insurance market by expanding the target groups they address. Billboards in public reveal the idea behind their marketing strategy: the concept of honouring your loved ones is used to attract those who have not yet signed up for family funeral cover, and the concept of caring for the future of children left behind appeals to customers' sense of responsibility (fig. 3).

Figure 3: Billboard advertising life covers, 2017

Source: Klocke-Daffa

What makes formal insurance so attractive to Namibians that they buy policies in large numbers, complementing public welfare, private rotating credit associations (ROSCAs), and informal support systems? As opposed to countries like Ethiopia, where ROSCAs are predominant and trust in financial institutions appears to be rather low (see contributions in this book), in Namibia, insurance has become an integral part of security provision and care. Three points stand out in particular: (1) *trust* – insurers are anxious to be reliable partners in the contract, and pay out punctually when the money is due and the need is there; (2) *face-to-face contact* – insurers try to keep good relations with their customers by appointing a personal consultant who can be approached at any time, knows his customer personally with all their individual peculiarities, and possibly calls on wedding days and birthdays; (3) the *image of modernity* – being part of the system of formal insurance makes people seem associated with youth, aspiration, and stylishness. The well-educated young generation aspire to a lifestyle that includes a good job, property ownership, and a household that is close to the Western 'nuclear family' of father, mother, and children. However, the image of the modern individual rarely corresponds to reality, even though the insurers tirelessly promote exactly this: making money, residing in one's own house, caring for the future of oneself and the children as a responsible adult, and living a good life. Such aspirations are hard to realize, not least because they compete with the concept of the care-giving *social person* that is very elaborate among many of Namibia's cultural groups (c.f. for example Klocke-Daffa 2001 for the Nama). This concept entails your social reputation being largely dependent on how much you give to others, how many people you support in your household, how much you care for your extended family, friends, or neighbours, and how much you contribute, for example, to a funeral (which may be very costly).

This is where funeral insurance comes in. More than any other form of saving, it allows people to provide for the future and build up their social reputation, since people openly talk among family and friends about their financial obligations towards funeral insurers, while they may conceal their life cover policy or disclose its existence only within the immediate family. Through *family cover*, elderly persons such as parents and grandparents (up to the age of 75)[6] as well as aunts, nieces, and nephews, and biological children from inside or outside of marriage can be included in one policy, provided that the policyholder is willing to pay for them. Emotionally, this ensures a high level of safety. As one interviewee said: "Security means, being able to care now and in the future [...] I want a decent funeral for my parents and for myself so that they [my family] must not suffer" (T., Windhoek, September 20, 2019: Interview).

As long as the policyholder pays, all are covered. The insurance is paid out within 24–48 hours after the death of any one of the insured persons. Many customers prefer the funeral money to be transferred directly to the undertaker. The only condition today is that the policyholder be insured themselves and be part of the same *family cover* he/she pays for. To make sure that everyone continues to be covered even after the death of the primary policyholder, waiver insurance is highly recommended. This constellation of requirements and options was not always available when the 'mass market' opened. Then new customers often requested *family cover* that excluded themselves so that they could save some money; this clearly highlights the social importance attributed to funeral insurances. The negative effect of this was that, at the passing of the person paying into the family cover, the policy lapsed and all members found themselves without cover, also the insurance company had no one to refer to. The insurers' new policy of urging policyholders to be insured

---

6   For Sanlam, one of the largest insurers in Namibia, additional people covered by the policy of the principal member must be younger than 75 years of age at the commencement of the policy (https://www.sanlam.co.za/namibia/personal/insurance/Documents/Namibia%2 oFuneral%20Brochure.pdf).

within the same contract as his/her family not only makes it easier for insurance companies to handle the contract, as they only have to deal with one person, but also reflects the principle of the underlying concept of the self-reliant individual, who should negotiate the adversities of life in advance rather than expect his descendants to find a solution.

The mismatch between individual interest and social obligations becomes all the more visible in the case of *life cover*. One of the points that makes it so attractive is the high level of interest (8 per cent and more per year[7]) that can accrue and contribute to remarkably large pay-outs of 500,000–20 million NAD and more when a death occurs. Many insurers point out the tempting prospect of such large sums. For example, one advert trumpets, "[...] protecting your dependants from large debts (like home, vehicle or credit loans) by paying a lump sum if you kick the bucket."[8] Such prospects tempt many of their customers, but there is another side of the coin: the paying out of large sums of money must be backed by large deposits to allow life insurance to function in the first place. The ability to depositing savings on a regular basis implies that these resources are redirected financial flows that otherwise may have been distributed for alternative purposes. There is a high number of needy persons that always demand and expect to be "given" (e.g., provided financial help), who now realize that the money that would usually have gone to them is no longer available to the same extent. Insurance customers may not be generous providers of support to anyone who asks for their help. Indeed, they try to limit their social obligations and channel financial donations into carefully constructed social networks. Taking out a life insurance policy is one of several means by which someone can save, care, and provide while escaping the ever-increasing demands of others. The rising number of insurance policies being taken out and wills being drafted indicate that customers today want to safeguard their own assets, save for the future of their own descendants, and ensure that their own preferences will be respected. The good life that many strive for may not materialize in the present, but at least they can take comfort in the fact that everything is taken care of.[9] Yet, at the same time, many customers are struggling with obligations towards relatives, descendants, and other people that need to be considered according to the traditional laws of inheritance and independently of their own preferences.

---

7   Interest rates were consistently high during the years of my research, so at least since the 1990s. It is not clear whether the high premiums could be maintained if interest rates were to fall dramatically.

8   Sanlam Namibia, "Life Cover + Quick Payout", https://www.sanlamindie.co.za/product-detai ls/life-cover (accessed August 23, 2023).

9   Sanlam for example announces: "Sanlam's life cover solutions can give you peace of mind that your family can take care of their needs and expenses if you pass away. This means your death will not place a financial burden on your loved ones" (https://www.sanlam.co.za/namibia/p ersonal/insurance/Pages/default.aspx).

Saving for the future and last wills and testaments

Problems may arise over life cover because insurance companies accept only a small number of nominees as beneficiaries and do not allow too many of the extended family on the list. This is generally not a severe problem for people of European descent, because they usually nominate the same people as beneficiaries of their life cover as would inherit according to national law, which prioritizes the surviving spouse and the biological children (or other next of kin) over more distant relatives. This is not the case with the cultural groups in Namibia, many of which want the rules of their culture-specific customary law also to be observed, and this does now always accord with national law. To mention only a few: *Nama* and *Damara* want as many people from the extended family to be considered ("everyone must get a share"). The *Herero* (for example, the Maharero of Okahandja or the Ovambanderu of Epukiro in Omaheke Region) distribute the movable and immovable property of a deceased man among his widow and children, including those born outside of marriage, with a remaining part to be distributed among his patrilateral family members, such as younger brothers, sisters, and nephews. People can also be inherited: "The widow is offered the option of being 'inherited' by a younger brother or nephew of her late husband" (Hinz/Gairiseb 2016:311). The matrilineal *Aawambo* (representing the majority of the Namibian population) pass on any inheritance to members of the matriline. This may lead to a situation where, when a man dies, his sisters' children come and take everything out of the house and claim the insurance money because they consider themselves his legitimate heirs (cf. Hinz/Gairiseb 2010–2016 for customary law in Namibia). It needs to be mentioned that many young people are barely aware of the regulations of customary law or simply do not care much about it as long as it is of no particular use to them. However, as legal advisers and lawyers have confirmed to me, some will bring a case to court if, in their opinion, they have a legitimate claim according to customary law.

In order to avoid quarrels amongst their heirs, people with high life cover try to care for as many people as possible and prevent all possibly claims from arising by setting up a last will and testament that merges national laws, bank and insurance regulations, and the requirements of traditional laws (Klocke-Daffa 2022:144–147). This is no easy endeavour, because the insurance policy might be subject to a mortgage (so the insurance money goes to the bank), or the farm is part of communal land that is not part of the inheritance. Some or even most heirs might thus end up empty handed and not particularly well cared for.

According to the Namibian Constitution, "both the customary law and the common law of Namibia in force on the date of Independence shall remain valid to the extent to which such customary or common law does not conflict with this Constitution or any other statutory law" (Article 66). In cases of conflict over claims to financial resources and estates, and where no testament exists, claimants can appeal to court. National law overrides customary law, but according to Section 13 of the Community Courts Act (No. 10 of 2003), customary law can be applied in courts by consulting cases or calling for oral and written opinions. Traditional authorities or elders of the respective communities can then be called as witnesses to testify to the regulations of customary law.

Despite all the adversities that may arise, customers prefer insurance as a means of caring for the future over other forms of savings because of its undoubtedly greater advantages: insurance money is protected from theft and third-party access; insurers urge customers to pay the monthly contributions and – as opposed to ROSCAs – will rigorously sanction non-compliance; and insurance agents are reliable partners, coming close to being clients' good friends. As such, insurers and their brokers or agents act as if they were part of their customers' informal social support networks (Klocke-Daffa 2016:218), albeit with less intimacy and a higher guarantee of not failing.

Analysis

To answer the initially presented research question, I will highlight a few points that appear pivotal for the analysis of the empirical data, and then refer back to the theoretical frame of this paper.

Cultural values play a decisive role in the demand for and the use of formal insurance if they are in line with social obligations and an individual's quest for reputation. Contractual savings allow customers to evade the risk of being destitute due to the ongoing demands of needy persons, and, to some extent, allow them to reconcile their individual aspirations and the social requirements of traditional law. In this regard, funeral insurance supports the requirement to be a responsible caregiver within the family network in a much more satisfying way than the more individualized life cover, which appeals to a single person providing for only a limited number of kin.

Trust in insurance institutions, however, is important, even the prerequisite, for customers' buying and saving behaviour. As long as insurers pay out punctually when their customers need help, and as long as no major corruption scandals shatter the image of the company as a trustworthy institution (like those regularly delivered by Namibian politicians), there is good reason to take out formal insurance as an additional way of ensuring safety. The same holds true for customer–bank relations, because banks are involved in every contract as the handling institution and may even be the owners of insurance policies that back customers' business and home loans. Without the cooperation of banks, no security-providing insurance would be possible. A most important role seems to be accorded to the brokers and agents as mediators between insurances, customers, and banks. Due to their commitment, customer relations may in fact resemble family ties: brokers stay in contact with clients and try to be reliable partners in cases of emergency. As one broker said: "It is like being married to your customers. You have to take care of them and be their friend. Otherwise, they blame you for everything that goes wrong with their contract" (A., Oshakati, September 12, 2018: Interview). As Herseman rightly pointed out, the face-to-face contact between customers and insurance representatives are essential for building trust in the "highly regulated hardcore business" of the life-insurance industry (2008:42).

Security in times of uncertainty with all associated contingencies does not appear to get lesser when linked with formal social insurances – at best they are a promise, but no guarantee. As such, insurance may be more or less as reliable as savings associations, but certainly has less advantages in regard to socializing. Insurance customers do not continuously meet or even know each other, nor do they have much insight into the overall financial performance of financial institutions. The lack of social ties and transparency on the part of insurers with regard to the overall development of finances, investments, interest rates, and the safety of deposits might well be among the reasons why private or communal saving associations are preferred in some countries. Where insurance companies do appear to be more effective in comparison to more informal savings associations is in the sanctions applied to defaulting clients. The threat of falling out of the system after defaulting on payments for three consecutive months weighs heavy on the customer, and does indeed keep most of them from falling short on their commitments, as Aliber has claimed (2010:136).

Payments for insurance policies have a direct impact on *gifting*. They mean that less money is available for one's investments (business, farm, animals, house) or the education of one's children due to the substantial *cash flow* that is redirected towards banks and insurance companies. But it also becomes obvious that insurance payments mean a qualitative reduction of social ties. An insurance-induced lack of financial resources means that support on the more informal level has to be decreased. The extended family which needs to be supported is scaled down to close relatives while external partners have to be content with what is left. Clearly, this leads to a reduction of social relations and possibly to an increase of poverty among those who are no longer co-funded (fig 4).

Time itself thus becomes a risk, because the *time of security* (should there be any) is delayed and relegated to the future if all goes well. With regard to funeral insurance, the policyholder can benefit from the security the policy offers, provided he or she has taken out a family cover. With life cover, it is quite different, because such policies in no way provide security for the policyholder. However, they do provide an opportunity to care for the future of descendants and other beneficiaries, which may otherwise have been impossible. The 'good life' in the present is reduced in the hope of providing more security for dependants in the future.

Figure 4: Life covers, insurance-customer relationship and the notion of time

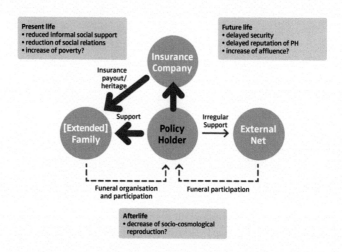

Source: Klocke-Daffa

Saving into insurance policies is a safe way to keep one's income for oneself. Particularly for the low- and middle-income groups, insurance companies appear to offer an escape from excessive social obligations. Savings accounts basically serve the same purpose, but are too easy for the accountholder to plunder if the pressure to respond to all the request for help from ever-present needy relatives, friends, and neighbours becomes too much. In this manner, even relatively small amounts subtracted and sent via the common phone-banking system may add up over the months, and "at the end of the day you sit with nothing", as many of my interlocutors would frankly admit.

The fact that a growing number of people are saving for the future – if only after death, whether their own or someone else's – not only reflects the increased incomes that have enabled people to afford insurance since independence came to Namibia, but also an increased awareness of uncertainty about what time will bring. Following Pedersen and Holbraad (2013), it becomes very clear that attitudes towards security and insecurity are intertwined with the perception of time – an inscrutable present and visions of an even more unpredictable future. In order to manage the future as best as possible, saving into insurance is one option out of many that ensures that provision so that nobody must 'suffer'. A sense of the danger of having to suffer seems to be deeply entrenched in many Namibians, but more research is needed to find out if this has anything to do with the difficult past of the population.

The delaying of security to the future may in some cases be accompanied by a delay in the reputation of the policyholder, because many family members do not even know that they have been chosen as future beneficiaries. Whether the insurance pay-outs increase affluence remains questionable, since most of the money is redistributed among the social network after the death of the policyholder. This occurs most certainly with regard to funeral insurance and may just be as true for life cover. Even if there is a last will that specifies what is to happen to the estate and from which many of the bereaved are to benefit, this still does not guarantee them a time of more security.

It also needs to be mentioned that there is a potential change in the concept of the afterlife (fig.4). Many Namibians strongly believe that the living and dead have obligations towards each other: the living are obligated to provide a proper burial for the dead, and the dead are responsible for protecting and blessing the lives of the living. This kind of reciprocal exchange relation seems to be disturbed by insurance. With insurance, it is now the dead who have cared for themselves (by the death benefit of their insurance policy) and for those left behind. For the surviving dependents, there is not much to do other than to organize the funeral. For external relatives and friends who used to share in the costs, the only thing left is to pay their last respects. This might be one of the reasons why funerals are tending to become more and more expensive, thus proving opportunities for the living to care for the dead, even though most of the costs have already been settled.

Conclusion: Caring for the future – Who cares? Whose future?

Saving for the future by way of formal social insurance may be a means of providing more security. However, unlike the Ethiopian *iddir* and *equb* organisations, which are private or communal associations acting on a face-to-face base, insurance companies are anonymous institutions. Even though some insurance brokers act like members of a social network, they do not even come close to the many social and spiritual functions connected with savings associations. Yet, there is more to insurance than just its economic aspects:

(1) The advance of the life insurance industry in Africa is clearly a sign of social transformation. Formal insurance is attractive because it enables customers to pool money and social obligations in order to care for their beneficiaries (if only after death) rather than spending it on the growing number of needy persons in the present. In this regard, formal insurance can indeed be conceptualized as a 'future-making practice'.

(2) Trust in the system is an important factor in this process. Everything runs smoothly as long as the financial institutions and their customers are reliable partners. Whether the flip side of this trust between formal institutions and their customers is a lack of trust between those customers and private savings

associations needs to be questioned, but informal savings associations are certainly not the predominant way of providing security in Namibia.

(3) Formal insurance challenges the notion of time and visions of the future: the time of security is not now but is postponed to the future. The hoped-for good life will at best start later. Death is the prerequisite for this.

(4) There is undoubtedly a social price connected to the growth of formal insurance, as it drains informal support networks and potentially undermines the socio-cosmological exchange relations between the living and the dead.

In view of the research question presented at the beginning, I can state that cultural values and trust in the financial institutions play a major role in terms of demand for insurance. Customers have confidence in their insurance agent because they act like a member of their social network: they, and the insurance they provide, are reliable, punctual, and provide help in case of emergency and death. Face-to-face relations are important factors in the process but are not the only point that matters in determining customers' buying behaviour. The real attraction of insurance is that it offers the option to blend individual aspirations to protect own resources and the need to meet the social obligations of caring for life and the afterlife.

Saving for the future is caring for the future. To do this by way of formal insurance entails a double burden but also a twofold promise. With monthly payments to the insurance company, which are usually subtracted from the bank account by debit, financial liabilities increase while social obligations within the informal support networks persist. To reduce this double burden, some may reduce their obligations towards needy persons. But the social price is high if those who were used to being cared for are relegated to other givers. What makes insurance so attractive nevertheless are the prospects and promises connected to them: if all is paid, insurance enables clients to pay for the costs of funerals without getting into additional debt, and it opens up the possibility of caring for the future of the next generation. With this a lot has already been achieved compared to colonial times, when the little people had had to be distributed to many, making the future appear not much brighter, and perhaps even darker, than the present. Today customers are trying to keep more for themselves and care for the future of those left behind by leaving some acceptable starting capital – much to the benefit of insurance companies and banks but to the detriment of the lower-income groups that might be thereby left out. More research is needed to find if this kind of individualized caring is acceptable to society on a broader scale, or if alternative ways of caring for the future are emerging.

Figures

Figure 1: "Funerals do not always come on payday". Advertising funeral insurance on the main street in Windhoek 2017

Figure 2: "Honour your loved ones". Advertising family funeral cover, 2018

Figure 3: Billboard advertising life covers, 2017

Figure 4: Life covers, insurance-customer relationship and the notion of time

Bibliography

Abels, Miglena (2016): *Pension Systems in Sub-Saharan Africa: Brief Review of Design Parameters and Key Performance Indicators*, Washington: World Bank.

Aliber, Michael (2010): *Rotating Savings Clubs and the Control of Dynamic Inconsistency. A South African Case Study*, Saarbrücken: LAP Lambert.

Ardener, Shirley (1964): "The Comparative Study of Rotating Credit Associations." *The Journal of the Royal Anthropological Institute of Great Britain and Ireland* 94, pp. 201–229.

Ardener, Shirley/Burman, Sandra (eds.) (1996): *Money-Go-Rounds. The Importance of Rotating Savings and Credit Associations for Women*, Oxford: Berg.

Ashong-Katai, Rahinatu (2011): Transition from a Stokvel to a Formal Business: A Study of Stokvels in Soweto, South Africa. Accessed March 5, 2024 (http://hdl.h andle.net/10539/9497).

Bähre, Eric (2007): *Money and Violence: Financial Self-Help Groups in a South African Township*, Leiden/ Boston: Brill.

Bähre, Eric (2011): "Liberation and Redistribution: Social Grants, Commercial Insurance, and Religious Riches in South Africa." *Comparative Studies in Society and History* 53/2, pp. 371–392.

Bähre, Eric (2012): "The Janus Face of Insurance in South Africa: From Costs to Risk, From Networks to Bureaucracies." *Africa* 82/1, pp. 150–167.

Bähre, Eric (2020): *Ironies of Solidarity: Insurance and Financialization of Kinship in South Africa*, London: Zed Books Ltd.

Bailey, Clive/Turner, John (2008): "Social Security in Africa. Brief Review." *Journal of Aging and Social Policy* 14/1, pp. 104–114.

Bonlife Assurance Namibia. Accessed March 5, 2024 (https://www.bonlifenam.com /).

Buijs, Gina (1998): "Savings and Loan Club: Risky Ventures or Good Business Practice? A Study of the Importance of Rotating Savings and Credit Associations for Poor Women." *Development Southern Africa* 15/1, pp. 55–65.

de Bruijn, Mirjam (1994): "The Sahelian Crisis and the Poor: The Role of Islam in Social Security Among Fulbe Pastoralists, Central Mali." *Fokaal: Tijdschrift Voor Anthrologie* 22–23, pp. 47–63.

de Bruijn, Mirjam/van Dijk, Rijk (2009): "Questioning Social Security in the Study of Religion in Africa: The Ambiguous Meaning of the Gift in African Pentecostalism and Islam." In: Carolin Leuthoff-Grandits/Anja Peleikis/Tatjana Thelsen (eds.), *Social Security in Religious Networks. Anthropological Perspectives on New Risks and Ambivalences*, New York/Oxford: Berghahn Books, pp. 105–127.

Dekker, Adriette (2008): "Mind the Gap: Suggestions for Bridging the Divide between Formal and Informal Social Security." *Law, Democracy and Development* 12/1, pp. 117–131.

Deubel, Tara F./Boyer, Micah (2020): "Building Benkadi. The Role of Trust in Malian Women's Community Savings Groups." *Mande Studies* 22, pp. 23–39.

Devereux, Stephen (2001): *Social Pensions in Namibia and South Africa*, Brighton: IDS Discussion Paper 379.

Devereux, Stephen/Getu, Melesse (eds.) (2013): *Informal and Formal Social Protection in Sub-Saharan Africa*, Addis Abeba: Organisation for Social Science Research in Eastern and Southern Africa.

Dorfman, Marc (2015): *Pension Patterns in Sub-Saharan Africa*. Worldbank Group. Social Protection & Labour. Discussion Paper no. 1503, Washington: World Bank.

Gillion, Colin/Turner, John/Bailey, Clive/Latulippe, Denis (eds.) (2000): *Social Security Pension. Development and Reform*, Geneva: International Labour Office.

Global Data (2023): *Namibia Insurance Industry – Key Trends and Opportunities to 2026*. Accessed March 5, 2024 (https://www.globaldata.com/store/report/namibia-insurance-market-analysis/).

Gockel, Augustine F. (1996): *The Formal Social Security System in Ghana*, Accra: Friedrich Ebert Foundation.

Golomski, Casey (2015): "Compassion Technology: Life Insurance and the Remaking of kinship in Swaziland's age of HIV." *American Ethnologist* 42, 1, pp. 81–96.

Gugerty, Mary Kay (2007): "You Can't Save Alone: Commitment in Rotating Savings and Credit Associations in Kenya." *Economic Development and Cultural Change* 55/2, pp. 251–281.

Herselman, Stephné (2008): "'Dabbling in the Market': Ideas on 'an Anthropology of Marketing'." *Anthropology Southern Africa* 31/1–2, pp. 39–47.

Hinz, Manfred O. (ed.)/Gairiseb, Alex (ass.) (2010–2016): *Customary Law Ascertained. 3 volumes. Volume 3: The Customary Law of Nama, Ovaherero, Ovambanderu, and San Communities of Namibia*, Windhoek: University of Namibia Press.

Horst, Cindy (2006): *Transnational Nomads. How Somalis Cope with Refugee Life in the Dadaab Camps of Kenya*, New York/Oxford: Berghahn Books.

ILO – International Labour Organization (2021): *World Social Protection Report 2020–2022. Social Protection at the Crossroads – in Pursuit of a Better Future*, Geneva: ILO.

James, Deborah/Rajak, Dinah (2014): "Credit Apartheid, Migrants, Mines and Money." *African Studies* 73/3, pp. 455–476.

Kedir, Abbi M./Ibrahim, Gamal (2011): "ROSCAs in Urban Ethiopia: Are the Characteristics of the Institutions More Important than Those of Members?" *Journal of Development Studies* 47, pp. 998–1016.

Kimuyu, Peter Kiko (1999): "Rotating Saving and Credit Associations in Rural East Africa." *World Development* 27/7, pp. 1299–1308.

Klocke-Daffa, Sabine (2001): *Wenn du hast, musst du geben. Soziale Sicherung im Ritus und im Alltag ben den Nama von Berseba*, Münster: Lit Verlag [You Must Give if You Have. Social Security in Ritual and Everyday Life among the Berseba Nama]

Klocke-Daffa, Sabine (2012): *Is BIG Big Enough? Basic Income Grant in Namibia. An Anthropological Enquiry*, Tuebingen: University of Tuebingen.

Klocke-Daffa, Sabine (2016): "'On the Safe Side of Life': Cultural Appropriations of Funeral Insurances in Namibia." In: Laila Prager/Michael Prager/Guido Sprenger (eds.), *Parts and Wholes. Essays on Social Morphology, Cosmology, and Exchange in Honour of J.D.M.* Platenkamp, Berlin: LIT, pp. 203–218.

Klocke-Daffa, Sabine (2017): "Contested Claims to Social Welfare: Basic Income Grants in Namibia." *sozialpolitik.ch.* Journal des Fachbereichs Soziologie, Sozialpolitik, Sozialarbeit, Universität Fribourg, 2, art. 2.3, pp. 1–26.

Klocke-Daffa, Sabine (2022): "Life Covers, Risk and Security – Anthropological Perspectives of Social Insurances: A Case Study from Namibia." *Anthropology Southern Africa* 45/3, pp. 135–152.

KPMG (2022): *The South African Insurance Industry Survey 2022.* Accessed March 5, 20224 (https://assets.kpmg.com/content/dam/kpmg/za/pdf/2022/life-insurance-industry-results-14.pdf).

Lindley, Anna (2010): *The Early Morning Phone Call. Somali Refugees' Remittances*, New York: Berghahn.

Midgley, James (2000): "Social Security Policy in Developing Countries: Integrating State and Traditional Systems." In: Franz von Benda-Beckmann/Keebet von Benda-Beckmann/Hans marks (eds.), *Coping with Insecurity. An 'Underall' Perspective on Social Security in the Third World*, 2nd ed., Yogyakarta: Pustaka Pelaja, pp. 219–229.

Mupedziswa, Rodreck/Ntseane, Dolly (2013): "The Contribution of Non-Formal Social Protection to Social Development in Botswana." *Development Southern Africa* 30/1, pp. 84–97.

Odén, Bertilo (1991): *Namibia's Economic Links to South Africa*, Uppsala: Nordiska Afrikainstitutet.

Pedersen, Morton/Holbraad, Martin (2013): "Introduction." In: Morton Pedersen/ Martin Hobraad (eds.), *Times of Security, Ethnographies of Fear, Protest, and the Future*, London: Routledge, pp. 1–28.

Pelham, Larissa (2007): *The Politics Behind the Non-Contributory Old Age Social Pensions in Lesotho, Namibia and South Africa*. Chronic Poverty Research Centre Working Paper, No 83, Washington: World Bank.

PwC (2018): "Ready and Willing. African Insurance Industry Poised for Growth." Accessed March 5, 2024 (https://www.fanews.co.za/assets/pdf_2018/africainsura nceindustryfinalwebsep2018.pdf).

Rohregger, Barbara (2009): "'Church Shopping' in Malawi: Acquiring Multiple Resources in Urban Christian Networks." In: Leuthoff-Grandits/Anja Peleikis/ Tatjana Thelsen (eds.), *Social Security in Religious Networks. Anthropological Perspectives on New Risks and Ambivalences*, New York/Oxford: Berghahn Books, pp. 146–165.

Signé, Landry/Johnson, Chelsea (2020): *Africa's Insurance Potential: Trends, Drivers, Opportunities and Strategies*, Rabat: Policy Center for the New South.

Swiss Re Institute (2020): "World insurance: Regional Review 2019, and Outlook." Sigma 4. Accessed March 5, 2024 (www.swissre.com/dam/jcr:864e8938–3d3c-4 8cc-a3d7–8682962971e7/sigma-4–2020-extra-complete.pdf).

Thomas, Elmar (1991): "Rotating Credit Associations in Cape Town". In: Elmar Preston-Whyte/Christian Rogerson (eds.), *South Africa's Informal Economy*, Cape Town: Oxford University, pp. 290–304.

Van Dijk, Han (1994): "Livestock Transfers and Social Security in Fulbe Society in The Hayre, Central Mali." *Focaal* 22–23/47, pp. 97–112.

Wallace, Marion/Kinahan, John (2011): *A History of Namibia. From the Beginning to 1990*, Sunnyside, South Africa: Jacana Media.

Weiss, Holger (ed.) (2020): *Muslim Faith-based Organizations and Social Welfare in Africa*, Cham: Palgrave Macmillan.

World Bank. 2022. GCI 4.0: "Life Insurance Premiums." Accessed March 5, 2024, (https://tcdata360.worldbank.org/indicators/hbae5670f?country=NAM& indicator=41438&countries=BRA&viz=line_chart&years=2017,2019).

World Data (2023): "Population Growth in Namibia." Accessed March 5, 2024, (https ://www.worlddata.info/africa/namibia/populationgrowth.php).

Zacher, Hans F. (1988): "Traditional Solidarity and Modern Social Security: Harmony or Conflict?" In: Franz von Benda-Beckmann et al. (eds.), *Between Kinship and the State. Social Security and Law in Developing Countries*, Dordrecht: Foris Publications, pp. 21–38.

Author's biographies

Abraham Asnake, born in 1987, is a lecturer and research fellow in the Department of Anthropology at Hawassa University, Hawassa, Ethiopia. He has conducted research on the indigenous early-warning practices of the agro-pastoral communities in southwest Ethiopia, and social unrest and the competing institutions of peace-making in the multi-cultural city of Hawassa. His research interests pivot around social networks and capital, ethnic federalism, inter-ethnic relations, state–society relations, traditional governance and conflict resolution mechanisms, traditional natural resource management, and linking technology with local innovations.

Alula Pankhurst (PhD), born in 1962, is the Ethiopia Country Director for the Young Lives longitudinal research project run by the University of Oxford. He obtained his PhD in Social Anthropology from the University of Manchester and taught at Addis Ababa University for 16 years. His research interests include migration and displacement, poverty and wellbeing, childhood and adolescence, minorities and social exclusion, customary institutions and dispute resolution, and the longer-term impact of development interventions.

Dagne Shibru Abate (PhD), born in 1975, is a social anthropologist at Hawassa University, Ethiopia. Dagne received his MA in Social Anthropology and BA in Sociology from Addis Ababa University, Ethiopia, and obtained his PhD in Anthropology (with a specialization in conflict and peace studies) at Andhra University, India, in 2014. Dagne served as head of Academic Program and Quality Assurance (2014–2017) and dean of College of Social Sciences and Humanities (2018–2022) at Hawassa University. Dagne is an active member and chairperson of the Ethiopian Society of Sociologists, Social Workers and Anthropologists, ESSSWA, South chapter. Dagne's research interests include conflict resolution and peace, federalism and ethnic relations, poverty and wellbeing, social institutions and development, and agriculture and pastoralism.

Hanna Getachew Amare (PhD), born 1979, is a social anthropologist in the Department of Anthropology at Hawassa University, Ethiopia. She received a PhD in Anthropology and Linguistic-Historical Studies from the University of Messina, Italy in 2014. From 2001–2007 Hanna worked as a curator and assistance researcher at the South Omo Research Center (SORC), Jinka. Since 2009, she has been engaging in curricular and extracurricular activities such as, teaching, research, and leadership at Hawassa University, Jinka University, Arbaminch University, and Wachemo University. Her research focuses on indigenous knowledge systems, museum and public education, Ethiopia–India relations, tourism and globalization, PhD trajectory & supervision in Ethiopia, women in conflict, and religion and development.

Kelemework Tafere Reda (PhD), born in 1971, is a postdoctoral researcher at the Frobenius Institute for Research in Cultural Anthropology in Frankfurt am Main, Germany. Reda has been working as an associate professor of Anthropology at Mekelle University, Ethiopia until he joined the Frobenius institute as a Gerda Henkel fellow in February 2022. He is also currently working on research projects based in Denmark and France. Between 2014 and 2016 he was a visiting scholar at the University of South Africa (UNISA), Pretoria, South Africa. His research focuses on migration, informal institutions, conflict resolution, and gender relations in apparel industries.

Kim Glück (PhD), born in 1986, is a social anthropologist specialising in Ethiopian studies. After studying social anthropology and history in Frankfurt am Main, Germany, and in Montpellier, France, she completed her doctorate in Mainz, Germany. For her doctoral thesis, she worked for several months with a professional dance group from Addis Ababa, studying dances and dance performances. She conducts research in Ethiopia as well as in the Ethiopian diaspora in the USA and Israel. Her research interests include migration and diaspora studies, performance studies and anthropology of the future.

Sabine Klocke-Daffa (PhD), born in 1956, is Professor of Social and Cultural Anthropology at Tuebingen University, Germany. She is member of the Collaborative Research Center on ResourceCultures (SFB 1070 RessourcenKulturen) at UT, funded by the German Research Foundation. Klocke-Daffa has done intensive fieldwork in Southern Africa, mostly Namibia, but has also worked in Madagascar and in Iran. Her research focuses on exchange relations, basic income grants, social insurances, the cultural dynamics of resources, migration, and children. In addition, she is engaged in applied anthropology, mainly science communication and anthropology in schools.

Author's biographies   229

Sebhatleab Tewolde (PhD) was born in 1957. Since 2016, he has worked as a lecturer at the Frankfurt University of Applied Sciences in Frankfurt, where he also is a member of the Institut für Migrationsstudien und interkulturelle Kommunikation (IMiK). He did his MBA at Strathclyde University in Glasgow, Scotland, and his doctorate at the University of Groningen, in the Netherlands. He worked as a lecturer at the Addis Ababa College of Commerce in Ethiopia and as an associate professor at the University of Asmara in addition to being Director of Administration and Finance at the National Board for Higher Education (currently Commission for Higher Education) of the State of Eritrea. He was adjunct professor at the Darmstadt University of Applied Sciences for 5 years. His current research focus is on the challenges and opportunities of the Eritrean communities in Germany.

Sophia Thubauville (PhD), born in 1979, is a social anthropologist at the Frobenius Institute for Research in Cultural Anthropology in Frankfurt am Main, Germany. Thubauville is an active member of the European Librarians in African Studies (ELIAS) and of the Commission for Migration of the International Union of Anthropological and Ethnological Science (IUAES). She is also spokesperson for the GAA working group "Family in the Field". In 2020 and 2021 she was a visiting scholar at the Africa Studies Centre at the University of California, Los Angeles. Her research focuses on migration, anthropology of the future, higher education, gender, and Ethiopia–India relations.

Worku Nida (PhD), born in 1963, is a sociocultural anthropologist teaching anthropological courses at the University of California, Riverside. He also taught at the University of California, Los Angeles for four years, where he received his PhD in Sociocultural Anthropology. Nida is an active member of the American Anthropological Association (AAA), Association of Black Anthropologists (ABA), Critical Urban Anthropology Association (CUAA), and Society for Anthropology of North America (SANA). In 2022, he was a visiting scholar at the Frobenius Institute for Research in Cultural Anthropology in Frankfurt am Main, Germany. Nida's research focuses on entrepreneurship, migration, identity, social change, African diaspora, ethnicity, and nation-making.

Yasmin Bushra, born in 1995, is an architect who studied at the Ethiopian Institute of Architecture, Building Construction & City Development. She completed her MA in Regional & Local Development Studies at the Institute of Development Research at Addis Ababa University. Her research interests include urbanism, service delivery, and spatial justice in cities of the South. She is a 2024 Prince Claus Building Beyond Mentee and took part in the Biennale College Architettura at La Biennale Di Venezia 2023.

Yohannes Tesfaye Getachew, born in 1983, is a PhD candidate in History at Addis Ababa University. He is a member of staff at the City Government Education Bureau of Addis Ababa. He conducts research in Ethiopia. His research interests include history, indigenous knowledge, and culture.

Zelalem Mulatu Demu (PhD), born in 1979, studied political sciences and international relation at Addis Ababa University. He is head of the City Government Education Bureau of Addis Ababa. He conducts research in Ethiopia and South Sudan. His research interests include political history, indigenous knowledge, and culture.